Idea•jacked \ī-'dē-ə, jakt\ past tense of idea•jack \-,jak\ vt [idea + hijacked] 1: an action in which an individual or company stole, from its legal owner, an idea that was protected by patent, copyright, trademark or proprietary rights 2: an action in which an individual or company prevented an idea's legal owner from selling products based on that idea 3: an action in which an individual or company took undeserved credit for another party's patented idea or invention — idea•jack•er \-,ja-kər\ n — Idea•jack•ing \ī-'dē-ə, ja-kiŋ\ n

IdeaJacked

Pat Kennedy

Marc,

Nice catching up
with you. Your passion
for EVs broad adoption is
a key ingredient for
success!

Pat

IdeaJacked is trademarked.

Pseudonyms are used in the book for a few individuals.

Visit the IdeaJacked Blog @ www.ideajacked.com

Library of Congress Cataloging-in-Publication Data
Kennedy, Pat

LCCN: 2009908895

ISBN   1-4392-5628-4

1.) Entrepreneurship
2.) Intellectual Property
3.) International Business
4.) Business Ethics

Available in Kindle format

KW-2 Media
Boulder, CO

October, 2009

To my three children: Erin, Matt and Brian.

Thank you for your understanding, inspiration and encouragement to pursue a life full of friendships and adventure - a life in which the IdeaJacked project was the latest chapter.

Table of Contents

List of Figures

Page

The process of writing *IdeaJacked* over the past several years was highly analogous to the process it takes to develop one of Cellport's patent portfolios. The experience was not straightforward, it took a vast amount of time and was far more expensive then I budgeted. And, much like building a patent portfolio, the IdeaJacked work product only succeeded thanks to the great efforts and contributions of many people. This book would not have been possible without the superb contributions of the three gifted editors, Alison Richards, Peggy Albright and Janine Allen. I am deeply grateful for their talent and tenacity in helping to make *IdeaJacked* a reality. Besides the numerous edits and research efforts that went into the drafting of the text, Alison Richards did a marvelous job with the drawings, creation of the book cover and distribution of over 50 draft copies to friends and family who helped critique earlier drafts. Finally, great appreciation goes out to Matt Olin and Sebastian Montealegre for working with Alison to make the final manuscript.

Over the years I have been blessed with the good fortune of having many wonderful friends who have once again aided me with their love — all of them caring enough to read through the early drafts of IdeaJacked and provide most helpful feedback. To all of you, thank you again for your critique and inspirational support that kept the IdeaJacked project flame burning. The following is likely an incomplete list of all those who helped review earlier drafts. If I have missed anyone, please forgive me — Alan Geller, Alf Naber, Axel Fuchs, Bernard Joseph, Bob Johnson, Bob Loeb, Chuck Spaur, Dale Hatfield, Dave Zinger, Dina Elder, Don Hume, Drew Kennedy, Eric Harman, Erin Kennedy, George Mansho, Hiro Sakurai, Janine Brown, Jay Plucienkowski, Jim Caile, Jim Schuster, Karin Eicher, Les Hatcher, Mark Berman, Mark Elder, Matt Azinger, Michael Braitberg, Michael Oakley, Mike Lewellen, Nancy Pierce, Philippe Vercruyssen, Sandra Diaz, Scott Axelrod, Sharon Glassman, Stan Lipton, Steve Smith, Susan McCrossin, Tammy Parker and Valerie Finberg.

President Obama has allocated vast amounts of government money to spur the American innovation engine; in fact, he recently stated that innovation is the best way to revive the American economy. Like most monies invested in research, not all the government stimulus funds will yield, but certainly there will be numerous important and maybe even a few disruptive inventions that will make their way from the research labs to factories and eventually to end-users. Hopefully the U.S. government will do an equally enthusiastic job of protecting these inventions by enforcing the resulting patents and the rules of the World Trade Organization. Unless the U.S. and other developed counties protect their innovators and producers from a world infested with IdeaJackers, we will continue to spend our research dollars and human capital to create — only to see more and more of these innovations produced in clandestine factories in marginally ethical parts of the world. If we do not commit to protecting intellectual property, our people will likely be forced to accept expectations for a reduced quality of life.

I suspect that President Obama has a deep understanding of the rhetoric between free trade and ethical trade. And I am hopeful he will lead a government that insists on the enforcement of the WTO rules and patent rights — for the world clock now runs on Internet time and unless it is understood that our new flat and filled-with-IdeaJackers world is a seriously dangerous place for inventors, producers and consumers, Americans and other citizens of the developed world will find our countries full of empty factories and fellow citizens with significantly diminished prospects.

For more readings on the topics of Innovation and Ethical Trade, please visit my blog on the Website, IdeaJacked.com.

Pat Kennedy

If it had not been so maddening, I might have enjoyed the irony. I had traveled across the world on business to visit a factory in the countryside near the village of Dabendorf, in what was the former East Germany. I saw my name posted on the company's welcome sign. The sight of balloons and streamers just inside the entry bolstered my hopeful mood.

It was December 2000. I had come to Dabendorf to persuade a local manufacturing company, one of Europe's most rapidly growing suppliers for the automobile industry, to license my company's inventions that make it easy and practical to add hands-free cellular phone systems to cars. I casually asked my hosts about the celebration and learned that the company had launched an initial public offering on the German stock exchange that very day. The IPO was more successful than they had anticipated because a line of hands-free products they manufactured for BMW and Mercedes Benz had turned out to be tremendously popular among consumers. While it was not mentioned, they knew, and I knew, that they had cloned their lucrative products from the inventions I was there to discuss.

The experience was starting to become familiar. Just a year earlier I had attended the Frankfurt International Auto Show, where a new Audi sedan, the A6, received enthusiastic attention and praise for an innovative hands-free cellular phone system its designers had incorporated into the car. I sought out the A6, got into the driver's seat and checked out the system. There it was: almost an exact copy of my company's invention, made by yet another manufacturer, a company I had never heard of.

The emotions that came over me during these experiences can only be described as a fuzzy blend of anger, flattery, disbelief, frustration, and despair. By 2000 my company, Cellport Systems, had spent nearly $10 million of investor funding and years of unflattering toil to pioneer and develop safe ways to use cellular phones in automobiles. We began specializing in this field in 1991 when my business partner, Hiro Sakurai, and I came up with our first patentable hands-free idea.

By 2000 our company had also invented the world's first Internet-connected car, which we were also trying to promote to automotive companies around the world. We had six patents and another four pending proving the authorship of our work, but no one was buying licenses from us.

Europe had a market but it was a reluctant one. The region was safety-conscious and many countries mandated the use of hands-free systems in cars. Automobile manufacturers on the Continent were eager to adopt our technology, but they did so by the world's least expensive method of research: reverse-engineering Cellport's products to create clones of our designs, and they did this openly. Several candidly told me that they would resist licensing Cellport's intellectual property for fear of helping create another technology powerhouse in America.

The U.S. was another story. For the most part, Americans were not yet absorbed with in-vehicle cellular phone safety issues and states had not yet enacted hands-free policies. The country's automobile manufacturers, historically slow to change, were reluctant to adopt technologies developed by outsiders. Ford Motor Company came close, but after placing an order for $8 million in product, changed course and cancelled the order in the midst of its corporate restructuring in 2002, forcing us to foot the entire bill for the $8 million in custom-produced inventory.

By then global firms had even less motivation to license Cellport's technology. Believing Cellport would collapse, mobile phone and automobile manufacturers expected us to auction our assets to pay off mounting debts. Our competitors began positioning to pick up the spoils: Cellport's seminal patents.

I recalled the words of one European IdeaJacker: "You are in the wrong country to develop such a great automotive technology."

Our First Big Idea | 1

1991
1992
1993
1994
1995
1996
1997
1998
1999
2000
2001
2002
2003
2004
2005
2006
2007
2008
2009

We entered the exquisitely marbled lobby of an ultra-modern glass and chrome Tokyo skyscraper. My business associate, Hiro Sakurai, and I registered with building security officers as invited guests and pinned on our visitor badges, indicators to the personnel that we needed an escort. We were inside the world headquarters of Nippon Telephone and Telegraph Corporation (NTT), Japan's most established telephone company. In just a few years, Nippon would launch one of the most powerful independent cellular phone companies in the world.

Our destination was a conference room on the "Labs Floor." It was spring 1991.

With precision promptness, a young Japanese woman dressed in a NTT company blazer and white gloves asked us to follow her. She led the way to a far bank of elevators that provided access to the labs floor. Upon our arrival, two more women wearing identical NTT escort uniforms greeted us. They bowed in unison, showed us our meeting room, and, of course, offered us the customary green tea.

These formal escort protocols were unusual even by Japanese standards and, combined with the panoramic view overlooking the Tokyo skyline and bay, put Hiro and me in anticipatory moods. After a brief wait, our host Mori-san entered the room carrying a box under his arm. He promptly greeted me with a handshake and warmly addressed Hiro in Japanese.

What we were about to experience would not only change my life, but Hiro's as well.

**

I traveled often to Tokyo in those days and always looked forward to a much-welcomed greeting at Narita Airport from Hiro, who was not only a business associate but a close friend. As I exited the final customs clearance area, Hiro's genuine smile acknowledged our close and historical friendship and instantly recharged my trans-Pacific jet-lagged batteries. The friendship that Hiro and I had built since we first met a decade earlier had grown into a true brotherhood, built on common interests, ambitions and, most importantly, the spirit of discovery and inventive optimism.

Despite the 6,000-mile distance and distinct cultural differences between us, we were cut out of a very similar cloth. We both majored in economics during our university days — in a time when economics was still considered "the dismal science": an arcane field of study that attracted mostly directionless intellects. (Fortunately much has changed since then to luster up the reputation of economic thought, training and its empirical contributions.) Immediately out of our respective university programs we both found career traction in the technology business and further opportunities in the bourgeoning field of wireless communication systems. We met in Las Vegas in 1980 when Hiro, then a wholesale electronics distributor, pitched some components to an electronics manufacturing company that I worked for at the time. We discovered a shared language efficiency afforded us by our common interests in economics. This gave us a framework, during endless business and philosophical discussions, for analyzing all types of business and social phenomena and extrapolating technology and market trends that were likely to emerge in the future. We also discovered that although neither one of us ever enrolled in an engineering course, most of our business associates and friends were geeks. Beyond that, we were both fascinated by wireless product development and system designs.

As with many great business friendships that endure over long periods, Hiro and I developed opportunities that kept us commercially engaged and we frequently introduced each other to new intellectual theories and commercial advancements of all sorts. In the late 1980s, I started Cellular Solutions, a cellular phone accessory product development company and catalogue distribution business that sold designer antennas for car phones and, for the new and growing mobile market: leather cases, battery packs, cigarette-lighter chargers, and a travel charger design that I invented. In classic fashion, immediately after I informed Hiro of this new business venture, he helped broker a supply relationship for us with Standard Electric, a Japan-based supplier of batteries, which happened to be our largest and most profitable product line.

This visit to Japan began routinely. Outside the Tokyo airport, we loaded my luggage into Hiro's trunk. Then he gave me the agenda for our week together. In textbook Hiro manner, he remarked, "I'm so sorry Pat, but as usual we have too much to do for such a short trip. This agenda is the best I could do given all the meeting opportunities. Please tell me what you would like changed, but," he slyly added, "everyone on the list is anxious to see you."

Nothing like leaving me an opening to change an already over-booked schedule! "Thanks, Hiro," I said with a smile, "I'm sure you did a good job — as usual."

We talked non-stop during a two-hour drive through intense traffic and into the concrete and glass canyons of central Tokyo, arriving at the Hotel New Otani, my home base for the next six nights. Hiro, as with most Japanese, values the comfort of relationship traditions. The Japanese, not typically physically demonstrative of their feelings, can be deeply passionate and emotional, which was very obvious to me once I became tuned in to their energy and values system. Hence, after I checked into my hotel and freshened up, Hiro always hosted a dinner with either his family or close business friends at a local restaurant as a formal ceremony to welcome me. The gracious warmth of a special dinner on the first evening after my arrival is the Japanese equivalent of a huge western style hug that one would receive from an old and dear college friend. On this trip, we dined with Hiro's wife and children, exchanged gifts, and caught up on the happenings of our respective families.

Hiro scheduled our first two days in the western Japan countryside at the Standard Electric battery factory, the company that was designing and manufacturing three new battery product models and cigarette chargers for Cellular Solutions to sell to the growing number of mobile phone users. I also used the visit to negotiate an expansion of my company's credit line to help Cellular Solutions finance its rapid growth in the exciting, new cellular phone accessory market.

With that part of our week's agenda completed, Hiro was ready to start what he considered "future fun" activities. He had scheduled three to four visits a day for the next three days with either the presidents or senior engineering staff members of various electronics companies. The firms we would visit ranged from the biggest Japanese technology players to very small operations, all with wireless business interests as the common thread and all looking for potential synergistic opportunities with my firm.

My good fortune was Hiro's ability to open countless doors for me in the closely knit Japanese society, where the success of one's family business and the stature of the university one attends generate more — and better — networking opportunities than they would in the states. In Hiro's case, his family had a high profile in the post-World War II electronic test equipment business and he himself had strong academic credentials, having graduated from Meiji University, one of Japan's top universities. Hiro was also blessed with tremendous energy and good looks that spilled over into a social charisma that Japanese men and women alike responded to.

My favorite relationships in life are with people who have what I consider balanced and high levels of these attributes: self assurance, idea-building skills, social caring, and the integrity to take the high-road in conflict situations. Hiro had these traits as well as a combination of Tokyo street smarts, a very capable intellect and comfort in his own skin — qualities that made him very enjoyable and stimulating to be with, both one-on-one and during family visits and business meetings. A natural marketer, he knew how to use his pedigree and social skills to build a network of contacts that, at the young business age of 41, made him a sort of hub in the dense mesh of Japan's business and social environments. That's why our week-long business agendas were typically tightly scheduled and fast-paced. To make the most use of our time, we would take a cab from one meeting to another. Our second host of the day would usually serve a bento box lunch. Then we'd be on to meeting number three in the afternoon with the final meeting of the day ending around 6:00 p.m. or evolving into a working dinner.

Prior to any company meetings in Tokyo, however, Hiro always scheduled a visit to the world's most densely packed retail and wholesale electronics district, Akiharbara, which occupies approximately six large city blocks. Akiharbara came to life in Tokyo after World War II as a business district specializing in the sale of vast quantities of surplus U.S. military radio parts left over from the war, and it continued in that vein after the Korean War. In the subsequent 60-some years, Akiharbara has evolved from arcade-like merchant store fronts that were roughly 4- by 6-feet in size or smaller to mega-sized electronics retailers fiercely competing to display the latest electronic components and consumer gadgets at the best prices. Some of the district's most savvy merchants are now today's electronic retail and wholesale giants in Japan.

The Japanese lead the world in product miniaturization and packaging designs that have created some of the most innovative consumer devices internationally, such as Walkman audio players, Atari and Sony video-game devices, and cellular phones. In the early 1990s these technical and packaging innovations, combined with a market hungry to use new mobile phones rather than fixed, in-car cellular phone systems, spurred the mobile phone market, particularly in Japan. In 1991, 80 percent of Japanese cellular phone users preferred mobile phones to car phones. [1] By comparison, consumers preferring mobile phones versus car phones in the U.S. represented just 37 percent of the American cellular phone market at the time. [2] By visiting the Akiharbara electronics district, Hiro and I gained priceless insights into the roles cellular phones and accessories would later play in other parts of the world. It was a stroll into the future for me, and, with hometown pride, Hiro enjoyed watching me react to Japan's brilliantly conceived merchandise.

The Japanese are much about relationship trust, and with Hiro as my ambassador-at-large, most of the week's meetings were very open and productive. By nature, most Japanese entrepreneurs and corporate executives we met tended to be very focused on their day-to-day missions, but they also had tremendous curiosity about other people's perspectives, especially on what the future would bring. Most of the sessions Hiro arranged were called "green tea meetings": meetings held in modest conference rooms, with each participant enjoying a small cup of the proverbial tea served by a female office staff member wearing white gloves.

After an exchange of business cards followed by a sometimes-awkward combination of handshaking and bowing, we'd sit down, ready to start our discussions. Hiro opened each meeting by giving a short briefing on the host company as well as my firm, Cellular Solutions, and what he thought the parties might find of common interest. Since most of the companies we visited hoped to either sell me some type of product for inclusion in our catalogue or to establish a joint venture like the one we had with Standard Electric, many of the meetings were fast paced and as the Japanese like to say, "open kimono."

Given my 50-plus visits to Japan, there are several general truisms that, as a gaijin (foreigner), I'm comfortable to state about the Japanese. First, the Japanese have mastered the concept of societal cooperation unlike any other culture I've come to know. As the second-largest economy in the world on a landmass about the size of California and with a population of 120 million people, the Japanese learned they must either cooperate as a people or stumble into chaos. Fortunately for the Japanese, they mastered the former paradigm. Today the Japanese certainly have their challenges, especially with a rapidly aging as well as now-contracting population, and the people are confronting new social issues caused by rapidly changing gender roles. On the positive side, the Japanese seem to genuinely care for and trust their fellow countrymen, which creates a unique social harmony. This harmony, in my opinion, is one of their greatest comparative advantages in the world economy.

For our second day back in Tokyo, Hiro had scheduled an afternoon meeting at NTT with Mori-san, an old friend of his who was a senior engineer in the company's advanced wireless design labs. My only insight into this meeting was that I would get the opportunity to look at mobile phone designs that were not yet available in Akiharbara and to learn about NTT's new product line, called MoVa.

Mori-san slowly opened the box as though it contained a glass crystal. He explained to us that over the past few years his design team had decided to create a specification for highly advanced mobile phones and to ask their manufacturers to produce phones conformed to that specification. It was a radical move in a time when product manufacturers controlled phone designs while the cellular operators, who did their best to try to sell the handsets to their customers, had little influence over the product characteristics. NTT's new approach would soon turn that operator-manufacturer relationship on its head. The sensation I felt was like a first-time father watching the birth of a child, except instead, this was a hot new product.

Much to my surprise, Mori-san pulled out a brochure with Bruce Willis's face on the cover. How anti-climactic was this? Not that I'm not a Bruce Willis fan, but a brochure dominated by pretty pictures was not what I was expecting; marketing materials of this type are considered "vaporware" in the high-tech business. As we turned the pages of the new MoVa brochure, we saw actual pictures of four amazingly small and beautifully well-designed cellular phones. Mori-san went on to explain to Hiro and me that NTT used its close ties with Fujitsu, Mitsubishi, NEC, and Panasonic to design this line of mobile phones. Their objective, in addition to contributing their own creative direction to the manufacturers, was to revolutionize how consumers use and relate to their mobile phones.

NTT designers mandated the phone's weight in ounces, not pounds, as was the norm in the global cellular phone market in 1991. Plus, they developed a common keypad and display that were clearly breakthroughs. As Mori-san spoke about their design efforts, I contemplated how the smart integration of silicon chips, combined with the quintessential packaging abilities of the Japanese to drive smallness, were huge factors in his team's concept work. Frankly, the designs were fabulous and my disappointment with this slick brochure quickly waned. As the hostess staff delivered us more tea and a small plate of rice crackers, Hiro and Mori-san engaged in a conversation in Japanese beyond my rudimentary understanding of standard tech-talk.

After they finished, I asked Mori-san if he would like to see the latest edition of my catalogue, which we customized for numerous mobile phone operators, and to discuss some of the accessories we pioneered for the needs of U.S. customers, such as our travel charger. Hiro interrupted me and politely said, "Yes, that's a great idea, Pat. But please, let's first see the four working models of new MoVa phones." I turned a few shades of red, fortunately a favorite color among the Japanese, and mustering the best recovery possible replied, "Of course. That's what we came here to see." The Japanese tend to be most graceful in general, and as Mori-san seemed to be particularly so, he did not let on that he noticed my faux pas.

Mori-san put his hand inside the box and pulled out four black velvet pouches that one might find in a fine jewelry store and carefully lined them up in front of us on the leather center section of the conference table. As one of the chief architects of the MoVa line of phones, he proudly removed the handsets, one at a time, from their velvet bags until all four were displayed. Hiro and I sat there staring at what seemed impossible for the year 1991: functioning cellular handsets that were slightly longer but half the thickness of a pack of cigarettes. My mobile phone at the time, a NEC model, was at least 50 percent greater in volume, almost twice the weight of these MoVa units, and it had a comparatively primitive keypad and display. The sensation that came over me when staring at the four models was a bit like visiting an auto show and feeling overwhelmed by the design and beauty of a Lamborghini, Porsche, Bentley or Aston Martin. As a product developer at heart I had dozens of questions, but I first asked if I could pick up the phones to examine them in greater detail. Mori-san was most generous and replied, "Yes, please be my guest."

Sure enough, these were real handsets, not the foam mock-ups I suspected when we first saw the product catalogue. I was extremely impressed with the elegant user interface and the ergonomic comfort of each lightweight device in my hand. After nearly a half-hour of study, I told Mori-san that his design team had hit a grand slam and they should be extremely proud of their great vision and effort. With classic Japanese modesty and in gentlemanly fashion, Mori-san, not taking direct credit for these four beauties, said, "Thank you, Kennedy-san. I will pass your compliments on to the design team."

Briefing Mori-san on my accessory catalogue by now was clearly a low-level priority. As I turned all four phones upside-down, to what's called the butt end, I became fixated on a surprising design aberration: Each handset had a unique connector interface, or port, where the cable from the automobile docking station attaches to the phone. How, I wondered, did NTT allow this to happen? Here was an opportunity to finally standardize on a common connector interface, and it was wasted! Why, I kept asking myself, didn't they make them all the same?

Usually in Japan I would hold off on a potentially embarrassing question, but I could barely constrain my curiosity about this. At one point, Mori-san stepped out of the room for a moment and I took the opportunity to ask Hiro if I could ask why NTT allowed these four portable phone producers to choose their own connector interfaces. Hiro said it might be a good question. "I suspect Mori-san has an answer, but why is that important to you?" he wondered.

I confessed a concern that as more people use mobile phones in their automobiles, there would be a greater need for hands-free car kits — hardware attachments that establish a phone's electrical connections to an automobile's remote speakers, microphone and antenna. Without a common port, manufacturers would have to produce customized car kits for each phone included in their product lines. This would limit the number and variety of mobile phones available for hands-free use and make quality car kits prohibitively expensive. Plus, we wanted to add hands-free car kit systems to our catalogue, and this approach was not good for sales. Hiro looked at me and said, "I see your point, but why are you just telling me about this now?" "Good point," I said. "I'll explain more tonight over beers."

As Mori-san reentered the conference room, I asked him why NTT allowed for each handset to have a distinct connector interface and did not take this design leadership opportunity to standardize this feature. "Your point was hotly debated both internally at NTT and then with the handset producers," he responded, "but after much consideration, we decided not to establish a standard connector interface — primarily because as phone designs continue to shrink in size, the connector must too. Plus," he continued, "as handsets become more complex, the electrical needs will change over time and those handsets will require different connectors as well."

Mori-san presented compelling examples of how, in a world of continuous design evolution, a connector specified in 1991 would most likely be irrelevant in 2011. I looked right into his eyes and said, "That's an excellent analysis and explanation. Thank you."

At that point, Mori-san got a call and needed to excuse himself for five minutes to address an urgent matter with his boss. After Mori-san left the room I looked at Hiro and said, "This is a design headache. The plurality of connector interfaces on handsets will keep a common car interface port from becoming a reality, which, in turn, hurts my business. And it will cause road safety concerns in the future since it discourages use of hands-free phones. We must figure out a way to go from a plurality of connector interfaces to a common port."

After Mori-san returned to the room, we wrapped up our questions on the MoVa line. I then gave him a brief overview of the Cellular Solutions catalogue and our business model. As I was briefing Mori-san, I noticed Mr. Personality himself, Hiro, had become quiet and looked very withdrawn, even sickly. As we got up to leave I asked him if he was OK. He just smiled and said, "Yes I'm feeling great, but we must go now. Please hurry."

We all walked to the elevators. I told Mori-san once again how impressed I was with his team's work and thanked him profusely for sharing the future with us. Hiro managed to mumble a polite thank you and goodbye in Japanese and off we went down the elevators with our white-gloved escort. As we descended toward the lobby, I again asked Hiro if he was feeling OK. Did he need to use the facilities in the lobby before catching a cab to our next meeting?

"I have a major big idea and believe what we really should do is cancel our last meeting," Hiro looked at me and said. "We must talk ASAP over some drinks at the Hotel New Otani."

This was uncharacteristic behavior for Hiro. He was always trying to add extra meetings to my schedule, not delete one. But historical friendship has its privileges, so I let him call our last appointment and heard him apologize profusely but nevertheless cancel the meeting. This was a first for Hiro.

Right after Hiro instructed our cab driver to take us to the side entrance of the Hotel New Otani, I said, "OK, let me hear it. This must be a good one." As Hiro proceeded to pull out his notebook from his attaché case, he started to break into a sweat and then warned me, "Maybe I don't understand the problem, so this idea may not be so good."

This must have been a line right out of some Japanese movie shown in elementary schools, promulgating their cultural modesty. "Please," I said, "when was the last time you cancelled a meeting? Let me hear it."

Hiro then proceeded to draw three cellular phones, adding a triangle, square and oval shape, respectively, to depict the distinct connector design at the bottom end of each device. With this display of primal artistry, I jokingly advised him that he needed to stick to commerce and skip any mid-life ambitions of becoming an artist. He then drew a separate cable-like line out of each of the different phone connectors, and on each cable line was a small box labeled "electronic phone-ID," which, in turn, was attached via a cable to a cylindrical-shaped connector. He labeled this connecter "universal port that interfaces to programmable control station." The electronic phone-ID circuit, he explained, would identify the needs of the make and model of the phone in use, and the universal port and programmable control station would establish the appropriate power supply and communications features needed to allow the attached phone to interoperate with the hands-free system installed in the car (see Fig. 1).

I was awestruck; this was a shockingly simple and clearly a clever solution to a very big problem. "You deserve a few beers for that epiphany, my friend, and I'm buying!" I said.

The rest of that evening, we brainstormed about the market impact of such a major innovation in the very young field of mobile phones and how it would solve such a big problem for both pre-installed and after-market hands-free car-kits. As Hiro went on and on about the "art-of-the-possible" of this design, I tried to find weaknesses in the concept. But not one weakness was obvious. This was truly a big idea by a very perceptive and smart guy.

Big inventive ideas that address enormously large markets are clearly crème de la crème spiritual events and rare in the high-tech world. In this instance, considering the combination of the fast-growing cellular phone market and the hundreds of millions of vehicles on the road, we could foresee growth opportunities and potential sales numbers that any marketer would love. At the time, only 6.4 million Americans owned cell phones. The forthcoming years would prove our hunches right: By mid-2008, 270 million cell phones in the U.S. were in service.[3]

The next morning Hiro met me for breakfast and, immediately after his good morning greeting, opened up his notebook and showed me some additional market and product design concept work he did during his sleepless night. We went through the motions of attending our scheduled meetings for the balance of the day, but clearly we were both preoccupied by the epiphany of the Universal Port design.

During each cab ride, out came Hiro's project notebook for further discussions. We were truly experiencing the wonderful euphoria that accompanies a major design innovation. This was going to be my last full day in Tokyo, so we decided to have dinner alone that evening and concentrate on the details of moving the Universal Port invention into product and market reality.

At the top of a long list of items to-do, we decided, was the importance of idea secrecy and the need to file for a patent before sharing the invention idea with others. Hiro felt strongly that a U.S. patent would be the most valuable, given the number of cars and the population in the U.S., which both eclipsed Japan's. Remembering that recently I met a bright engineer back in Boulder who seemed to have a strong background in patents, I promised to research the patenting process as soon as I got home. Given that neither one of us had ever filed for a patent before, this clearly had the makings of a new and exciting learning adventure.

Traditionally during my final day in Japan, Hiro would join me for a long debriefing breakfast in the scenic Garden Lounge at the Hotel New Otani and then drive me to the airport in time for my late afternoon flight home to the states. On this beautiful spring day the schedule was the same, albeit our trip debriefing was limited to one topic: advancing the Universal Port concept as a patent application and then into product reality.

As we reviewed the Universal Port to-do list, I began to realize that our collaboration over the past few days would change the nature of our relationship forever. Hiro would no longer play the exclusive role of a trading agent but would gain a particular status that a pioneer of intellectual property and company founder enjoys in Japanese society. And together we would now become partners with a common ownership and mission. This was huge! Hiro noted that this would be a great benefit of our inventive work together and that we must work shrewdly together, as wise old men. It was a special bonding moment. We shook hands and committed to do our best as new partners for both of our families and, in a larger sense, to promote the safety benefits our product idea would give to society.

After all, we both grew up as post-World War II baby boomers and although we were capitalists at heart, we shared a deep sense of the importance of delivering contributions that will repay society for the fabulous freedoms and opportunities we both enjoyed.

The final leg of my weeklong adventure in Japan ended much like it began, in Hiro's car, albeit now we were headed back to Tokyo's Narita Airport. Hiro's debriefing style took on added complexities and subtleties during the drive. Unlike our pedal-to-metal ride into Tokyo the past Sunday evening, today, as with our past drives back to the airport, trucks passed us with ease. This was Hiro's way of adding minutes to our treasured discussions. Today it was especially meaningful because of the importance of our new partnership to advance the Universal Port design.

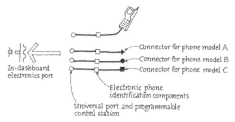

Custom cable and connector assembly for each phone

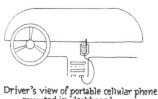

Driver's view of portable cellular phone
mounted in dashboard

Figure 1: The Universal Port

This drawing illustrates Hiro Sakurai's original rendition of the Universal Port idea that allows various types of mobile phones to operate with a hands-free docking station in a car via the use of an adaptor cable. The cable contains a circuit that identifies a phone's particular operational needs and a universal connector that plugs into the hands-free docking station.

As we drove, I took out my project to-do list one more time and realized we needed a name for this new design idea, business concept, connectivity architecture, Universal Port, and vehicle safety system. Suddenly it hit me. "Let's call our new idea and company "Cellport," I said.

"Perfect," he replied. "That says it all. It will be easily understood in the U.S. and other countries too." I modified my notes to read, "Cellport to-do list." It felt so natural to write the word Cellport. And this wonderful naming idea seemed the natural end to a most stimulating week with a dear old friend and now the start of what we both hoped for: a successful partnership together.

As I checked in for my flight back to the states the airline agent said, "Mr. Kennedy, this is your lucky day. We have a free upgrade for you in business class." I smiled and said, "Thank you. It has actually been a very lucky week."

"Good for you, sir. Travel well!"

2 | The Founding

1991
1992
1993
1994
1995
1996
1997
1998
1999
2000
2001
2002
2003
2004
2005
2006
2007
2008
2009

A business card highlighting the words, "Engineering and Patent Consulting," held my gaze. I was in my office, the first day back from Tokyo, trying to take care of the many business matters that accumulated in my fast-growing Cellular Solutions company while I had been overseas. It was no use. I was so preoccupied thinking about my patent application promise to Hiro and our Universal Port idea that I was not functioning efficiently at all. So I called the engineer and patent consultant listed on the business card, Michael Braitberg. The call was short and to the point: I had an important idea and I wanted to meet with him ASAP to understand whether the idea was worthy of a patent application.

The next morning Michael came to my office and we had what the Japanese would call "a super green tea session," though our beverage was several cups of coffee, not tea. I began the briefing by explaining my deep-rooted belief that one day nearly all cellular phones would be mobile and that they were sure to grow rich with functionality.

Further, I believed that cell phone usage in automobiles would become commonplace and a public safety issue. I then showed Michael a NEC hands-free kit in my car and explained to him that while it was great for safety and convenience, it only worked with my NEC mobile phone. Eventually, if I wanted to upgrade to a new phone model, I would also need to replace the entire hands-free unit in my car to the tune of more than $300. The system had no flexibility to accommodate another phone, not even another NEC design. All hands-free car kits on the market around the world, regardless of manufacturer, had the same drawback.

Back in my office, I showed Michael the cellular phone samples we had at Cellular Solutions. Motorola, NEC, OKI and Nokia handsets all had different connector interfaces. I also showed him the pictures of the MoVa phone from the NTT brochure that Mori-san gave me a week earlier. Michael quickly understood the unnecessary costs that phone-specific hands-free kits for vehicles would place on the cellular phone and hands-free markets. He also understood that each successive generation of technology would likely have different interface connectors, so that any solution to this problem had to be future-proof. Michael saw right away that our Universal Port could revolutionize hands-free solutions in vehicles. While he thought our idea promising, he explained there was much work to do before we could even file a patent application.

Much to my delight, Michael turned out to be a bit of a renaissance man. An electronic storage systems engineer with very diverse interests, from archeology to the repair and restoration of automobiles, he was well aware that vehicle technologies were primitive compared to fast-changing communications technologies and cognizant of how far automobiles could potentially advance in the future. Because he had such an eclectic background and keen interest in inventions, I was hopeful that Michael would add another dimension of highly creative and visionary thinking to our young but promising invention team. We spent the balance of our morning meeting discussing the details of preparing for and filing a patent application along with, as Hiro brought up, the importance of keeping our idea an absolute secret and working diligently to develop this exciting kernel of an invention to its utmost potential.

During our meeting, I took four pages of copious notes on all the steps needed to turn an idea into a patent application filing. Clearly

I was about to embark on a major project that would be full of very new life experiences. That day I decided to hire Michael as a project consultant and tutor in this new world of patents. As Michael explained, converting an idea into a meaningful government-issued patent would be a big accomplishment — but it would require a lot of research, further development to refine the idea, extensive documentation and expense. Plus, we would eventually need to hire a patent attorney to finalize the application and to negotiate its way through the U.S. Patent and Trademark Office.

Michael and I agreed to meet a few hours each week to review our respective accomplishments on a patent project checklist and to exchange updates with Hiro weekly, via fax, on his advancements as well as ours. I committed to find all the hands-free products on the market, past and present, along with available schematics showing how the electronic circuitry works in these devices. Michael would search all prior invention artwork at the patent office for both U.S. and international filings to make sure our epiphany hadn't been invented by others. We assigned Hiro to help with drawings of our Universal Port invention and to search for past and present products in Asia that may have accomplished the hands-free function too. As I reviewed the patent project list, I was shocked at the amount of work required to file what Michael called "a seriously professional patent application." A week earlier in Tokyo, Hiro and I had estimated it would take two months and cost under $5,000 to apply for a patent. That was our first partnership snafu. In reality, we were looking at a filing date five to six months out and an overall project budget of $15,000 to $25,000.

At home that evening, I reviewed my four pages of notes and found that I kept reflecting on one of Michael's most profound statements: "Ownership of an intellectual creation was part of America's constitutional fabric, a citizen's right, written into the Constitution by our founding fathers to promote innovations that could be both shared and owned by the inventor."

Ownership of intellectual creations as part of the U.S. Constitution was a bold concept with economic implications that I had completely missed in my 39 years of academic studies, readings and day-to-day learning. My new awareness of this was an early and delightful consequence of our invention project. The exciting discovery exercises in Tokyo that led to our invention were now opening up truly expansive and new intellectual frontiers for me. I decided to spend time that weekend learning more about why and how ownership of intellectual creations was so important to the United States' founding fathers.

That Sunday, I dedicated myself to spending the entire day at the University of Colorado law and engineering libraries in Boulder. The history of patents was far broader and richer than I imagined, predating the founding of the U.S. The concept of a patent is a mystery to most people, as it was to me in 1991, and although patents can be complex and confusing, they are based on some fairly simple concepts. At the highest order, a patent is a license to own a monopoly on a novel idea for a limited time. The government issues a patent in order to provide protective incentives and economic advantages to an inventor but it also publishes the invention to make sure society has an opportunity to benefit from broader understanding of the innovative art.

For the past six centuries there have been two primary types of patents: royal and innovative. Fortunately, royal patents were phased out in the seventeenth century in favor of today's innovative patents. The first royal patents were issued primarily by monarchs in Europe as a means to transfer technology or skill across countries. For example, in the fifteenth century, parts of Italy were home to advanced and high-tech glassmaking guilds that produced colored and clear glass used in building construction, lamps, domestic ware and jewelry. The royal courts of France and England offered patent monopolies to individuals or groups in the Italian glassmaking guilds as an economic incentive to leave their home countries and relocate, bringing their skills and wealth, to their patrons' regions.

Initially, both European monarchs and society benefited from this system; however, some monarchs corrupted it over time. In the sixteenth and seventeenth centuries some monarchs issued patent licenses to craftsmen and merchants for the right to trade basic goods such as salt, soda, certain types of cloth and wine in exchange for royal favors, such as land or privileges. Some of these early royal trade patents provided little to no incentive for craftsmen to innovate, and because these patents were monopolistic in nature they tended to drive costs higher, thus bringing about a negative social value.

**

In the 1620s, the leaders of the young British Parliament forced common-law control over England's much-abused royal patent system and created the Statute of Monopolies in favor of a patent law system that would encourage commercial innovation [1] [2]. This statute declared royal monopolies void but allowed the issuance of patents good for 14 years to "true and first inventors" or "new manufacturers." Today's innovative and incentive theory of patents can be traced to this bold and insightful action. Many historians and economists credit the British patent system shift with ushering in the Industrial Revolution that helped make England the most powerful political and economic empire in the seventeenth, eighteenth and nineteenth centuries.

One of the often-overlooked — and perhaps one of the most important — societal benefits of innovation patents is the requirement that an inventor publish specific details about the invention in order to receive a patent monopoly license for a limited time period. The publishing of the knowledge resulting from an invention is far more advantageous to society than if the knowledge is obfuscated or kept secret. A wonderful example of this are the inventions for an improved and much more effective method of creating and harnessing steam power. Starting around 1760 a Scotsman named James Watt began more than 40 years of development work in advancing several core patents focused on steam power systems. After the shrewd addition of a partner who added industrial and legal savvy, Watt delivered to the world a monumental contribution — a vastly improved steam-powered engine.

In the Watt case, the patent bargain worked as follows: Watt received a limited-life patent monopoly to build or license his vastly improved steam power systems, in exchange for publishing specific details about his innovation. Watt's ideas were therefore made available to other inventors, who in turn used the Watt steam power system to create derivative applications and improvements lasting for centuries beyond the life of the patent monopoly he was issued —applications such as using the system to power steamships, locomotives, and factories. The success of Watt's industrial innovation and the resulting steam-powered systems that both fueled Britain's bourgeoning factories in the Liverpool and Manchester industrial belt and led to the development of world-class steam-powered transportation laid the foundation for the Industrial Revolution and Britain's sustained role as a global powerhouse. [3]. The Watt patents are a classic example of the win-win incentive structure the patent system offers inventors and society alike.

The economic power of patent incentives was not lost on the early American colonies. Prior to the founding of the United States, many colonies had the ability to grant patents, albeit only for their limited colony-wide geographic areas. In the 1780s, once independence from England seemed assured, the American constitutional framers sought to create a strong patent system for inventors and industry that the new federal government would manage and apply across all states. The founders understood that, at the most basic level, the country's citizens would be motivated by both need and competition to use their talents and labor to provide for their families and that this foundation of talent and labor, what we now call the economics of "human capital," is what would build and sustain the new nation [4]. Thus in September 1787, members of the Constitutional Convention unanimously adopted Article 1, Section 8: "The Congress shall have the Power...To promote the Progress of Science and useful Arts, by securing for limited Times to Authors and Inventors the exclusive Right to their respective Writings and Discoveries." During an early session of Congress, the country's first lawmakers — carrying out their constitutional role — passed the Patent Act of 1790 [5].

I was inspired to learn that two leading advocates of a strong patent system were Thomas Jefferson, the first Secretary of State, and Alexander Hamilton, the first Secretary of the Treasury. As a farmer and leading statesman, Jefferson was highly inventive himself and an early champion of the idea that "ingenuity should receive liberal encouragement." He became America's first patent examiner. Alexander Hamilton was one of the country's early economic geniuses, and as

Washington's first Secretary of the Treasury he understood well that encouraging inventions would drive production and trade of manufactured goods, which in turn would increase tariff revenues for the highly indebted U.S. Treasury. The combined brilliance of these two men, despite their differing motivations for promoting innovation and industry in the new country, was highly influential in ensuring that a means to reward inventors with limited-life patents became a material component of the U.S. Constitution.

History shows that patents have indeed played a significant role in the advancement of wealth in U.S. society. Since Congress passed the first patent statute in 1790, the United States has evolved from a backwater colonial economy to its preeminent roles in the international economy and technology community [6]. Industrialized economies in general have increased their economic productivity more in the past two centuries than in all of human history, an achievement that is attributed, in part, to the economic forces unleashed by innovation patents [7].

In the last couple of decades, the number of patent applications filed annually worldwide has grown dramatically, increasing at an average annual rate that reflects the average annual growth in the world domestic product. The World Intellectual Property Organization, which tracks patent activity by country, believes applicants are using the system as it was intended, "to stimulate innovation and promote economic activity." And because we are an increasingly global economy, more and more of these applicants are seeking patents in multiple countries [8].

Many of America's greatest businesses launched or grew at an accelerated pace upon receiving their first patents. The belief in the power of patents explains why a leading technology company such as Qualcomm displays engraved plaques for many of its more than 5,000 patents on the wall at the entrance to its corporate headquarters. It explains why Motorola recognizes its inventors for their patent contributions not only through financial rewards but also by giving individual inventors special status in the company based on the number of patents they've received. The revenues gained from licensing patents, by these and other companies such as Genentech, General Electric, and

IBM, allow the firms to maintain higher margins, pay better salaries and continue to invest in research and development.

To receive a patent in the U.S., an inventor must submit an application to the U.S. Patent and Trademark Office (PTO) and propose to demonstrate that he or she has developed a novel, useful, and non-obvious process or product. The inventor has no proprietary right to the invention until the patent is reviewed and issued by the PTO, but once the patent is issued, he or she has the exclusive right — for 20 years retroactive to the initial filing date — to build products or license others to build products that use the patented idea. Since the creation of the U.S. patent system more than 215 years ago, more than 7.4 million patents have been issued in this country.

After better understanding the history of patents and how the patent system has worked as an economic tool in advancing science and industry over the past few hundred years, I was ready — with added enthusiasm, vigor and a deep respect for the philosophy and practice of property ownership — to help Michael and Hiro complete our Universal Port patent application.

By July, three months into the patent application project, Michael, Hiro and I were encouraged that our research into prior art and similar product inventions indicated that our invention was truly unique. Luckily, Marco de la Torre, the head of our Mexican joint venture at Cellular Solutions de Mexico — always a helpful and gracious partner — provided research assistance that ultimately turned up some critically important technology intelligence for us.

Cellular Solutions de Mexico was affiliated with a large Mexico City-based cellular phone operator that had electrical design schematics for manufacturers' hands-free systems for use by company technicians in case consumers might need to return the products for repair [9].

Ordinarily manufacturers such as Motorola, OKI, NEC and Nokia would not have released these custom-circuitry blueprints to outside companies, preferring to fix their products at their own company repair shops. That approach was impractical, however, when it involved shipping products across the Mexico border, because customs procedures and the country's tariffs created unwanted delays and fees for customers. Therefore, the phone manufacturers gave their operator partners in Mexico these sensitive schematics to facilitate local repairs. This fluke of international business was our good luck, yielding us a look at the state-of-the-art of hands-free designs and allowing us to compare, for patentability purposes, our Universal Port idea to these proprietary device-specific solutions. After reviewing how the internal electronics enabled these various hands-free kits to work, we were convinced that our invention was clearly an innovation and potentially of great economic and societal value. Michael had proved to be a real patent sage. His insistence on conducting good research was already starting to pay off and our diligent work added more patentable ideas and sophistication to our original epiphany of only four months earlier.

Our goal was to start drafting the patent application by August and happily we were on schedule [10]. We already had more than 20 pages of drawings and text nearly ready for submission. As Michael liked to point out, it is incumbent on the inventor to submit a thoroughly compiled application and for the patent office to reciprocate with like diligence and study of an invention that is worthy of a patent award.

Because the U.S. patent and trademark system has been in business for more than 215 years, it has had time to refine its processes to promote well-intentioned applications and reviews. Given that the majority of patent examiners are engineers or scientists, they do not take kindly to hucksters or whimsical types who might try to fool the system or undermine its integrity. In conducting its review, the Patent Office expects the inventor to demonstrate that he or she has conducted a sincere effort to ensure the innovation has not been published or described in any prior art and to present convincing explanations — on technical, market and societal grounds — that the invention is indeed meaningful and unique.

Knowing his experience, we asked Michael to pull together our small invention team's research findings, inventive improvements, drawings and text and compile a rough draft of our patent application that we could submit to a patent lawyer for final research and completion. In early September, Michael presented to us the first draft of our Universal Port patent (see Fig. 2). This was clearly a moment of great pride and anticipation. We all agreed that in a week all first comments were to be due to Michael and after a few more modifications to the draft, we'd submit the application to a patent attorney that Michael recommended. By late September the patent lawyer was reviewing and further enhancing our application for an October filing. The Universal Port patent was submitted to the U.S. Patent Office on Oct. 19, 1991, with Michael Braitberg, Patrick Kennedy and Hiroshi Sakurai as the three inventors of record.

**

During the months we were focused on the Universal Port patent project, and throughout 1991, Cellular Solutions continued to grow. In December of that year we learned that the company's lead venture capital investor wanted to shut its Boulder office and divest its Colorado holdings. This news prompted our Board of Directors to hire an investment banker to help sell the company. Selling Cellular Solutions' hybrid distribution and product design businesses in the hot cellular market was not too difficult. Within six months we consummated the sale of our Mexican partnership, U.S. catalogue sales and our Japanese product development joint venture with Standard Electric [11]. By the summer of 1992 the investment banker was left with a sole asset, ownership in Cellular Solutions' Universal Port patent application, which Hiro and I proposed to buy. And we did, which further ratcheted-up the partnership commitment we had toward one another.

**

In August 1992, I started a sabbatical. The only other time I had experienced a sustained break to ponder life and explore new territories without work or school obligations was the summer going into my junior year of college, 18 years earlier. At that time, two school friends and I set out to ride our bicycles, loaded with tents, sleeping bags and limited clothing from Virginia Beach, Virginia, to Los Angeles in eight weeks. After seven weeks of biking into the prevailing winds and visiting a few too many college campuses along the way, our pedaling stopped in Colorado, more than 1,000 miles short of our intended destination. One of the most memorable aspects of that summer in the mid-1970s was that the free time, combined with the many new experiences I had and stimulating people I met, opened my mind to greater ambitions. During that 1,800-mile bike trip, we met farmers and small-business people deeply focused on producing a good living for their families, but who were also interested in our backgrounds, our motivation for travel and what we had learned along the way. From these people, I learned much about regional styles and the varying degrees of economic interconnectedness they felt. This, for me, sparked a deeper curiosity in comparatives — comparatives like culture, education, government, skill, and ethics, for example, between city and rural people, other countries and the U.S. and so on. This interest in comparatives helped me decide to focus my studies in economics more on international themes, including studying abroad. Upon returning to the University of Buffalo that fall I did shift my coursework in that direction and 12 months later started a year of international study at EAFIT University in Medellin, Colombia, where I studied international economics and marketing as well as Spanish.

In my studies in Colombia, I gained my first shocking market insight that things in international trade are often not what they seem. Working as an intern at the U.S. consulate, I helped Colombian businessmen research potential trading options with the U.S. Through this avenue I encountered the Colombian powerhouse businessman Jacobo Lerner. A Romanian Jew who immigrated barefoot to the country fleeing the Nazis in the 1930s, Jacobo quickly established himself as an innovative entrepreneur. At the consulate, he sought my help and ultimately hired me to investigate possible routes to advance his trading ambitions with the tobacco giant Phillip Morris USA.

Over the next eight months as Jacobo paid and mentored me in the empirical side of international business, I found myself decoding an incredible fraud. Ninety percent of Marlboros — the "Marlboro Americana" type of cigarettes sold on the streets by kids — were smuggled in at night, I discovered, from two tariff-free islands. Condemningly, the trail from this illegal contraband scheme led right to Phillip Morris executives. I flew to New York City to meet with the executive vice president of Iberian and Latin American sales at Phillip Morris and threatened to leak the story to *The Wall Street Journal*; ultimately, the V.P. agreed to meet with Jacobo to discuss a trade concession. The whole experience of decoding unethical trade served both to break my innocence and naiveté when it came to international economics and to contrast deeply with the theoretical and scholarly world of economics I was engrained in as a student. Frustratingly, the lesson that business on an international scale often strays from my engrained ideas of right and wrong was a lesson I would encounter again.

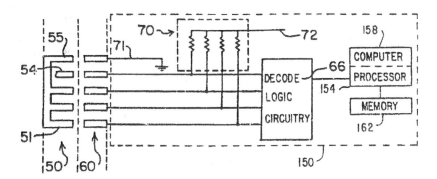

Figure 2: Detail from the Universal Port Patent

This drawing from the Universal Port patent illustrates the "brains" of the technology, the logic or "phone identification" circuit that identifies the power, charging and audio needs of the specific phone in use. It conveys this information via a circuit in the cable to the universal connector, which establishes the appropriate electronic and communications features needed to allow the attached cellular phone to interoperate with the hands-free system's docking station.

I welcomed the opportunity to embark on my second sabbatical in 1992 and again used the time to plan my next moves in life, although this time, with my children still in school and a commitment to coach my oldest son's junior soccer team, adventurous travel was unlikely. Most mornings I would ride or run four miles to my athletic club for a two-hour calorie burn that I desperately needed to counter balance all the catch-up lunch commitments that seemed to fill my early afternoons. After a few months of steady workouts and lunches, I was ready to find something more intellectually focused. Prior to starting Cellular Solutions, I had been vice president of business strategy at a small Boulder-based telecommunications consulting firm called Hatfield Associates.

The Hatfield firm was well regarded in the telecommunications industry and its offices were a great place to visit, for the working partners tended to be geeky bright, insightful and full of optimism.

As I reflected on a laundry list of business opportunities, the Universal Port idea that we called Cellport kept on surfacing as a market opportunity that was both sizable and offered room for technical and market expansion. By October, I put together a list of founders to help build the Cellport business concept. I put Hiro Sakurai and Michael Braitberg at the top of the list. Next were Dale Hatfield and Dick Chandler of Hatfield Associates. Dale, a nationally known telecommunications expert, had held leading policy positions at the Federal Communications Commission and other federal agencies prior to starting his own firm. In the mid-1990s, he would go on to become chief of the office of engineering and technology at the FCC. Dick Chandler was a networking guru. He possessed not only an advanced degree in engineering but, prior to joining Hatfield Associates, had spent years conducting research at the world-renowned Bell Labs. The next founder was Les Hatcher, who had been chief financial officer at Cellular Solutions. In addition to his business administration and legal smarts, Les, born and raised in Texas, had an MBA from Texas A&M and had been a Navy Seal in Vietnam. The roster of founders made for a well-balanced team. Now I needed to meet with them to discuss the charter, or mandate, of our Cellport business.

**

Beginning in early October, the Cellport founders, with the exception of Tokyo-based Hiro, met at the Hatfield offices at 6 p.m. each Thursday for two hours of discussion and my dinner treat: a steady diet of pizza. We discussed potential business charters, plus the structure and timing of our launch into the market. As the disparate group of founders became more comfortable with one another, several common threads emerged. Everyone thought it was important to continue pursuing innovative designs and patent applications focused on the eventual convergence of wireless phones and automobile systems.

This was a perfect extension of our Universal Port invention and pending patent application. The founders also felt very strongly that it was important to commit to an open licensing model in which, typically, a company promises to license its current and future technologies to anyone without prejudice and to charge a reasonable royalty, generally around 5 percent and certainly less then 10 percent of the retail price of a product and/or service that uses the patented innovation. We rejected the notion of a closed licensing model, in which a company licenses its innovations to a limited number of select customers who are willing to pay higher, sometimes even exorbitant royalties; we believed, like most advocates of the open approach, that the latter scheme stifles further innovation and progress in the market [12]. We named the business Cellport Labs, in part after the audio licensing powerhouse Dolby Labs, which was a successful proponent of the open-licensing approach.

Funding was the next key consideration. Because a technology and patent development firm can take years to mature, delaying payout for 10 or more years, we agreed to avoid relying on venture capital firms because they generally have shorter time-horizons for getting a return on their investments. The individuals sitting around the Cellport Labs founders' table agreed to become the primary source of capital, self-funding the business with both sweat equity and cash. When I described my new business charter and philosophy to my father, he said a career in the French Foreign Legion might be easier. Little did I appreciate my father's insight.

One day in early December of 1992, Les Hatcher called me at home with exciting news. "We received wonderful news today from the patent office," he said. "They have granted us three independent claims and, with some negotiating, we should be able to add even more claims."

This was indeed very big. I immediately called Hiro in Japan with the patent award news. His first reaction was, "My family will be so proud that I am a U.S. patent holder. This is second only to a Nobel Prize in Japan." During our historic call I informed Hiro that I would ask Les Hatcher to start the documentation necessary to incorporate the company. By month's end we had secured new office space for our new company, Cellport Labs.

1991
1992
1993
1994
1995
1996
1997
1998
1999
2000
2001
2002
2003
2004
2005
2006
2007
2008
2009

Starting a new business is a process full of prolonged nervous excitement. It produces an energy thrill well suited for an adrenaline-seeking entrepreneur.

All through the December holiday break I anxiously awaited the start of January 1993 and planned the official launch of Cellport Labs. I listed our top priorities that required immediate focus. First, we needed to find licensees who shared our enthusiasm for the Universal Port idea and second, if we were to connect wireless devices to vehicle systems as successfully as Dolby Labs had brought audio enhancement technologies to recording studio, movie theater, home and car environments, Cellport Labs needed to develop additional meaningful inventions.

As I considered our founders' skill sets in light of the potential technical challenges we would encounter, an idea hit me: Michael Braitberg had a strong knowledge of both automotive systems and computer networks and Dick Chandler's expertise in communication system architectures was profound. If I could effectively develop "what-if" scenarios to identify ways in which consumers could eventually use wireless devices in cars and, at the same time, inspire Michael and Dick to expose the missing or sub-optimal links between wireless and vehicle systems that had to be resolved to make the envisioned consumer applications work, we should be able to establish a platform for further inventions. I was confident that while the challenges would be easier to articulate than solve, these two tenured engineers would be able to find novel ways to make wireless-to-vehicle connectivity enhancements a reality. And since we were all founders of a start-up and working without salaries, we had the motivation to work efficiently and fast. Finding technology transfer and licensing partners and developing "what-if" scenarios thus became my primary contributions to Cellport. These two roles, happily, still exist for me today.

My first objective was to get organized. I started a project folder that I titled, "Vehicle Connectivity," and set it up to hold files for the information, notes, and other resources I expected to compile in my forthcoming work — not bad for week one at our new company Cellport Labs. My second objective was to meticulously scrub my extensive business card file of nearly 1,000 wireless industry executives and search for those who might be interested in licensing our technology.

Next, I needed to begin spending time identifying the connectivity hurdles between wireless devices and vehicle systems in order to challenge Michael's and Dick's invention skills. I found I was most prolific at the "what-if" architectural work in the early mornings or after a noon-time bike or run, so I made sure I always allocated time for this work during those parts of the day.

With a patent assured for our Universal Port invention, I felt at liberty to explain the concept to potential customers and seek technology licensees. After a few months pitching the idea to cellular carriers and phone manufacturing executives, the pioneering founders of McCaw Cellular Communications and Mexico's Grupo Iusacell said they would sign up as anchor customers for a consumer hands-free product based on our Universal Port concept. Both were noteworthy customers. My primary senior contact at McCaw Cellular was Bob Johnson, an old friend who completely understood the significance of our invention and product vision. McCaw Cellular was the leading cellular phone company in the U.S. at the time and its founder, Craig McCaw, strongly believed that use of cellular phones in automobiles would eventually become a public safety issue. When Bob and I began pitching Cellport's universal hands-free proposal to McCaw, it was like preaching to the choir. Iusacell, which had been Cellular Solutions' partner in Mexico prior to purchasing Cellular Solutions' portion of our joint venture, was part of a vast industrial conglomerate that just two years before had given us the hands-free car kit schematics that helped us enhance our Universal Port invention. Its parent company, IUSA, was owned by Carlos Peralta, a gifted visionary and technologist who ran the conglomerate's business supplying high-volume wiring harness systems to the car industry. Carlos understood the importance of Cellport's Universal Port technology from both the cellular and automotive industries' perspectives and believed very strongly in it.

Having these early wireless carriers on board as customers was a critical first step; now I needed to find a manufacturer to license the technology, build the product and take it to market. This led to our first semi-setback. We learned that mobile phone manufacturers did not like the prospect of a universal hands-free product because it would compete with their high-profit, device-specific car kit sales. The cellular phone carriers, on the other hand, loved our solution but they weren't in the business of building products and they were not in the habit of telling their manufacturers to produce specific designs, as NTT had begun doing in Japan. At a meeting of Cellport's founders, Michael and I raised the possibility that Cellport might need to find a way to design and produce commercial products itself in order to serve its two new customers. We went back to the strategic drawing board.

**

Concurrent with my search for licensees, Michael, Dick and I began meeting twice a week to find enhanced techniques for connecting wireless devices to vehicle systems. Although the three of us have fairly different personalities, we were pretty compatible, making us more likely than not to work productively together. The connectivity-bridging exercise proved to be a tough challenge, primarily because the cellular and automobile industries had essentially opposing ambitions. The cellular industry, which was growing at an exponential rate, was already ambitiously seeking ways to expand the applicability of its technologies to new environments. Yet the auto industry, needing to protect communications systems that could involve a car engine computer, the transmission, airbags or other vital performance and safety technologies, considered it essential to maintain a firewall around its network and keep its network protocols secret. The incompatibilities between these two industries seemed unworkable.

Like a monk reciting a mantra, Michael kept repeating that these are ideal problems. "Tough problems make an ideal Petri dish for novel inventions," he insisted. Michael's enthusiasm was great, but it didn't put food on the table.

About a month into our bi-weekly invention sessions, Dick said he had had an epiphany that would solve our quandary. He went to the white board to explain his big idea, which would give wireless mobiles in a hands-free car kit or embedded in the vehicle new electronic circuitry and intelligence capable of communicating with the automobile's networked components as well. Not only would the invention allow communications with vehicle systems, it could connect to mobile phones via our Universal Port technology, thus taking advantage of, and expanding the use of, our first invention. Michael understood the brilliance of Dick's idea within a nanosecond. He got up and gave Dick a high five — both men were smiling and bright-eyed.

The energy that this inventive camaraderie generated truly signified good progress but personally, I needed more details. In fact, I needed a tutorial, for advanced networking courses weren't offered to economics majors. Fortunately, Dick was an adjunct university professor and accustomed to teaching slower students like me. He graciously went to the white board and listed, in three separate columns, the various challenges preventing advanced networking between wireless hardware devices and automotive network systems (automotive network systems are systems in which the communications network inside the vehicle uses a proprietary interconnection method and software protocol to send information from one electronic module to another.) He then methodically illustrated a set of new components, including a car kit controller that would provide the interface between wireless and vehicle electronics and that would control the transmission of data to and from a car's electronic modules via the vehicle's network system (or bus) and a new systems design that could make it all work together as an extension of a wireless network. Not only would the wireless and vehicle systems work together, the invention would make it possible for a cellular phone to transmit data to and from a variety of electronic modules in a car, such as a GPS positioning device, CD-ROM, video display, speech recognition system, car alarm or vehicle engine monitoring system.

His diagram essentially listed what would become the claims of the invention. It would complement our other efforts to commercialize our Universal Port idea while establishing Cellport as a specialist in communications between wireless devices and automobiles. We called our new invention a "Dynamic Digital Bus" and spent the rest of the day brainstorming other possible ways to extend it to even other inventions (see Fig. 3).

**

After Dick and Michael departed for the day, I happily relabeled the Vehicle Connectivity project folder "Digital Bus" and created a file for it that I labeled, "Patent Application Work." I worked on the project with an intense level of energy until late into the evening and drafted a plan to guide us through the process of refining our Dynamic Digital Bus idea and preparing our second patent application. Although I was completely happy with my new team of gifted thinkers, Thomas Edison's famous words, "Genius is one percent inspiration and 99 percent perspiration," were very present in my mind. Cellport's Dynamic Digital Bus advancement would take much work to patent and build.

Michael was particularly excited about Dick's big idea. He said building a company with one patent is very difficult; great companies have a portfolio of complementary patents. I looked at him and sighed, "Now you tell me." We all laughed, but my chuckle was only half-hearted. Fear of failure keeps entrepreneurs working hard. While I was confident we had entered untapped inventive territory, I knew that building hardware solutions to bridge these two different worlds would be both expensive and time consuming. This idea would also take us deeper into the automotive industry, which was new to us. The encouraging part was that the team had demonstrated its ability to work and produce together.

**

As we entered the second quarter of our new company, excitement was running high. I focused on finding a licensee to manufacture products based on our Universal Port patent. A quarter of the way into a run one early morning, I thought of an ideal prospect: Allan Batts and his company, Hello Direct. I had met Allan when his company bid on buying Cellular Solutions the previous year. Allan was the CEO of a rapidly growing consumer telephone equipment catalogue company and we got along very well. As a result of Hello Direct's due diligence work toward bidding on Cellular Solutions, I knew that Allan wanted a cutting-edge strategy for his cellular accessory business. I was confident that if we secured large formal purchase orders from McCaw and Iusacell for products based on the Universal Port patent and coupled those anchor orders with a Hello Direct license to create the products, we could have a win-win-win situation.

That morning I called Allan and introduced the idea. I told him that I could get multimillion-dollar orders from two leading carriers. Allan responded, "Pat, I should have bought your company last year. This idea is great, and," he added, "it gives us another way to work together."

The next week Allan was in Colorado on some other business and met with us to frame the forthcoming relationship. He told us that Hello Direct was 100 percent on board, but before he would sign a license he wanted to see written purchase orders for a minimum of 30,000 units. He also wanted the Cellport Labs team to lead the product design effort. This changed our business charter. We now had to convert the patent first into a design and then into a working product prototype before Hello Direct would assign the product to its primary contract manufacturer, which was based in South Korea.

In less than three months we secured purchase orders from McCaw Cellular and Iusacell for 25,000 and 10,000 units, respectively, 5,000 more than Allan's minimum requirement. With more than $5 million in purchase orders, we could now sign Hello Direct as our first licensee.

I visited Hello Direct's headquarters in San Jose, California to present the purchase orders, scope out the product design tasks and finalize the patent license. I learned that one of Hello Direct's key motivations for our transaction was that they planned to go public within a year and wanted a hot product to enhance their IPO.

After a couple days of planning and negotiations and evenings spent faxing contracts back and forth with Les Hatcher and our attorney in Boulder, we were getting close to consummating the deal. I was reluctant to add Hello Direct's product design responsibilities to Cellport's core charter of specializing in invention work and Allan knew this. A skilled negotiator, he sweetened the agreement by allowing Cellport to have exclusive ownership of all new inventions that we might discover during Hello Direct's product development. As reluctant as I was to expand our charter, Allan's offer of invention funding was too good to turn down. During my third day at Hello Direct's offices, we finally came to an agreement. We signed the license and product development contracts and Hello Direct wrote Cellport its first five-digit check.

The timing was ideal. We were nearly finished working on a patent filing for the Dynamic Digital Bus, so we had available time and energy to take on the Hello Direct design project. It turned out to be a bigger challenge than any of us expected but at the same time it suited our inventive aspirations, for there were still plenty of connectivity design problems to solve. To keep our costs low, we contracted several well-regarded firms in Boulder to help us design the electronic, software and hardware aspects of our first commercial product, which we happily called the "world's first universal hands-free kit" for cellular phones.

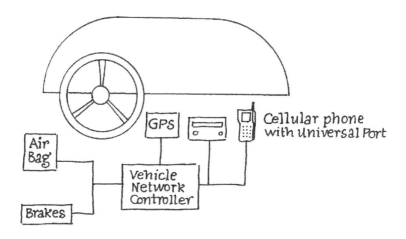

Figure 3: Dynamic Digital Bus

The Dynamic Digital Bus invention is an advancement of the intelligence used in the Universal Port technology. It makes it possible for a wireless device to transmit data to and from a variety of electronic modules that are connected to a network-style computer in an automobile. Such devices can include (but are not limited to) an engine control unit, air bags, brakes, a display or a GPS positioning device.

Within a few weeks we ran into our first major design challenge: how to hold mobile phones in place in a car in a manner that could accommodate any one of a variety of connector configurations a mobile phone might have. The solution we came up with was to produce a plastic phone adaptor with a built-in logic circuit that would be specific to a phone and that would, in turn, attach to the Universal Port and the hands-free kit's universal docking station. As Michael and our contract teams worked to design these phone-specific adaptors, they identified several patentable aspects of this solution. This was really fun pioneering design territory. By this time we had filed our Dynamic Digital Bus patent and we were back at the drawing board with what looked like our third and fourth patent applications—the "Phone Adaptor Holder" (see Fig. 4) and the "Phone Adaptor with Charging." The latter invention provided techniques to connect the universal docking station to a power source in a car; it could also be used to charge a handset in a stationary environment, such as on a desktop.

Given both the strength of our inventive team and the fertile area of universal wireless connectivity that we were addressing, I was comforted by a thought that our patent attorney, Dave Zinger, was the managing partner at a very reputable law firm and a most gifted lawyer with deep knowledge in the patent field. His descriptions of our inventive ideas in the specification and claims sections of the patent applications were exceptionally articulate. Working with lawyers like Dave Zinger taught me a valuable legal lesson: analyze the quality of crafted legal work first and the rates second. His work was instrumental in bringing Cellport's patent concepts to fruition.

In October 1993, I was finally ready to introduce Cellport and its Dynamic Digital Bus achievements to senior executives at several cellular phone companies in North America. I visited an old friend, Chuck Parrish, who was senior vice president of marketing and strategies at GTE Mobile Communications in Atlanta, a company that is now part of Verizon Communications. Parrish was a kinetically charged, brilliant visionary. I gave my old friend and his senior staff a presentation on Cellport's progress designing the Hello Direct Universal Hands-Free kit and our now patent-pending Dynamic Digital Bus architecture. A quintessential 30,000-foot visionary, Parrish displayed great interest in Cellport's decision to specialize in developing technologies to connect wireless and automotive electronic networks.

He enthusiastically approved of Cellport's open licensing model and liked the accomplishments we had made during our short history. As a visionary, he recognized the importance of our work to the wireless industry, especially if the automotive connectivity challenges could be radically improved. After the briefing, he asked if I could push back an afternoon meeting I had previously arranged with BellSouth so we could discuss an issue in private during lunch. I agreed, a gesture that recalled Hiro's last-minute meeting cancellations that day in Tokyo two years earlier when he urgently needed to discuss his first big idea. During lunch, Parrish informed me of a large technology initiative in the U.S. cellular industry called CDPD, or Cellular Digital Packet Data, that would make it much easier to use data applications on wireless phones and create an entirely new generation of phone capabilities for wireless users. CDPD was a brilliant architectural idea created by IBM researchers. Parrish was leading a new team at GTE that would launch a CDPD system across its vast cellular network.

Parrish said that a consortium of eight wireless carriers had committed to spend hundreds of million of dollars to add CDPD services to their then-analog cellular networks. The companies would first offer it commercially to large corporate customers, particularly companies that had vehicle fleet dispatching applications (such as United Parcel Service) and agencies that could use remote data services (such as law enforcement and public safety organizations.) Eventually, CDPD would be deployed to provide service to every consumer's portable handset.

He believed the CDPD carriers would understand the great benefits of adding Cellport's vehicle connectivity moxie to these wireless data products and would want to play up our technologies' capabilities in their advertisements promoting the value of adding wireless data to fleets of vehicles. CDPD packet data capabilities sounded great, but it was just being transitioned out of IBM's research labs and we needed to explore how to use it with our technologies. Fortunately, Parrish had already thought through that challenge. He said that if Cellport proposed a comprehensive study on how CDPD data services could be extended into vehicles, he was certain he could help get most, if not all, the CDPD carriers to sign up to fund the research. Along with a warm thank you, I shook my old friend's hand and committed to get a proposal to him within a month. Since Michael was tied up with the Hello Direct design project, I committed to Parrish that I would personally lead the planning and drafting of Cellport's proposal.

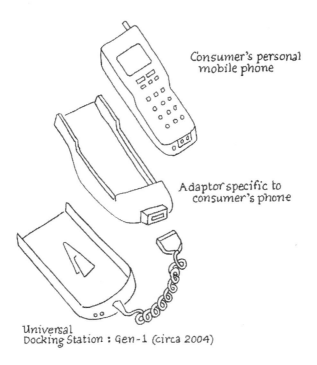

Consumer's personal mobile phone

Adaptor specific to consumer's phone

Universal Docking Station : Gen-1 (circa 2004)

Figure 4: Phone Adaptor Holder

The Phone Adaptor Holder is a plastic cradle, specific to a phone, that makes it possible for the phone to interface with one or more connectors and to hold the mobile phone in a car. It attaches to the hands-free docking station. The adaptor holder and the docking station incorporate Universal Port technologies, enabling consumers to use a variety of mobile devices with the hands-free docking station.

During my flight back to Colorado I was filled with a sense of euphoria, for in just under a year Cellport was winning complex design and technology study projects. But upon returning to the office, I learned that Michael was too busy with the Hello Direct project to give the

CDPD-to-vehicle study any serious time at all. Fortunately, Dick Chandler was available to orchestrate the study, but due to his consulting commitments he could only participate part-time. In 11 short months, I went from fear of failure to being overly booked: This was either great progress or bad planning.

It was time to add capacity to our small but popular company. Simply put, I was looking for a very bright person who understood complex network issues, who could look at our wireless-to-vehicle technical challenges with fresh eyes, and who was so highly creative that even gifted technical people would consider this individual an exceptional architectural analyst. It was a tall order, and fortunately our crème de la crème patent attorney, Dave Zinger, made a spot-on recommendation. Dave introduced us to Chuck Spaur, a 30-something communications design specialist who had a master's degree in computer science from Johns Hopkins University and several years of experience developing highly classified computer networks for U.S. intelligence agencies at the school's applied physics laboratory. Now in Boulder, he worked with the National Oceanic and Atmospheric Administration developing cutting edge satellite networking architectures. Chuck's networking skills were strong but he lacked expertise in vehicle systems that would be required for the CDPD project. Michael and Les Hatcher persuaded me that if I led the study of automotive design issues, gave Chuck responsibility for leading the networking research and had Dick Chandler oversee the work, we could develop the CDPD study nicely. I hired Chuck Spaur as a consultant for the project to advance our Dynamic Digital Bus invention.

By December 1993 we had a proposal for a study that would take 15 months to complete and cost several hundred thousand dollars. We sent it to Parrish, and he called back within a week, saying, "I will support your proposal and I'll recommend the other carriers participate.But you'll need to consummate a research funding agreement with each carrier separately."

Selling seven other carriers on the study certainly posed a challenge, but the opportunity to get this level of exposure and money was an effort worth pursuing. After tens of thousands of airplane seat miles and countless presentations to the individual companies, and with terrific support from Parrish, we signed on six cellular phone carriers — GTE Mobile Communications, McCaw Cellular, AirTouch Communications, Ameritech, Bell Mobility and Bell Atlantic — enough companies to support the start of Cellport's "CDPD-to-Vehicle Connectivity Project" [1].

Meanwhile, Michael and our product design consultants were making good progress on the Universal Hands-Free kit design project for Hello Direct. Unfortunately, it was becoming clear that Hello Direct needed to dedicate more resources to get the product ready for production and cellular carrier sales. They were too heavily dependent on both our technical and market expertise. We addressed the need for more financial resources with Allan Batts and he supported our request. However, he confessed that the launch of the Cellport product and the marketing campaign were two-times over what had been a straw-man budget. Yet there was no turning back now because Hello Direct's investment bankers were excited about the Cellport project. For an organization of only three full-time people, Cellport had a lot of balls in the air, a classic case of "when it rains it pours." Fortunately, along with our growing popularity came enough monies to start paying salaries and travel expenses. This was timely because we now needed to present our growing expertise in wireless connectivity at industry conferences.

By April 1994, Chuck, Dick, Les and I scheduled once-weekly meetings dedicated to the now-funded CDPD-to-Vehicle Connectivity Project. And twice a month I would travel to Detroit to participate in a nationwide research project established by automotive leaders who wanted to develop internal vehicle communications systems that would function like computer networks, using so-called Intelligent Transportation Systems Data Bus technology, or IDB. While attending the IDB Forum meetings in Detroit, I discovered an unfortunate cultural difference between our two industries. As a wireless technology pioneer, my nature was to always strive for the art-of-the-possible in technology discussions, yet the senior members of the automotive community who attended the meetings seemed to have a "not invented here" mindset that precluded consideration of approaches offered from outside of their industry. Now I understood why so many of my colleagues in the wireless community were happy to see Cellport take the lead role in working with the automotive community.

As we prepared to make an interim report to the CDPD research consortium, it became obvious to us that the wireless industry would eagerly accept our connectivity enhancement recommendations, but that the segment based in Detroit would pose a much more difficult challenge. We were very surprised and delighted to see many CDPD industry representatives show up at our interim report meeting in Boulder that August. We learned at this meeting that the CDPD community identified a target market of 13 million public safety and delivery vehicles and that they considered our vehicle connectivity research a key to tapping that sizable market. During this CDPD interim report meeting we committed to our funding sponsors that, as difficult as it was, we would work diligently to get greater cooperation from the vehicle community to develop wirelessly connected vehicle solutions.

In November 1994, Michael's Universal Hands-Free kit team completed its design. They were getting it ready for field testing and helping Hello Direct prepare to send the product to its Korean manufacturer to build some working prototype units. Our carrier customers and a few distributors tested the early hand-built prototype products, with very encouraging results; after a few small design changes, Michael and his team would be ready to hand the product over to Hello Direct's manufacturing contractor for an initial production run of 10,000 units. It was great timing for Hello Direct, which needed the additional revenue and product exposure to bolster the demand for its forthcoming IPO shares.

We looked forward to 1995, expecting a third straight year of good fortune for Cellport Labs. The Hello Direct product would begin broader sampling by January and the CDPD-to-Vehicle Connectivity Project was scheduled for completion in May. Just after the new year began, however, we started to see some of the downsides of working with an IPO-bound small company like Hello Direct. Their staff resources were still spread too thinly, which affected their ability to prepare adequately for the launch of our Universal Hands-Free kit, a product they branded "CellBase." They made a couple of fundamental mistakes. First, they sent the product to South Korea for manufacture without personnel to oversee production, and the CellBase products were inconsistent in quality. Secondly, because they were short staffed, they sent the first production units to McCaw Cellular and Iusacell in boxes that lacked proper installation instructions. They offered to provide technical support, but only over the phone. Hello Direct did well selling CellBase directly to consumers through its catalogue operation, but its early relationships with McCaw and Iusacell were in serious trouble.

Realizing we had a world-class debacle on our hands, that spring I committed to help Hello Direct patch up the badly bruised relationships with the carriers. It turned out that Hello Direct's catalogue mindset was not going to work with the service- and quality-intensive needs of these carriers, who expected Hello Direct to provide a level of support and hand-holding they would get from vendors in multi-million dollar phone supply agreements. Plus, the CellBase end-users needed help installing the aftermarket car kit docking station and antenna in their cars, which was a fairly complicated process. Hello Direct unfortunately, distracted by its IPO, had not planned adequately for the vital business relationships that a successful launch of this product required.

To further complicate these major challenges, in the 18 months since the purchase orders had been issued, McCaw had been sold to AT&T and Iusacell was being sold to Verizon Communications. The mergers added unforeseen variables to these relationships.

When a series of accidents happen concurrently, the chances of an escalation toward disaster increase exponentially. One solid lesson I had learned in my early business career was that an accident could often be repaired and corrected for the better, but a series of accidents can easily spiral out of control. Clearly, considering the carriers' changes of ownership and Hello Direct's early quality debacles and its "cataloguer's mindset," the carriers were not likely to purchase the volumes they signed up for initially.

In the pit of my stomach, I knew we had a major disaster on our hands and as the technology licensor, I felt strangely helpless. Allan Batts and his team worked hard to fix the situation, for they had invested several million dollars in the design, production and marketing efforts, but it was clear to me that they were not up to the task. A tenacious optimist, Allan reported to me that Hello Direct had recently received orders for several dozen units from German customers who had seen a quarter-page advertisement for CellBase in a Delta Airlines magazine. He thought perhaps his company should look to foreign markets for sales. The CellBase Universal Hands-Free kits would only work with phones sold in the Americas, however. I speculated that the German customers most likely had vacation homes in the U.S. and wanted the products to use while driving in the states. A small market of wealthy foreign visitors clearly would not justify the multimillion-dollar investment Hello Direct made in CellBase.

Thus 1995, which began with so much promise, was shaping up to be a year of challenges on many fronts. And as if the Hello Direct challenges weren't serious enough, our CDPD-to-Vehicle Connectivity Project was now in jeopardy. While Cellport's work on the project would soon be finished, the automotive community refused to cooperate and two carriers dropped their commitment to launch CDPD services on their wireless networks, deciding to wait instead for the next generation of cellular networks and phones that would use digital technologies and provide a more efficient way to send packet data over networks. Ongoing work with CDPD thus looked highly unlikely. Although I had developed a fair amount of agility in the technology industry to overcome substantial challenges, the prospect of two major crises hitting Cellport Labs at the same time made it feel like we were going into a death spiral.

By late spring, the now publicly owned Hello Direct was receiving too much pressure from bankers and shareholders to improve its quarterly results and it decided that maintaining the mis-launched CellBase product would not be good for its stock price. By mid-May, Allan Batts asked me to come to San Jose to help figure out how they could phase out the product and wind down its relationships with McCaw Cellular and Iusacell. This was a big failure for both our firms. To

Allan's credit, he took the high road and fulfilled all his existing customer and supplier commitments. Nevertheless, the CellBase product did not appear in the June edition of the Hello Direct catalogue. Fortunately, in our original agreement with Hello Direct, Les Hatcher had anticipated the possibility that Hello Direct might abandon the project, and in addition to the contractual terms giving Cellport ownership of any inventions that might come out of the partnership with Hello Direct, he worked in a provision ensuring all design and product rights would revert to Cellport as well. But without any way to distribute the products to the market, our organization was ill-prepared for this setback.

The CDPD initiative also unraveled when, in early June, we delivered our final presentations and recommendations on the CDPD-to-Vehicle Connectivity Project to the project sponsors. We received flattering comments on the quality of our research and report but the project had no future. Chuck Parrish aptly summarized the situation: "The key obstacles we are all facing today are political and economic," he said, referring to the automobile industry's opposition to the project and some cellular phone carriers' decisions to not pursue CDPD. [2] Cellport now had no revenues and its patent applications and other financial obligations, such as rent, would soon eat up its remaining cash.

**

As I've told many of my fellow entrepreneurs over the years, the one conversation scenario you want to avoid is the one that forces you to sit down with your family and tell them that your business failed and the dream is over. Without income or customer prospects, I privately prepared to break the news of Cellport Labs' failure to my family. This was a conversation that I clearly wanted to avoid, particularly because my children were having fabulous Little League baseball seasons and everyone was looking forward to a beach vacation in Southern California. And I could not imagine giving up working with such a great group of people who had made so much progress in such a short period of time. I went back to my business card files, looking for industry leaders who would understand the importance of Cellport's wireless connectivity solutions and perhaps help save the company. As I developed a list of prospective partners, I thought of Bob Johnson and his boss Steve Hooper, two of the McCaw Cellular visionaries who stayed on with the company after AT&T Wireless purchased McCaw. Both Bob and Steve had been the key drivers behind McCaw's purchase order for 25,000 Universal Hands-Free kit units and McCaw's decision to fund the CDPD-to-Vehicle Connectivity Project. Fortunately for Cellport, Steve had just been promoted from chief financial officer to president of AT&T's new wireless unit and he had kept abreast of Cellport's progress on both the CDPD study and the Hello Direct CellBase design. Bob suggested that I call Steve's office to request a meeting — I did, and was surprised and delighted when his assistant called back within an hour and said, "Steve has you on his calendar for two hours the first week of July."

Steve Hooper and I had plenty of common interests. Like me, he was very concerned about cellular safety and the lack of consumer-friendly hands-free solutions on the market. Plus, AT&T Wireless still planned to launch CDPD services on its network. I rallied Les and Michael to help write a proposal for a corporate equity investment by AT&T Wireless in Cellport Labs. Throughout the month of June, we rethought our business structure and objectives in favor of a win-win funding partnership. We were sure that Steve would look to Cellport to revive the Universal Hands-Free product launch, plus he would likely want us to build a product that would enable cell phones to connect to vehicles more effectively via CDPD. We crafted both objectives into a partnership funding proposal.

As we finalized the document preparation, we needed to decide on two critical numbers: How much money we would ask AT&T Wireless to invest and Cellport's valuation. We determined the investment amount primarily on the amount of capital we forecasted needing to launch the two products: $2.5 million. But the valuation amount was much trickier. Considering Steve's financial expertise we needed to take care not to appear too greedy by overvaluing the company or too naive by picking too low of a company valuation number. Traditional companies would be valued at 7 to 10 times earnings or a number equal to sales, but those valuation mechanisms would price Cellport at just north of zero.

We did have assets: two issued patents and two more pending. I decided to call Dave Zinger, our trusted friend and lead patent counsel, to seek his valuation recommendations. Dave tended to be conservative, so I prepared myself for a low valuation. To my surprise, he said that solid core patents in large markets like cellular could be worth tens of millions of dollars apiece. He said our research on behalf of the CDPD consortium had value as well. This was delightful news, although Dave warned me that such numbers are subject to many variables that could increase or, more likely, lower the amounts.

After sleeping on Dave's most helpful insights, I told Les and Michael that, given our close and lengthy friendship with the McCaw team, we should offer them a very fair valuation discount. Les Hatcher looked at me with an expression that read loud and clear: "OK, give me the bad news." I then said, "Given that we have two core patents and have forecasted needing $2.5 million, we should sell AT&T Wireless 20 percent of Cellport for a total valuation of $12.5 million." The room fell silent and after a few minutes Michael said, "Pat, you are the trophy rabbit hunter. Let's see if you can pull a rabbit out of a hat that size."

That afternoon we printed 10 copies of the investment memorandum that included the freshly set valuation figure, and sent six copies to Steve for his review in preparation for our meeting the following week at McCaw's headquarters. Every time I answered the phone that week I prayed it wasn't Steve Hooper's assistant informing me that Steve had decided to cancel our meeting because Cellport had crafted an unrealistic valuation. Luckily, Friday afternoon came and went without a meeting cancellation notice. The anxiety I suffered in that one week aged me at least a year.

I traveled to Steve Hooper's office outside of Seattle just after the Fourth of July holiday. While waiting for the meeting to start, I sat peacefully in his conference room overlooking a marina and beautiful Lake Washington, with Mount Rainier in the background. The breathtaking view put me in a high-energy mood to deliver my presentation in a meeting that would clearly determine the fate of Cellport Labs. Attending the meeting with Steve Hooper were vice president-level lawyers and technology executives. All the attendees had copies of our investment proposal and asked very good questions about our technology visions, strategies and the well-known challenges of trying to penetrate the automotive community. Much to my surprise, no one discussed our proposed valuation price, but they did want to know how we would spend the requested $2.5 million in funding.

At the end of our two-hour meeting, Steve stood up and said, "I like the proposal. Cellport's innovation and open licensing philosophy are important to the wireless industry. If there are any dissenters let me know by the end of the week." As we said goodbye, Steve and I shook hands firmly. For the next several hours I was overwhelmed with an adrenaline-fueled feeling of ecstasy. This was certainly one of the most exciting moments I've had as an entrepreneur.

That Friday afternoon I nervously called Steve's office to learn the outcome of AT&T Wireless' decision. Steve was out for the day, but his assistant gave me the great news that they planned to move forward with Cellport's proposal. Steve had requested that his CFO, John Thompson, and AT&T's lead transaction attorney, Andy Quartner, begin preparing investment documents with Cellport. Steve's assistant said she thought we should hear from them by early August. This was not only great news but also a great cultural fit, given that many of the AT&T Wireless executives had "cut their teeth" in the highly entrepreneurial and empowered environment that founder Craig McCaw fostered.

By early August, John Thompson contacted me to discuss an investment term sheet he was preparing and said that Andy Quartner would work with Les to finalize the legal documents for the transaction. Within a week, John faxed me a term sheet that chiseled our funding and valuation numbers down by a gentlemanly 20 percent. The document simply stated, "AT&T Wireless intends to invest $2 million to buy 20 percent of Cellport Labs and will attempt to close the prospective transaction within 30 days." Wow! AT&T Wireless' investment offer valued Cellport at $10 million!

During the next several weeks, I shifted into planning mode while Les worked with Andy Quartner to finalize the investment documentation. As Michael and I playfully modeled key research projects and hiring plans for the renewed and soon-to-be well-capitalized Cellport, Les was becoming grumpy under the stress of working with AT&T Wireless' Andy Quartner. Les assured me that AT&T's intention to invest in Cellport appeared assured, but Andy was a "lawyer's lawyer" when it came to deal details and structures and it was driving Les crazy.

It all worked out, however. After numerous document exchanges, on the third Friday of September 1995, Cellport Labs consummated a vital $2 million investment agreement with our new partners. AT&T Wireless requested in the agreement that we resume our CDPD-to-vehicle connectivity research and that we go even further and build a working prototype of a product that would make it possible for automobiles to connect to the new CDPD network and handsets. It also wanted us to pick up the Universal Hands-Free system that Hello Direct had abandoned. Cellport was back in business.

4 | The World's First Internet Car:

IdeaJacked!

1991
1992
1993
1994
1995
1996
1997
1998
1999
2000
2001
2002
2003
2004
2005
2006
2007
2008
2009

Within minutes of receiving the investment funds via wire transfer from AT&T Wireless into Cellport's bank account, I called Chuck Spaur and made him an offer to join Cellport as our lead network systems designer.

Chuck was ready to leave his comfortable government job designing satellite systems and excited to join our young, bleeding-edge technology firm. He had the right traits for Cellport: he was an out-of-the-box thinker and an "architect's architect", just our style. He also had an Iowa farm family history, which was even more important to us than his advanced degree in computer science from Johns Hopkins. During the years when Chuck was growing up and living at home, his father had routinely experimented to create new farm equipment designs and, along with Chuck's assistance, often took disparate pieces from a variety of farm implements to make completely unique and reconfigured tools. The farm invention experience was not on Chuck's resume but it was highly pertinent for his new role at Cellport. His first objective was straightforward: to design and build a working prototype of a CDPD wirelessly connected automobile for demonstration at the national cellular phone industry trade show in April 1996, just seven months away.

Not only would this demonstration prove our ability to meet AT&T Wireless' expectations, it would serve our belief at Cellport that work solving the arcane problems of connecting wireless devices to vehicle networks would yield core pioneering patent opportunities and, eventually, generate royalties that would become the foundation of a long-term business. This was, after all, our core charter.

Chuck joined Cellport officially in early October 1995 and hit the ground running. He reviewed the papers from our CDPD-to-Vehicle connectivity research project and the notes from the IDB Forum meetings I attended in Detroit and came to the conclusion that it would be impossible to persuade companies in the automotive community to either a) open up their proprietary network interfaces to create communications compatibilities between wireless systems and automobiles or b) cooperate with one another to achieve this. He had to find another approach. Given the scope of the challenge, Michael and I decided to give Chuck plenty of space and met with him only weekly to review his progress.

During the morning of November 1, Michael walked into my office and asked, "Do you have time to hear the mother of all big ideas? Chuck has knocked the cover off the ball." This was intellectual seduction at its finest. Of course I would make time! Within minutes our entire company, all five of us, gathered in the conference room to hear about Chuck's epiphany.

Chuck delivered to us an idea that not only changed Cellport's destiny but also the way in which the world would deal with the closed and disparate natures of automobile communications networks. Essentially, Chuck proposed that we abandon our previous strategy of trying to customize wireless devices and user applications to accommodate each type of vehicle and vehicle network that might adopt the technology. Instead, he proposed using the then-nascent language of the Internet, TCP/IP, to process wireless data communications as needed and to send all data and applications through an in-car electronic black box, or Web server. The server would then, working in conjunction with the Dynamic Digital Bus, convert the data or applications into vehicle-specific languages (see Fig. 5). Chuck's Vehicle Server was a hugely innovative idea and its use of the open Internet proto-cols gave it universal applicability. It also turned the automotive indus-try's paradigm of proprietary vehicle communications on its head and made the problem of customizing each system according to car type obsolete. It was a brilliant extension of our 1993 Dynamic Digital Bus invention and it helped our friends in the cellular CDPD community tremendously because they, too, decided to use the Internet's TCP/IP communication language to make application development easier (see p325 for a diagram of the MNT Portfolio).

Chuck's Vehicle Server idea was particularly well-timed. Earlier that year, in April of 1995, the U.S. Government had finally allowed com-mercial and consumer applications full and unrestricted access to the Internet, which until then had been limited to government and edu-cational researchers. And in August 1995, the web browser pioneer, Netscape Communications, launched its wildly successful IPO that, by displaying the tremendous groundswell of support for new and revolutionary commercial Internet innovations, launched the boom-ing Internet economy. Cellport's creation of a Vehicle Server, which made it possible to represent an automobile as a node on the Internet, occurred in these early days of Internet innovation.

We had all expected Chuck to be a great fit and contributor to Cell-port's vision of "open-connectivity," but hearing of such a major breakthrough so early in his tenure was sheer delight. After a lunch break, we decided to dedicate the afternoon to laying out a compre-hensive plan to guide the engineering design effort to produce the Vehicle Server technology, to establish procedures and a schedule for pursuing a patent application filing, and to build the prototype Vehicle Server into an automobile for the wireless trade show, now less than six months off.

**

One of my greatest enjoyments is to help assess the business and tech-nical challenges that occur during the inventive process and to then find ways to motivate and help my colleagues on a creative design team turn novel ideas into reality. It was pure pleasure to work with the all-star cast of Chuck, Michael and Les on this paradigm-shifting innovation and to build the Vehicle Server prototype for public demonstration. I learned long before: the kernel of a great innovative idea often comes from a highly creative individual like Chuck, but the framing of the opportunities and challenges — the framing which sets the stage for discovery — is often done by other members of the invention team. Approaching the project from distinctly diverse backgrounds, they are the ones that stimulate the breakthrough of the innovative idea. Cellport's Vehicle Server innovation was a stunning result of this dynamic process.

From this point on, as the primary developer on our Vehicle Server team, Chuck dedicated the bulk of his time to developing a prototype wireless-to-automobile network ecosystem that would enable the Vehicle Server to convert Internet-based applications to a car's proprietary network. Chuck also assisted Michael, whose primary role was to work with our patent attorney, Dave Zinger, to draft a patent application for the Vehicle Server, our fourth core technology architecture invention. Les and I signed up to find an appropriate demonstration automobile and to manage a contract integration engineering team we hired to help build what we now proudly called "the world's first Internet-connected vehicle." If we were to successfully produce this radically new and complex technology in less than six months while preparing a patent application and gearing up to market the Vehicle Server product, all the team members would work very long hours, especially Chuck.

Cellport was still flying under the radar of the mainstream cellular and automotive industries, but it would soon rattle the world with its new wireless connectivity innovation. As a licensing company in favor of open architectures, we typically allowed advanced product design engineers from automotive, software and wireless companies to visit us for briefing sessions on new technology advancements we were pioneering. But these times were very different.

It was imperative that we file the Vehicle Server patent, build the equipment prototypes and then write real software applications that we could use in an actual automobile to demonstrate the capabilities and performance of our technology before we disclosed our vision and technology to anyone.

Les searched for a suitable vehicle to use for the demonstration and selected a white Ford Bronco, in part because it was sizeable enough to accommodate a Vehicle Server and Dynamic Digital Bus, a GPS receiver, and other needed equipment.

Also, through crafty research, Michael was able to dig up scarce technical documentation that gave us enough information to establish limited communications with the Bronco's data bus, which was essential for the demonstration. We obtained a short-term lease for the Bronco in just enough time to complete, install and test the Vehicle Server system. We had to be 100 percent heads-down on the tasks at hand to avoid any and all distractions. This degree of focus, while certainly stressful, was vital if we were to meet our critical near-term objectives.

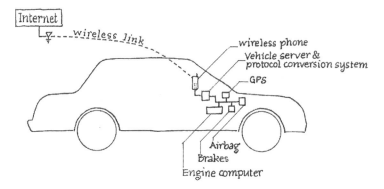

Figure 5: Vehicle Server

Cellport's vehicle server patent, referred to as "MobileWeb," made it possible to build the world's first Internet-connected automobile. In a typical usage scenario, Internet resources are used to transmit data via a wireless network to a wireless phone that is in turn connected to an Internet server installed in the vehicle. The vehicle-based web or Internet server converts the data into a vehicle-specific network language to communicate with the engine control unit, airbag, brake system, GPS receiver and other electronic car devices.

By February 1996, we filed the patent application and Chuck's 60-hour weeks were paying off. The world's first Internet Vehicle Server, which we affectionately called "MobileWeb," was encased in a black box crammed full of complex electronics, powered by an Intel 386 processor. The excitement at Cellport was completely high voltage. Chuck made a few technical refinements and then gave the MobileWeb black box to the Ford Bronco integration team and application developers, who were very anxious to install the prototype in the automobile. Much to the delight of the entire CDPD data phone community, Chuck succeeded in connecting one of the first CDPD mobile phones ever produced, a PCSI handset, to the MobileWeb black box, which in turn communicated to the vehicle's network.

At least once a day, I asked Chuck to show me a demonstration of the MobileWeb system and to explain in granular detail how the various components and complexities of our Vehicle Server technology worked. I desperately needed these drill-down tutorials as preparation for the various press releases and brochures and the launch of Cellport's Web site, which all had to be ready in time for the cellular industry trade show in April. I was also trying to understand as much as possible about the technology and the benefits of its applications so that I could explain it to lay audiences. It was not easy to articulate how an Internet-connected vehicle works or why it was important for society. In 1996, most people had heard of the Internet and the World Wide Web, but there were only about 100,000 Web sites in service [1] and society was still a long way from experiencing it. It would be a year before even one-fourth of U.S. adults had access to the Internet, and practically half of those would have access only while at work. [2] The market was not familiar enough with the Internet, Web or even mobile phones to readily understand the notion of an Internet-connected automobile.

By March 1996, our contractors built six MobileWeb server units, enough to allow both the application engineers and the vehicle integration team to finish their critical work. Chuck and Michael decided we should demonstrate three diverse applications at the trade show to illustrate the value of both the MobileWeb gear and connecting automobiles to the Internet. We decided to demonstrate that a computer running a Netscape Navigator Internet browser could send an application or information to the Internet, which in turn could route the information to the CDPD cellular data network, which could then transmit the Internet applications wirelessly to a CDPD phone for transmission to the MobileWeb server in the Ford Bronco. The MobileWeb server would then convert the Internet applications to the communication needs of the vehicle network system and other devices.

We used the system at the April show in Dallas to control several devices in the Ford Bronco. For example, we invited attendees to put their briefcases on a weight scale in the back of the vehicle; the weight of the briefcase would show up within seconds on the screen of a computer that was located some distance away inside our booth. We proved we could lock and unlock the doors of the Bronco remotely by sending a command from an Internet-connected personal computer to the Bronco's CDPD phone and then through the Vehicle Server technology and the vehicle's network to the door locks. We used a GPS application, in conjunction with some software simulations, to show the Bronco's location on a map.

The Ford Bronco — the centerpiece of Cellport's booth — created a sensation among attendees for the three hectic days of the trade show. The most common comments we heard included, "Now I've seen everything," and, "Why in the world would anyone want to communicate with their vehicle?"

The highlight of the show for me occurred when I asked Jim Barksdale, then president of Netscape Communications, to walk over to the Cellport booth with me to see how we had used Netscape's market-leading browser technology to demonstrate the world's first Internet-connected vehicle. After I gave Jim the demonstration, he looked at me and said, "You know, Pat, this Internet phenomenon has endless possibilities. Thanks for showing me another great one."

I was thrilled, as well, when AT&T Wireless' CFO, John Thompson, who became a Cellport Board member when AT&T invested in the company, told me that at an executive wrap-up session for industry leaders he attended, Cellport's Internet-connected vehicle was credited as being one of the wireless industry's best new innovations. This was a fabulous compliment to come so early in my relationship with John. Along with the pleasure I felt from hearing this, the recognition our technology received at the show gave John added confidence in Cellport's work, which would prove invaluable in the near future.

After all of the preparation leading up to the convention and then the successful debut of our Internet-connected car, the members of Cellport design team were totally exhausted and certainly needed a break. I told everyone they deserved time off and to take a three- day weekend to recuperate. During the drive to the Dallas airport after the show I had my first chance in three days to check my office voice mail. Much to my delight, I had more than 40 messages from people who saw our demonstration or read about us in the press. Many of the calls were from our early cellular industry CDPD supporters offering us congratulations. And nearly a dozen companies wanted to schedule visits to Boulder to learn more about our MobileWeb breakthrough. It looked like the best I could do was to take the weekend off. Given that just nine months earlier Cellport was on the verge of collapse, I had to keep our "deal heat" alive.

During the next few months we hosted many companies at Cellport. Most visitors came more for a tutorial on our newly launched MobileWeb technology than to give us near-term business. Two fellows from Daimler-Benz's Research and Technology Center in the U.S., who visited Cellport late that spring, became an important exception to this pattern. Dr. Axel Fuchs and his boss, Paul Mehring, had recently opened up the research center in Palo Alto, California, with the objective of finding U.S. technology partners that would benefit their parent company in Germany.

Axel and Paul were fairly recent newcomers to the U.S. and brought with them many European perspectives and terminology. We learned from them that European automotive companies were starting to give the convergence of wireless phones and automobile networks more research consideration. The industry had even developed a catchy name for this new phenomenon: telematiks. As they explained this term to us, "tele" stood for telecommunications and "matiks" stood for computing. They called Cellport's new technology "MobileWeb Internet Telematiks." The term, of course, is now well known, though businesses in the U.S. tend to use the spelling "telematics."

Axel and Paul were also the brightest and most sophisticated auto executives we had ever met, and they completely appreciated our MobileWeb solution. After a short demonstration and technical briefing, Axel said, "Great. I love this new telematics technology. Can we buy some MobileWeb units for our research department to play with?"

Sophisticated, well-funded and enthusiastic buyers were exactly the type of customers we hoped to meet. Better still, in the mid-1990s, Daimler-Benz was clearly a technology leader in the automotive industry. It was one of the first car makers to use electronics to optimize engine and transmission performance and to use vehicle bus technologies to control the functions of peripheral devices in a car. A potential relationship between Daimler-Benz and Cellport Labs would be a partnership made in heaven. As Axel and Paul prepared to leave that day, Paul asked, "Does Cellport need any additional investment money? Your business model of innovations and open licensing represents the kind of company Daimler-Benz is looking to invest in." I replied, "Thank you. But," I added, "at the present time we have plenty of funds, courtesy of our strategic supporters at AT&T Wireless."

Within a few weeks of that meeting, Les Hatcher and Axel Fuchs ironed out a purchase order for Daimler-Benz. They wanted four MobileWeb boxes and four of the Cellport Universal Hands-Free kits that we were just starting to resurrect — as well as a nine-month contract for Cellport's engineering teams to provide technology integration support to the Daimler-Benz staff in Palo Alto. Throughout 1996, Cellport sold a number of similar product and design support contracts to companies such as John Deere, which wanted to turn farm machinery into Internet-connected nodes for a host of agricultural applications, and the Union Body Truck Company, which sought to add Internet-based dispatching and logistical capabilities to its customized delivery vehicles [3]. It was a very busy period for our

MobileWeb development and design team.

Throughout these months, another segment of very fundamental work was taking place at Cellport, and that was a revival of the Hello Direct CellBase product for AT&T Wireless. As soon as we had signed the agreement with AT&T Wireless in the fall of 1995, I had begun searching for a counterpart to Chuck to lead the effort to commercialize our Universal Hands-Free technology. After months of searching, Michael introduced us to a young engineer by the name of Ralph Poplawsky, who was ideal for the job. His background was similar to and as eclectic as Chuck's. Ralph was trained in physics as well as electrical engineering, and he spent much of his free time modifying car designs.

Having worked closely with engineers for the past 20 years, I have come to the conclusion that there are fundamentally two types: those who are born engineers and those who become engineers during the course of their university studies. The people who are born engineers are those who, as young children, are frequently compelled by a strong, innate curiosity to dismantle their families' televisions, kitchen appliances or cars in order to see how the devices work, only to reassemble the products again. For the type of work we engaged in at Cellport, I found that natively skilled engineers are much more productive and compatible with my way of working than are university-made engineers.

Ralph was an engineer by nature and another gifted geek. He was just what we were looking for to help us develop new design architectures and products. He joined Cellport in late 1996 with a charter to find technical solutions, markets and sales opportunities for a Universal Hands-Free system. He proved to be a great complement to our other "born engineers": Michael, Dick Chandler and Chuck.

In many ways, Ralph's challenges were more complex than the MobileWeb team's because he inherited a product that was originally designed for Hello Direct's catalogue and carrier customers. Within months, after very careful product and market analysis, Ralph was already developing a strategy to re-create the Cellport Universal

Hands-Free kit product line. He was convinced that the optimal target market for the product was not the aftermarket segment of parts and accessory suppliers, but the automobile manufacturers themselves, who could provide a superior, less expensive and safer product by embedding the Cellport Universal Hands-Free technology in cars so that their customers could use their personal mobile phones in hands-free fashion. In the five years since Hiro, Michael and I had created the first Universal Hands-Free technology, the cellular market had changed so dramatically that by the end of 1996, the vast majority of cellular phone sales — about 85 percent of the U.S. market and 90 percent of foreign markets — came from mobile handsets, not in-car phones [4]. Due to the popularity of mobile handsets and the expense and inflexibility of existing device-specific hands-free car kits, more and more people were using handsets in their vehicles without hands-free capabilities.

The shift away from vehicle-installed phones to mobile phones by consumers was not lost on two industry-leading vehicle interior systems and components suppliers to the automotive industry: Lear Corporation and Prince Automotive. In 1996, after extensive discussions, we signed technology-use licenses with both companies to allow them to utilize Cellport's Universal Hands-Free products. We also signed technical support agreements with both companies to help their engineers integrate our Universal Hands-Free kit into vehicle interiors. The deals with Lear and Prince, both Michigan-based companies, represented our first tangible opportunities to help the automotive industry develop hands-free products that would be offered to consumers as standard production options in cars. Both programs were real eye-openers for tiny Cellport. The primary insight I gained from the experience was that these companies approached the market from a supplier perspective first and customer perspective second. This was quite different than the wireless industry's approach. Ralph's extensive exposure to these large automotive suppliers' technology requirements and to the business styles these large-scale companies had also helped the small and technology-oriented Cellport mature into a more learned organization.

**

The year 1996 was coming to a close, and while it had been an exciting and productive time, we had less than $500,000 in the bank and we knew that Ralph's Universal Hands-Free business would need significant new investments in the next year. The Cellport Board decided that it was important to raise another $2 million or more. Given Cellport's commitment to a long-term research and product development strategy rather than a strategy that would require a near-term return-on-investment for shareholders, we agreed that, as before, the best course was to find an investment source that avoided traditional venture capital funds. We already benefited immensely from the AT&T Wireless partnership, not only from our partner's financial support but also because our two companies had compatible innovation values and synergistic ambitions. AT&T Wireless could be patient and allow us time to focus on developing the best possible systems and physical designs that would benefit both our companies, consumers, and society at large.

AT&T Wireless' CFO and new Cellport Board member John Thompson had become a big fan of our progress since his company's investment just 14 months earlier. John was a tax lawyer by training and despite his substantial responsibilities and workload as the CFO for the multi-billion dollar AT&T Wireless, he had graciously given Cellport legal and financial guidance since becoming involved with our company. He proved, during Cellport's funding strategy discussions in 1996, to again have very practical and valuable advice.

John was one of dozens of young executives that Craig McCaw hired in the 1980s to help build McCaw Cellular into the largest independent wireless carrier in the U.S. When Craig McCaw sold McCaw Cellular to AT&T in 1994 for $11.5 billion, the executives who helped him build his company each earned millions of dollars from the sale of their generous stock option positions in the company. John suggested that since many of the former McCaw executives likely followed Cellport's appreciable progress and understood its technology and needs, that we should offer those individuals an opportunity to invest in the company's second investment series, in what was called an "angel" round. Within a few weeks we finished an investment memorandum and, with help from John and others, started offering and selling shares of Cellport Labs to angel investors. During the next several months we raised more than $2 million. Fortunately, we avoided a drama similar to Cellport's near-collapse in mid-1995.

**

With our treasury replenished, we were able to resume our existing Universal Hands-Free car kit business strategy. We took this work forward by building phone adaptors for several new handset models that Ericsson, Motorola, Nokia, and Panasonic introduced to the market. Concurrently, Chuck Spaur and I resumed work on an interesting "what-if" scenario we discussed occasionally during the past six months. The discussion began one day while we were driving to lunch. I said to Chuck, "If I am a police officer with both a CDPD cell phone and a traditional two-way radio system in my vehicle for communicating with headquarters, how would I decide which one to use for MobileWeb applications?" He said, "Good question, we should think about that."

After that day, we tried to figure out how someone in an automobile could use a variety of wireless connections in optimal fashion, depending on the needs and applications at hand. We had clearly framed a real problem that would emerge in the near future, but we lacked a clear technical solution. We did have a name for the solution, however: We called it "Link Select."

During a breakfast meeting with fellow Cellport founder Dale Hatfield, I introduced the link select issue and explained that we were stymied by it. Dale agreed that the concept would be important but even he, a nationally recognized cellular industry pioneer and technology expert, did not have a clue on how to solve the challenge. Dale suggested that I contact a fellow University of Colorado professor, Ken Klingenstein, for technical assistance. Shortly after, I contacted Ken and asked if he would consider helping Cellport, on a consulting basis, to help solve the link-select challenge.

Ken loved complex technical challenges and agreed to help us. He was a high-energy, can-do technology intellect who was well-regarded nationally as an Internet systems expert. In addition to his academic work, Ken served on a variety of national research commissions that developed and managed technical aspects of the bourgeoning Internet system. In our first meeting with Ken, Chuck described the Link Select "what-if" scenario and explained how we had struggled to find a solid technical resolution for it. Within minutes, Ken stood up and went to the white board. He explained that the next generation of the Internet would have a new addressing scheme, called IPv6, which would make it possible to assign an Internet address to every cellular phone or mobile device, even an Internet-connected car. If the device in the car simply possessed more than one Internet address, one for each possible network it might use, a consumer could simply choose which network to use. Additionally, the network or device could be programmed to automatically choose which network is best based on network traffic, cost, location, bandwidth or other parameters. With Ken Klingenstein's sage insight, we pursued a patent application for Link Select, filing it in January 1997 (see Fig. 6). We listed Ken as a fellow inventor.

We filed the Link Select patent just days before the 1997 International Consumer Electronics Show in Las Vegas. While attending the convention, I approached the trade show booth of the mighty Motorola.

Considering the booth's enormous size and its complex array of many types of products, I studied how best to vector into the booth crowd and try to establish a relationship with Motorola. Within a few minutes I noticed a senior executive in his mid-50s. He was not interacting with anyone at that moment, so I quickly approached him. I introduced myself and met Jim Caile, who was the corporate vice president of marketing for Motorola's cellular phone subscriber business. After giving a one-minute overview of Cellport's products, I asked Jim my most critical question: "How might I begin to develop relationships with Motorola's product development teams?" The company was a potentially ideal partner: Motorola started business in the 1930s as a car radio supplier, then evolved into a U.S. leader in consumer electronics, semiconductors, and other products, including cellular phones and network equipment. They supplied the automotive industry some of the earliest embedded mobile phone solutions.

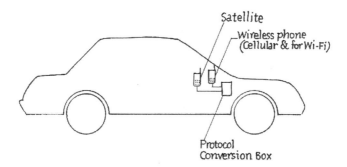

Figure 6: Link Select

We developed the Link Select invention to give consumers the ability to select from and use various types of wireless networks that connect to their mobile phones, for the purposes of transmitting data. Link Selection makes it possible for a consumer to choose which wireless network to use or for the device to automatically choose the best available network based on network conditions, connectivity costs, bandwidth availability or other parameters.

Jim laughed and said, "That is not an easy question to answer. We are so large and diverse that it often takes me too long to figure out the same question." When Jim noticed that I was from Boulder, he asked if I knew Dale Hatfield. I told him that Dale was a Cellport founder. Jim said, "Let me think about your question and I'll call you." As I excitedly walked away from my first-ever contact with a senior executive at Motorola, Jim called out to me, "Wait a minute, I'll be in Boulder in a few months for a conference. I'll make a note to call you for a follow-up meeting."

**

On April 29, 1997, while reading *The New York Times* during breakfast, I was startled to see an article on the front page of the business section titled, "Daimler-Benz to Exhibit an Early-Stage Internet Car" [5]. With great anticipation, I plunged into the lengthy story, eager to read about Cellport's core contributions and role in making this prestigious Internet car a reality. Halfway through the article my blood started to boil. I realized that Daimler-Benz took credit for our innovation. I kept asking myself, "How could our charming friends at Daimler-Benz Research completely disregard Cellport?" The article did give credit to other companies, such as AT&T Wireless, which provided the cellular phones; a well-known wireless data equipment vendor at the time, called Metricom, which provided another, proprietary wireless modem that could also be used with our system; and U.S. Robotics, which provided a Pilot handheld computer. Not a single word mentioned Cellport or its MobileWeb server that was at the heart of the Daimler-Benz Internet car system. Nor was there a mention of Cellport's Universal Hands-Free kit, which was featured prominently in the photo of the Mercedes-Benz vehicle in *The New York Times*. In shocking desperation, I reread the article again and became not only dejected but angry, as well, that two senior representatives from this company, whom we had helped so sincerely and intently over the past 11 months, had "IdeaJacked" my young company.

When I arrived at my office that morning, I called the offices of Axel Fuchs and Paul Mehring to demand an explanation for their failure to credit Cellport's role. Their assistant explained they would have to get back to me in a few days because they were traveling around the U.S. on a press tour, introducing Daimler-Benz's new Internet car technology to the media. The news that Daimler-Benz was flaunting their Internet car prototype — that was 100 percent enabled on Cellport's MobileWeb technology —without giving us any credit felt like a real stab in the back. If Cellport had received credit that it deserved for its contributions of not just one, but both core technologies used in this Internet car — technologies that we had spent millions of dollars developing — the company would have received huge, international media exposure. This level of media exposure has unimaginable value for a small company. Instead, Daimler-Benz claimed the first coup in the national media for delivering a futuristic Internet car.

The next week Daimler-Benz did return my call, but I received two slightly different stories explaining how and why Cellport Labs was not mentioned in favor of the three other companies, which each clearly made far lesser contributions to the Internet car's success. Paul Mehring, while polite and apologetic, said that Cellport was too small of a company to be of interest to the national media. I didn't buy this explanation. I thought it might be germane in Germany, where large industrial companies tend to draw prevailing media attention, but I knew the U.S. well enough to believe that the media appreciate and like to publish stories about small companies that have done noteworthy things.

While concluding my call with Paul Mehring, I learned that Axel Fuchs was on another line, also returning my call. Axel was younger and a super straight shooter. I suspected his story would be more accurate than Paul's. It turned out, however, that Paul's story was actually generally true. Axel said that in preparation for the press release and national media tour, Paul and the research staff in Palo Alto had briefed the New Jersey-based Daimler-Benz marketing crew on how they conceived of and built their Internet car. He said Cellport was at the center of the entire story. Axel's opinion, he said, was that the marketers in New Jersey decided to leave Cellport completely out of the entire press release because they wanted the story to focus on Daimler-Benz's cutting-edge research, and not on a small innovative tech company in Boulder, Colorado. Axel expressed his sincere apology. He assured me that both he and Paul felt badly, but he reiterated that mistakes like this happen in large and political companies.

Daimler-Benz continued to take credit for the accomplishment. In 2005, their new parent company, DaimlerChrysler, published an article in its technology magazine that claimed that the company had built the "first Internet-connected car, a Mercedes-Benz E-Class" sedan. Again, it failed to mention any of Cellport's contributions or Cellport's demonstrations that predated theirs by more than a year [6].

1991
1992
1993
1994
1995
1996
1997
1998
1999
2000
2001
2002
2003
2004
2005
2006
2007
2008
2009

Aside from the Daimler-Benz marketing debacle, Cellport had plenty of new business opportunities in the spring of 1997 and the future looked rosy. More and more companies were pursuing the new field of telematics, a field in which Cellport had invested millions of dollars and five years of struggle to pioneer and develop essential core system patents. Yet the Daimler-Benz incident became, in retrospect, the harbinger of an 18-month series of difficulties at Cellport.

Shortly after the eye-opening *New York Times* article appeared, Cellport exhibited at a wireless industry trade show in San Francisco, excitedly displaying an expanded line of Universal Hands-Free phone adaptors and MobileWeb products that now had the added functionality of new Link Select capabilities. As the trade show progressed, I developed an uneasy feeling that the Daimler-Benz setback was not our only problem. I learned that Chuck Parrish, Cellport's early supporter from GTE, had left that company to become cofounder of a hot new start-up in the cellular phone industry called Unwired Planet, which was trying to make Web applications work on the small screen of a cell phone [1]. I was not surprised that Chuck jumped out of his corporate role for a more entrepreneurial opportunity, but I feared that the loss of his leadership at GTE would certainly hurt a CDPD technology roll-out. To make matters worse, several technology-savvy wireless insiders confirmed to me at the show that some additional wireless carriers, beyond those that had dropped their interest in CDPD in 1995, might also abandon the technology and put their wireless Internet strategies on hold to await the next generation of cellular phone systems that would use more efficient digital technologies.

A collapse of the CDPD industry would have grave consequences on Cellport's ambitions for a rapid market rollout of its MobileWeb products. The potential situation could be likened to the circumstances a company like eBay would find itself in if, just as it was ready to commercialize its service, Internet service providers and consumer electronics companies decided to delay widespread availability of broadband networks and digital cameras.

While it was too early to panic, I thought of the countless stories I had heard over the years about the risks technology pioneers take to create new markets and break into new commercial territories, only to find that companies that come along later, entering the new market after it has been established, are better positioned financially to compete. Often, these later-arriving companies are capable of unseating the early market leader. One of my primary tasks at Cellport was to craft a strategy that would make sure we would become a surviving pioneer regardless of the number of arrows we might take along the way. As the CEO of an advanced technology development organization, I needed to keep one eye on the near term and my other eye scanning two to seven years into the future for market needs, opportunities, and risks — like CDPD's troubles.

Cellport's MobileWeb business development team certainly did not seem to share my concerns. The MobileWeb product attracted new levels of interest at the trade show, some from very large entities such as the U.S. military's advanced field research laboratories, Chrysler Motors' test organization, John Deere's new products team, several companies that had been members of the IDB Forum, such as Motorola, as well as dozens of smaller organizations. And at the show I learned one development, in particular, that I thought would accrue to MobileWeb's favor: a new Internet-centric wireless data technology — which would later become known as Wi-Fi — was expected to become an internationally recognized technology standard in the coming months. The new standard would make it possible to develop high-speed wireless local area networks that could provide Internet and data services for businesses and consumers, and because it was based on Internet technologies, it could be very inexpensive. While intended for use by stationary computers or wireless devices, I theorized that if appropriately networked, MobileWeb devices could be mounted in automobiles to provide Internet access in garages and installed in fleet vehicles for use within small geographic areas, such as maintenance garages, car rental lots or warehouses. Wi-Fi could open up new applications for Cellport's MobileWeb. We needed to consider how this new technology might complement our MobileWeb plans.

On the last day of the trade show, an Italian fellow came up to our booth and talked to Les Hatcher about our Universal Hands-Free products. I heard only a portion of their conversation because I was engaged in another discussion, but what I did hear triggered a hauntingly scary flashback to a conversation I had had with Allan Batts of Hello Direct two years earlier. I caught up with Les after the show to gather more details. I learned from Les that the fellow said he had seen a Universal Hands-Free product, offered by a German company, which was almost identical to ours. Les did not seem too concerned, but I was now convinced that some of the kits that Hello Direct reported selling to Germans in 1995 did not end up in their U.S. vacation homes but in a counterfeiter's design lab. We spent weeks searching the Web for any products like ours distributed by German firms, but to no avail. Les did his best to convince me that the Italian visitor probably did not understand the details of Cellport's Universal Hands-Free systems, but I did not buy his confidence.

On my flight home to Colorado, I reflected on the various unwelcome developments that occurred at the trade show. I perceived a few too many parallels to the string of unfortunate events we had encountered during the spring of 1995 and committed myself to find ways to avoid another series of accidents. While we currently had plenty of money in reserve, we needed to be cautious considering we now had a faster cash burn rate and a new threat of additional IdeaJackers. Instead of being completely open with our cutting edge technologies and open licensing business models, Cellport needed a more defensive plan.

During the flight I developed a list of high-priority strategic objectives that I, personally, needed to pursue to help shift the company toward a more protective posturing. My new objectives included the following:

A)   Find a bright and passionate business contract attorney to join Cellport as our in-house counsel. Believing that the telematics market would soon begin to mature, I expected more companies would encounter Cellport's patented technologies and I was in no mood to be out-lawyered. The right individual would draft more comprehensive and more defensively structured business and licensing contracts for Cellport.

B)   Diversify our market exposure to find customers outside the U.S. My experiences in Japan throughout the 1980s and early 1990s had taught me that seeing the world from an international perspective fosters important additional insight, creativity and new relationships. We needed to be more tuned-in to telematics markets, technology trends, and business practices in other parts of the world.

C)   If German companies had knocked-off our first generation Universal Hands-Free system patents, we should leapfrog them with a vastly improved second-generation design. I would begin working with Ralph immediately to find ways to accomplish this.

Of course, delivering on these new objectives would be easier said than done. As Hiro and I discussed over the years, when striving to achieve the art-of-the-possible — or in this case, the desirable — it is advantageous to view oneself as a dynamic hub-like structure that moves around in space and time within a stratified business networking environment, linking to other hubs of synergistic value that, in turn, lead to new associations and new opportunities. A hub can be an individual or an organization. Relationships provide the linkages between hubs.

As I looked at my list of three new objectives, I noted the relationships (linkages) that could help us find needed resources (hubs) to help further enhance Cellport's business prospects and competitive position. Cellport, with its two core technologies, founders, investors and Board of Directors, provided several hubs. Hiro in Japan was a separate hub. The relationships formed by these hubs extended Cellport's reach out to additional hubs that included, for example, Cellport's suppliers, research sponsors, Dale Hatfield's telecommunications consulting firm, and automotive companies. [2]

Thus to find a talented lawyer to hire as our in-house counsel, I would contact Cellport Board members, investors and dozens of associates for a list of recommendations. To expand our perspectives outside the U.S., I would reach out again to Board members and investors as well as vendors that had international operations. Finally, to start a new generation of our Universal Hands-Free car kit design, I would reach out to employees, particularly Ralph, as well as to founders. Cautiously, I would also approach trusted vendors for their respective insights.

The following Monday, as I began work in my office toward pursuing these new objectives, I received an email from David Holmes, a senior engineer at AT&T Wireless and an old friend and supporter of Cellport. David said that the Cellular Telecommunications Industry Association (CTIA) was growing very concerned about criticism of the safety risks from cellular phone use in vehicles, the reported increase in the number of accidents caused by drivers using cell phones, and intensifying media focus on these issues. Therefore, the association wanted to form a standards committee to create a specification for a Universal Hands-Free solution for automobiles. CTIA asked David to lead the standards effort. Given that Cellport had the only known universal solutions and that AT&T Wireless supported Cellport's work in this field, David said he would propose the industry adopt use of Cellport's Universal Hands-Free technology for this new standard.

The standards committee was set to meet once a month and AT&T Wireless requested that I assign an engineer to represent Cellport's technology and business interests on the committee. I confessed to David that I knew very little about standards processes, but that I would have Michael Braitberg and Ralph Poplawsky attend on our behalf as he requested.

Over the course of the next several months, Michael and Ralph attended the CTIA Universal Hands-Free standards meetings. After only the second meeting, Michael reported with great enthusiasm that all the technology discussions and product examples cited at the meeting had centered on Cellport's pioneering work and that committee membership was already growing as word of its charter began to spread throughout the industry. Because we obviously favored the notion that businesses worldwide might adopt Cellport's patented Universal Hands-Free technology, and because our open licensing model was completely compatible with the standards committee's objectives, I decided, for my own edification, to attend the next meeting with Michael. In contrast to the first few meetings that were almost exclusively attended by wireless carriers and phone manufacturers, this meeting included new participants from the automotive manufacturing and supply industries. As the meeting progressed, I recognized several old faces from the automotive community. I whispered to Michael, "This is a déjà vu of the IDB Forum meetings I attended in Detroit back in 1994 and 1995." My optimism started sinking fast. Sure enough, Michael said the meeting was the least productive since the committee had begun its work.

**

Meanwhile, my proactive networking endeavors to diversify Cellport's business and build exposure in international markets began to bear fruit. Hiro Sakurai came through in classic fashion with an interesting opportunity in Japan. One of Hiro's business colleagues was a newly appointed business development manager at Nissho Iwai Corporation, a multibillion-dollar Japanese trading company. Nissho Iwai wanted to diversify its business to add telecommunications technology development to its strategic investment portfolio and was interested in studying a potential collaboration with Cellport. To move these discussions forward, Hiro asked if Michael and I could visit Tokyo to attend an exploratory meeting with Nissho Iwai's development staff. For the first time in several years, I traveled to Japan to visit with my old friend and partner, Hiro, and to participate in green tea discussions with the fellows at Nissho Iwai.

Japan's leading trading companies are famous for shrewd commodity and merchandise deal-making as well as logistics management, and each of the major trading companies in the country facilitates the sale of tens of billions of dollars a year in global material goods. Much to my delight, Nissho Iwai's telecommunications staff appeared to possess the savvy of the firm's traders and a solid knowledge of the wireless telecommunications market. During a series of meetings over a three-day period, we briefed them on Cellport's technologies and discussed the market needs that interested them. At the end of our session, we struggled to develop a particular opportunity, but they seemed fond of us and offered Cellport a contract to support them in a study on how they could launch our Universal Hands-Free technology in Japan. At the conclusion of our meeting, we agreed to participate. Hiro would negotiate the terms and closing of a relationship agreement.

**

Back in the states, Michael and Ralph attended the next CTIA Universal Hands-Free standards committee meeting. As I had feared, they reported that with the automotive community's increasing influence on the committee, the group's work toward adopting any standard had grown rancorous, and particularly so for any standard involving patents. During the next several meetings, the discussions began focusing on creating a new design that would shift the envisioned hands-free system's connectivity technology away from the fast-moving wireless industry's technologies and toward the less-than-nimble but cohesive automotive community's perspective. The standards meetings became more like the confrontational IDB Forum sessions. The wireless participants' attendance dropped off and the attendees from the automotive community took control of the agenda. The automotive contingency promised David Holmes that they would draft a specification that would meet the criteria for a universal wireless interface and bring it to the next meeting. I bet Michael a beer that they would not deliver on their commitment. My skepticism came from my experience attending the IDB meetings in Detroit circa 1994, plus my understanding that other than the air pressure valves on tires, gas input orifices and trailer hitch connectors, the U.S. automotive community has consistently failed to agree on any other standards.

Around this time, I was thrilled to receive a call from Motorola's Jim Caile, who asked to set up an appointment to visit Cellport following a conference he was planning to attend in Boulder. Jim allocated two hours for our green tea session. It was extremely important to me that I make a superb first impression with this Motorola corporate vice president. Small companies like Cellport rarely receive attention from executives in any of Motorola's business sectors. To now have two hours of face time with one of their top executives in the cellular sector was huge. To keep the meeting from getting too technical, I decided to focus our first meeting on Cellport's products, innovations and business licensing model and to ask Jim a lot of questions about Motorola's telematics strategy and possible interest in working with Cellport. Les helped me prepare for the meeting by arranging for all the PowerPoint presentation materials, drinks and snacks. We were out of pretzels and peanuts, the typical snack in the office, so I decided to run out to a local store for something special. I decided on a can of fancy cashews. Little did I know that Jim had skipped lunch to accommodate the meeting schedule and that he had a weakness for cashews!

Jim was very interested in Cellport's telematics connectivity approach and provided several helpful insights into Motorola's existing telematics efforts and emerging trends in cellular phone design. Jim explained that Motorola's telematics business was structured to sell embedded analog phones to automakers, but that this effort clearly needed to be given more attention. Within five years, he believed, very few traditional cellular sales outlets would carry embedded mobile phone technologies for automobiles. This was particularly interesting to me because I was beginning to consider the art-of-the-possible for our next-generation Universal Hands-Free architecture. Jim also believed that soon, better industrial design approaches and manufacturing techniques would make it possible to produce radically smaller and more power-efficient cellular handsets, but that the expected introduction of new features — such as color screens, back-lit displays, vibration alerts, sophisticated user-interfaces, and the ability of a phone to operate on more than one cellular network — would continue to compromise battery life. This issue played right into our hands-free solution, namely because our solution automatically charged a phone's battery. Plus, just as Mori-san said at NTT in Tokyo six years earlier, Jim said he believed that handset designs were evolving too fast to standardize on one or more connectors. The conversation led me to wonder, "How many other sages are there at Motorola?"

I had no doubt that Motorola could be a powerful business partner, and as Jim astutely pointed out, Motorola's competency in both wireless and automotive electronics gave them a big advantage over other companies that might crave a piece of the bourgeoning telematics market. Jim made it clear that establishing a relationship with Motorola would take a great deal of persistence, but he promised that the company had a history of respecting its partners' intellectual property.

The meeting went by quickly. As it was drawing to a close, Jim said he would follow-up by sending me the contact details for several Motorola colleagues whom, he expected, would have an interest in our Universal Hands-Free design. He believed it was strategically important for both of our companies that Cellport spend time developing relationships with his colleagues. Two days later, I received a FedEx package from Jim's office containing the names and contact information for three Motorola employees along with descriptions of their job titles and roles. The package included a one-pound bag of gourmet cashews. Jim Caile's attention to detail was nothing but impressive.

✸✸

In classically short order, Hiro finalized contract negotiations between Nissho Iwai and Cellport for a collaborative research study to evaluate the potential market for our Universal Hands-Free system in Japan. During the next several months we conducted numerous meetings with Japanese wireless carriers, phone manufacturers and automotive producers, who were all eager to help us understand their market needs. We learned through this research that Cellport's current first-generation Universal Hands-Free car kit design was physically too large to gain appeal in the highly miniaturized Japanese consumer electronics market and that the electronic components did not perform with the speed or agility needed to run applications that were expected to become popular in the Japanese market. Ultimately, the brief market research assessment was inconclusive and, at first blush, somewhat disappointing for both parties. However, the Japanese tend to be very gracious as opportunities cool off and, as I was learning, they have a cultural propensity to take a long-term view of relationships. At almost all costs they try to avoid burning bridges. Thus the Nissho Iwai executives said they were confident the cellular phone market would move in the direction of Cellport's hands-free and Internet technologies and they wanted to develop a long-term relationship with us. They asked to participate as an investor through a new venture arm in the company, which we welcomed. Another primary benefit from the study was that we were able to share our new insights with Ralph, who was developing a list of potential improvements for our next-generation product.

**

During the course of the next few months I asked Michael to keep us updated on CTIA's efforts to adopt a Universal Hands-Free system standard. Ultimately, the committee's contingent from the automotive industry failed to bring forth a design alternative for committee review, as it had promised. Michael surmised that either the Michigan automotive participants themselves could not come to a consensus or, if they had favored a design, found it would cross one or more of Cellport's three patents for a Universal Hands-Free system, in which case — acknowledging the automotive community's aversion to paying royalties — they likely did not submit the design. Later, substantiating this conjecture, several of the automotive industry's members told me privately that they believed Cellport's hands-free system was the most future-proof of the available approaches but that their first ambition was to design around any method that would incur patent fees. By this time the committee lost many of its participants. Without a design alternative, AT&T-Wireless' David Holmes resigned as chairman and the standards committee dissolved shortly thereafter [3].

The Cellport team was greatly disappointed in the standards process, for not only had the company invested money and executive-level participation in the effort, but we had delayed work on a next-generation design until the committee settled on a direction for the industry. The main lesson I gained from the experience was that beyond my opportunity to collect a beer from Michael, it was now fully obvious that the cultural differences between the wireless and automotive communities were as wide as the Grand Canyon. While the wireless industry, motivated by the promise of royalty fees, thrives on innovation, the U.S. automotive community, avoiding royalties like the plague, delays the introduction of new innovations for its customers.

**

In the fall of 1997, I was invited to speak at an investment banking conference in New York City featuring young companies that were developing unique technologies for the bourgeoning Internet. Cellport's MobileWeb telematics solution was well recognized as a category leader in Internet applications — it seemed like I was speaking every other month at these types of conferences. John Thompson had been most helpful introducing me to prospective in-house counsel candidates for Cellport and, knowing that I was speaking in the city, suggested that I meet with Gary Friedman, a founder of a medium-sized New York corporate law firm, and most importantly, one of Cellport's angel investors.

Gary graciously scheduled an hour-long briefing to learn about Cellport's progress. During our meeting I expressed to Gary my growing concerns that as more and larger companies entered the telematics business, we would experience additional IdeaJackers like Mercedes-Benz. I owed it to our shareholders to not let potential customers like Motorola, Nokia and Microsoft, which seemed headed for the distinct areas we pioneered in the telematics market, to out-lawyer us. As a fellow investor and experienced business attorney, Gary fully understood my concerns and said he would discuss a few ideas with John Thompson and call me in a week or two. The very next week, Gary called me and said that both he and John thought that I should meet with Andy Quartner of AT&T Wireless about the in-house counsel position. Gary noted that Andy had invested in our angel round and was planning to leave AT&T Wireless at year-end. Gary thought Andy might be interested in helping Cellport. If Andy was indeed a possibility for the in-house counsel position, this could be the turn in fortunes I was looking for in Cellport's organization. Not only was Andy already an investor, but also, as we knew from his tough and unforgiving work with Les Hatcher during the contracting process with AT&T Wireless, he was exactly the kind of attorney Cellport needed on our side.

The next day I called Andy at his office in Washington D.C. to introduce myself as well as Cellport's needs for in-house counsel. After a brief discussion, Andy confirmed that he was indeed leaving AT&T Wireless and was interested in learning more about the Cellport opportunity. I told him that in December I would be going to the East Coast, where I was scheduled to make yet another presentation at an investment banking conference, and that I would try to schedule a lunch with him during that trip.

I immediately called John Thompson and gave him the good news. I asked him dozens of questions about Andy and his background because, even though Andy had been an investor in Cellport, I never met him personally. John said that Andy had joined McCaw Cellular in the mid-1980s and that he had been instrumental in negotiating and structuring billions of dollars in financing packages and acquisitions while McCaw, leading the industry's consolidation in the U.S., was buying wireless carriers of all sizes. Andy had also been a key player when negotiating and structuring the $11.5 billion sale of McCaw Cellular to AT&T in 1994. John also shared insight on Andy's relationship with his boss at McCaw, Wayne Perry. John said that Andy and Wayne had developed a close business and personal relationship over the years and that Andy had enjoyed reporting to Perry, who was McCaw's cerebral and influential vice-chairman. As the conversation continued, it became clear to me that Andy was bright, honest and negotiated hard for his side, all traits I was looking for. Plus he knew the wireless industry well. As soon as we finished our conversation, I adjusted my December East Coast trip itinerary so that I could make a stop in Washington, D.C. to meet Andy Quartner and recruit him to be our desperately needed in-house lawyer.

Andy Quartner asked me to meet him at a restaurant near his office, usually a nice neutral venue for an introductory meeting. Andy didn't seem either ferocious or overly lawyerly. In fact, he seemed most interested in our technology and the applications it enabled. Further, he seemed rather geeky, just the type of colleague I like to have. If this was his tactic to win me over, it sure was working. During our two-hour lunch we spent little time discussing legal issues and the vast majority of our visit talking about technology, markets and the big-picture opportunities as well as challenges facing Cellport. Throughout the lunch Andy spoke fondly of his mentor and former boss at McCaw Cellular, Wayne Perry. There was little doubt that Andy was leaving AT&T Wireless because he missed the frontline action that Wayne and the McCaw entrepreneurial environment had provided prior to the company's sale to AT&T. The longer we talked, the more Cellport's challenges and opportunities intrigued him and the more I became convinced that Andy was the right person and that he would have a passionate commitment to Cellport's legal as well as the fundraising work. We agreed to talk later that week to see if there was a way to work together.

As I drove away from the lunch I started to reflect on the depth and breadth of the resources Andy would bring to Cellport. I was comforted that not once during our meeting did he flaunt his undergraduate schooling at Yale, nor his graduation from Columbia University Law School. He seemed very self-actualized and confident, which were important ingredients for good team play. It was obvious Andy was interested in learning more about joining Cellport. Now I needed to offer Andy a role and compensation package that would get him to say, "Yes, I'll join the team."

I learned long ago that independent of recognizing a person's career success or capabilities, understanding and addressing their personal ambitions helps tremendously when building meaningful new relationships. I talked to John Thompson for advice on how best to secure Andy's interest in Cellport. John helped me understand that Andy was looking to broaden his role from one that was strictly finance and contracts to one that offered more holistic business influence, especially in strategic planning. During the discussion I asked John if he thought offering Andy a general counsel position as well as a vice chairmanship role would help him realize how serious I was about getting him on the team. When John heard of my plan he laughed and said, "That would pull Andy even, at least title-wise, with his good friend and mentor Wayne Perry. That's an excellent strategy."

I secured support from the other Cellport founders for offering Andy an aggressive stock-option package, a semi-meager salary and a significant leadership role in the company and was then ready to make him an offer. During eight months of searching, I met plenty of lawyer candidates, but none was as ideal as Andy Quartner. Now I just needed to land him.

In preparation for the call to Andy, I decided to leave the vice chairmanship offer until last, figuring I could make him an attractive offer to move him toward the close of the negotiation and then I would sweeten the deal with an "Oh, by-the-way, we'd also like you to sit on our Board as vice chairman" suggestion. As storybook scripts go, Andy seemed open and excited, hearing me describe both legal and fund-raising opportunities at Cellport. He seemed satisfied with our generous offer of stock options and I sensed that he was excited about the terms. When I gave him the "Oh, by-the-way" line, he said, "You've got a deal, I'll draft our agreement tonight and you can study it in the morning." His agreement to become our vice chairman and general counsel marked a significant day in the history of Cellport, much like the day in 1995 when Chuck Spaur joined the company.

Andy joined our small team in January 1998 and within weeks Cellport began to reap the benefits of having an experienced lawyer who was well connected with the dozen of McCaw alumni investors. Although Andy continued to live in the Washington D.C. area, he traveled to Boulder often and frequently went on the road with us to visit customers. Andy's presence in strategy sessions brought new perspective on licensing and financing goals. Plus, having a lawyer present at customer meetings tended to accelerate contract discussions.

In the business planning arena, Ralph and I proposed that we phase out our first-generation Universal Hands-Free kit and work on a radically improved design that would anticipate changing handset trends and add the capability to transmit data and host a new family of software applications. We also committed to build our MobileWeb design staff to enhance Cellport's abilities to serve its growing list of highly demanding customers. As the team member who had the freshest eyes on the business, Andy suggested taking a more formal approach to our MobileWeb customer agreements, which he would lead, and to bring in additional funds from his McCaw brethren, whose support would give us critically needed additional time to architect the second-generation Universal Hands-Free design.

During the first half of 1998, with Andy's and John Thompson's help, Cellport secured supplementary funding from some additional McCaw alumni, which gave us time to draft a formal business plan and funding document and to hire an investment banker to lead our next funding round, in which we proposed seeking $5 million.

**

During this time, our MobileWeb sales team was led by Tom Kubancik, a creative market maker who joined the company as director of sales development in the spring of 1997. Tom was another one of those lucky personnel finds for Cellport. He came to the company directly from a role he held as sales manager for the Rocky Mountain region for Netscape. Because of his work at Netscape, Tom understood better than most how ubiquitous the Internet would grow to be. He fully expected that someday, Internet-connected vehicles would become an essential market and a huge opportunity for companies selling Internet technologies. He had a passionate belief in Cellport's work and, serendipitously, happened to live in Boulder within a short bike ride of our office. He thought the coincidence was uncanny and that joining Cellport was meant to be.

Tom quickly made extraordinary progress in some very exciting collaborative projects with companies from the automotive industry that began showing renewed interest in using wireless devices to deliver

Internet applications to a vehicle's networks via the IDB technology. The projects, sponsored by an IDB Forum committee, brought together representatives from companies like Cellport, Motorola, Chrysler Motors, Ford Motor Company, General Motors, and others to contribute technologies and expertise to build several concept cars that could connect to the Internet. Several of the automotive companies donated brand new cars for the demonstrations, including a GM Cadillac, which we modified to deliver MobileWeb applications.

One of the benefits of this project was that it gave Cellport a very worthwhile opportunity to work side-by-side with experts in the automotive side of Motorola's telematics business, which also contributed vehicle network interface components to the Internet-connected cars. I had begun a relationship with the telematics team at Motorola in December 1997, thanks to Jim Caile, who had informed me that Motorola wanted to expand its telematics business in response to the market's increasing interest in the technology. By 1997, Motorola, previously the worldwide leader in mobile phone sales, had lost its position to Finland's aggressive competitor, Nokia. To say that Motorola was both in turmoil and a bad mood from this situation was an understatement. Loaded with billions of dollars in cash, Motorola was desperately anxious to regain its former luster. It decided to invest aggressively in growth markets and the promising new telematics segment was one of those.

The IDB demonstration project also gave us an opportunity to work closely with with General Motors, which donated the Cadillac for the IDB and MobileWeb showcase. GM's help had very practical value in building the demonstration telematics platform and the company also gave us the technical details we needed to enable the MobileWeb to communicate with the vehicle bus. Our work with GM was a wonderful opportunity for Cellport to show off a physical representation of its intellectual property and talk publicly about it. The project kept the kinetically charged Tom Kubancik busy managing this work and promoting Cellport's role at venues such as the Detroit Auto Show, the International Consumer Electronics Show and other events from 1998 through late 1999.

Cellport made fundamental advancements in its Universal Hands-Free design by the summer of 1998, when Ralph and I finished a high-level architectural design for the next-generation Universal Hands-Free systems. First and foremost, I wanted this new design to have a powerful digital signal processor in the docking station to resolve two issues we had in the first-generation system: background noise from the vehicle and the need to be able to support voice-activated dialing. Secondarily, I wanted the next-generation hands-free system to take advantage of smaller and more consumer-like mechanical designs. With the concept formulated, we could now begin formulating a plan for creating our next-generation's innovations and designs.

**

That summer Cellport's internal identity changed a bit when it encountered the departure of one of its founders, as Les Hatcher announced his desire to retire by year end and move back to his home state of Texas. Though he had always been a stalwart executive and advocate for Cellport, Les felt it would take the automotive industry another decade to get around to allowing wireless technologies to connect to vehicles. The loss of Les was a reminder that our company was now five years old yet it was years away from the type of success we had all hoped to accomplish in just a few short years after founding Cellport. It was sobering for me to realize that developing technology architectures, securing the resulting patents and finding markets for all our pioneering work required more patience and money then any of us had anticipated.

6 | Deal Heat

1991
1992
1993
1994
1995
1996
1997
1998
1999
2000
2001
2002
2003
2004
2005
2006
2007
2008
2009

Fortuitously, on one October morning in 1998, I received a call from a Frenchman by the name of Bernard Joseph. I had never met Bernard, but he certainly knew a lot about Cellport and me. He said that Cellport was well known among European telematics companies and well regarded for its pioneering inventions in the field.

Bernard invited me to speak at the InCarTech telematics conference in Paris that December. Bernard was organizing the conference and round table discussions and selecting speakers and his familiarity with Cellport's technologies was flattering and persuasive. After a half-hour discussion, I agreed to accept two speaking positions at the conference, one to deliver a presentation about Cellport's MobileWeb technology and the other to participate in a panel discussion of future technologies, including technologies that make it possible to use cell phones safely in vehicles. Clearly, this type of international exposure was exactly what we needed, but considering that Cellport did not have enough money to design our envisioned second-generation system and hardly had enough to send me to Paris, we could not afford for this publicity investment to fail. By deciding to go, I was taking an intuitive gamble — as I had done so many times during the past five years — based on my deeply rooted belief in Cellport's technologies and its charter to pursue wireless connectivity designs for automobiles. I realized that if our current equity fund raising efforts to raise $5 million were not successful, my trip costs would become not a business expense but a burden on my family's bank account instead.

We had plenty of innovative telematics technologies to present in Paris but decided to focus on just two: our Vehicle Server technology and MobileWeb, and the concept of our newly architected Universal Hands-Free system. We were sure we'd create a sensation among the technology enthusiasts at the Paris conference, but the company-betting question was: Would the exposure pay off financially? (see p323 and p325 for diagrams of the HCS and MNT Portfolios.)

The first hint that Bernard's invitation might yield something magical for Cellport came when we realized that Gaston Bastiaens, the president of a Belgium-based company called Lernout and Hauspie (L&H) — a global leader in the speech-recognition technology industry — would appear on the very same panel I was scheduled to address at the Paris conference. Gaston had also recently shown an interest in our investment documents. Could this be the lucky break we needed? Perhaps, but we needed to tailor my presentation precisely to address Gaston's particular concerns and needs. After extensive research on L&H, we learned that their speech-recognition technology was an ideal application for our new hands-free concept, which would have a powerful computer processor that could run their speech-recognition software. We also learned that they were seeking to build their technology into high-volume consumer products. Our design was perfect for them. Our two companies were a perfect match, at least in theory. We tailored my presentation so that the strategically valuable synergies between our two companies would be obvious to Gaston as well.

As I drove to the Denver International Airport on a cold and snowy December Sunday morning for my flight to Paris, Andy called to inform me that if we didn't secure funding by month's end, our accountants would most likely declare Cellport insolvent and we'd have to sell the patent portfolio at auction, which typically means selling cheaply. This was one of those quintessential calls with Andy, who tended to counterbalance any entrepreneurial optimism I might offer with cold, only-the-facts, lawyerly logic.

After hanging up with Andy, I realized my stomach was tied in knots and I was clenching my jaw for fear of losing my business and, even worse, having to say those dreaded words to my family: that I had failed in the pursuit of my dream and that money would be scarce for a long time. I boarded a nearly empty plane to Paris on this gloomy and bitterly cold day. It was a long, sobering flight, despite the free jug wine the flight attendants offered to those of us flying in coach. How could Cellport be so underappreciated? Did Les know something I needed to better understand — that it was time to move on? Perhaps all our hard work developing and patenting pioneering designs that were sure to change the world for the better was based on an illusion! But in my heart, I knew Cellport deserved to survive so we could continue to design innovative products for society and, eventually, share the success of a big payday with our investors. After the long and depressing flight I finally landed in Paris, which was at least 15 degrees warmer than Colorado, although it was even more overcast and wet.

The next morning, after a delicious warm croissant and a few cups of strong European-style coffee, I was ready to meet Bernard Joseph at the Palais des Congrès, the venue for the InCarTech conference. Within minutes of meeting Bernard, I felt that he was the real McCoy, Parisian style. Obviously a well-educated and successful businessman, he was disarmingly down to earth and seemed very sincere. Bernard briefed me, along with several other speakers, on the rules of presentation at the conference and helped us prepare for the events of the next two days. I thanked Bernard for placing me on the same panel as Gaston Bastiaens and told him I intended to pursue a funding relationship with L&H. In the Parisian version of a New York minute, Bernard turned to his assistant, said something to her in rapid-fire French regarding Messieurs Kennedy and Bastiaens, and away she went. Unfortunately, my French vocabulary in those days was less then 25 words, which included the numbers one through ten. I was unable to interpret Bernard's business-savvy instructions to his assistant and the jet-lag fog I was in didn't help my cognitive abilities. As it turned out, Bernard had instructed his assistant to rearrange the panel so that I would be seated next to Gaston and so my presentation would follow immediately after his. If Bernard had been an American and I had understood his astute and strategically clever instructions that morning, I would have wanted to give him a high-five.

I felt wonderfully upbeat that day in Paris, considering that I was the CEO of a nearly insolvent company. I met with dozens of European technology and car industry executives, which was most enlightening. They all seemed to know much more about Cellport than I knew about their companies. A great feeling of optimism swept over me, allowing me to forget the fear of auctioning off our beloved inventions and designs. Looking for an opportunity to salvage my business in this city of beautifully designed edifices, avenues and well-dressed people was just what my spirits needed.

That afternoon, just prior to the panel discussion, the conference management staff told me that the hall assigned to our panel was overflowing with attendees and that I had only 10 minutes to take a seat at the panel table. As I approached the table of six presenters I saw my name plaque and, adjacent to it, the name plaque for Gaston Bastiaens. Bernard had come through with magnificent attention to detail; this seating arrangement was a deal-seeker's dream come true! During his presentation, Gaston summarized L&H's growing capabilities in speech-recognition software and he said that incorporating this technology into the cellular phone automotive hands-free product market was one of his company's top strategic goals. Gaston's message was the equivalent of a perfectly pitched ball across home plate to me. Taking the podium, I then told the audience about Cellport's newly architected Universal Hands-Free system, making a special effort to explain that its powerful new computer processor was ideally suited to run speech-recognition software and that the combined use of the two products could help enhance safe cell phone usage in automobiles.

As I sat down following my presentation, Gaston leaned over to me in cinematic fashion and said, "Please come to see me in Belgium. I have the funding you need to launch Cellport's brilliant design." While trying my best not to do cartwheels on stage, and while maintaining the type of poker face one needs when holding only a pair of deuces, I looked him in the eyes and said, "That sounds great. I'll be up to see you in Belgium on Thursday." Gaston shook my hand. He promised that his staff would assist me with travel logistics and give me a warm welcome.

Our panel's question-and-answer session ran over the allocated time by 20 minutes due to the European audience's strong interest in cellular hands-free solutions. Road safety concerns appeared to be very important to European drivers and pedestrians, especially in the northern countries. In fact, I learned that several European countries had adopted laws mandating hands-free use of cellular phones in automobiles and that more countries were expected to join this trend soon. Already, many automotive producers were responding with plans to offer hands-free systems with their automobiles. Clearly, from a regulatory perspective, Europe was more ideally suited to appreciate Cellport's Universal Hands-Free product than the U.S. was. I also heard from an audience member that a German automaker was planning to offer a Universal Hands-Free system for its customers. I couldn't get any specific details about this, but I made a note to myself that this might be an interesting opportunity to pursue once we closed our next round of funding. Fortunately, the majority of the audience's questions for our panel were directed at me; this had to help reinforce Gaston's confidence in our second-generation Universal Hands-Free system and its value for potential investment.

During the balance of the day, I learned that the InCarTech conference, which was heavily subsidized by the French government, was as much a technology transfer fair as it was an exhibition for telematics businesses and technology leaders. The French government had a clever motivation for the conference: They wanted to establish leadership in the young telematics market, seek ways to bring new research and technology ideas that have promising commercial value into the country, and encourage businesses, especially U.S. companies, to relocate to France. As chairman of a Paris-based software development firm and a graduate of École Polytechnique, France's equivalent of MIT, Bernard Joseph was ideally suited to help the French recruit foreign business executives like Gaston and me to the country. During much of the balance of that afternoon and dinner as well, I heard sales pitches from nearly a dozen economic development officers, representing various regions of France, who all attempted to convince me that Cellport should establish research and production facilities in their respective regions. These meetings barely left me enough time to call our investment banker, Mark Connell. I instructed Mark to send, via an overnight delivery service, a half-dozen copies of our investment prospectus to Gaston's office in Ieper, Belgium. I would need these for my meeting with Gaston's staff in just two days.

The next day at the InCarTech conference, I gave my presentation on Cellport's revolutionary Internet-connected Vehicle Server technology and our MobileWeb product. Both were highly popular with the attendees, especially the French technology intellectuals. As much as I loved promoting our MobileWeb product to the enthusiastic crowd, I was preoccupied thinking about my upcoming funding meeting with L&H and how I should best craft a pitch to L&H for funding to support development of our new Universal Hands-Free design. I did my best to avoid the regional economic development officials during the second day, but they were well-trained, professional promoters and several more succeeded in getting a bit of my time. If any of these well-intended regional development people had offered me funding for my cash-starved business, I would have agreed to open an operation in France right then and there.

During my final day at the conference, Gaston's assistant called me numerous times to work out the logistics of my trip and she also requested that I stay in Ieper. The meetings would take place on both Thursday and Friday. I began to feel a rush of adrenaline as well as confidence that I might soon be able to close our third and desperately needed funding round.

On Thursday morning I boarded the high-speed TGV train at Paris' main train station, Gare du Nord, for a two-hour ride to the Lille station on the France-Belgium border. As the TGV train sped through the manicured countryside of northern France, I intently studied a copy of the Cellport investment prospectus that Gaston's office should have received that morning. As soon as I stepped off the train at the small station in Lille, I heard a young man's voice call out, "Monsieur Kennedy, I'm the driver hired by L&H. Please let me help you with your bags." We then motored off in his new Mercedes van toward

Ieper, Belgium, world headquarters of L&H speech technologies. During our 90-minute drive through the beautiful farmland and storybook villages of Belgium, my driver, like a well-educated docent, briefed me on Belgium's history — especially of the town of Ieper. I learned that Ieper was the epicenter of some the longest and bloodiest battles of World War I. More than a million lives were lost in and around this small town during the war.

The driver also briefed me on the history of L&H. He said that the company founders, Jo Lernout and Pol Hauspie, were as famous as rock stars, having brought both employment and U.S.-style technology-driven wealth to the Flanders region of Belgium. My driver said that the unemployment rate in the area prior to L&H's recent growth was more than 12 percent. While helping alleviate unemployment, L&H helped solve the even bigger problem of stagnant living standards. Since L&H had gone public two years earlier, salaries skyrocketed and the people of the Flanders region were feeling much more optimistic, especially for their youth.

As we arrived at my destination, the Regina Hotel in Ieper, the driver told me that all transportation expenses during my stay would be picked up by L&H and that right after lunch he would drive me to meet my hosts at FLV. "FLV? I'm sorry," I said, "There must be a misunderstanding. I'm here to meet with Gaston Bastiaens' staff for a technology collaboration and investment matter." My driver smiled and told me not to worry. FLV was the money arm of L&H. I was scheduled to spend the afternoon as well as all day Friday at their facility.

My lunch in the hotel dining room was completely unproductive: Fear of failure had set in once again. This was no time for me to make a mistake by spending three precious days and expenses, which I could ill afford, in who-knows-where Belgium, especially while my business was facing insolvency back home. The adrenaline high that I had thoroughly enjoyed for the past three days had vaporized. Was it the air in Paris? I went into a mantra that I chant to myself in times of crisis: "It's rally time, Pat. Don't lose the ball. Score the goal."

Promptly at 1:50 p.m., my driver picked me up for the 10-minute drive to the L&H campus just outside of Ieper. Strangely, as we approached the main building of L&H he made a sharp left and parked in front of a nondescript old house. Posted on the door was a contemporary sign that read, "The FLV Fund."

The interior of this building was quite the opposite of the ordinary exterior. It looked like it was just recently remodeled by a Scandinavian designer who had little concern for budget. My driver walked me into a well-lit and beautifully furnished conference room, instructing me to help myself to a coffee and telling me that the investment managers from FLV would join me shortly. I poured a cup of freshly made coffee and sat there waiting for an audience. Fifteen minutes later, like a well-practiced army unit, five smiling men in suits walked into the conference room and introduced themselves in English, though they all had Flemish accents.

As we sat down, each of the FLV representatives pulled out the copies of the Cellport investment memorandum that Mark Connell had sent to Gaston's office. Maybe the paranoia I had just suffered through during lunch was for naught. There was no doubt that these FLV bankers had a very real tie to L&H. During our introductory discussions that afternoon, I learned that FLV stood for Flanders Language Valley — a play on America's famous technology region, the Silicon Valley area south of San Francisco — and that it was the former investment arm of L&H prior to being spun out in a public offering. The FLV Fund was now an independent and publicly traded venture investment firm that concentrated its investments in the area of speech technology applications.

For the next four hours the fellows from FLV asked questions about Cellport's history, technology and future plans as well as how we might use L&H speech software in our next-generation Universal Hands-Free design. The only oddity of the meeting was that the majority of the FLV "investment managers" appeared to have engineering backgrounds. They were much more interested in our technology and product roadmap than most venture investors, who are primarily concerned with their valuation expectations and establishing exit strategies. Frankly, they acted like the type of strategic investor we had found with AT&T Wireless back in 1995: one that would have the patience to support us while we pursued important core inventions. After the afternoon session we all agreed to resume our business discussions at 9:00 a.m. Friday. Then two of the meeting leaders, Philip Vermeulen and Philippe Vercruyssen, invited me to join them for dinner in the historic town of Ieper.

Over dinner that evening we talked about the histories of Cellport, L&H and the FLV Fund. Philip and Philippe were very curious about Cellport's entrepreneurial culture. What was it about Cellport, they wanted to know, that enabled such a small company to continue to lead the world's telematics architectural innovations? How was Cellport able to extrapolate, from current technology and business trends, inventions that would be valuable in the future? I gave my standard answer to this question: We motivate bright people from disparate backgrounds to work with us and we encourage all of the principal inventor team members to discuss "the-art-of-the-possible" in a positive and collaborative environment.

Philip and Philippe shared with me colorful stories about L&H's founders, Jo Lernout and Pol Hauspie. While receiving government grants to fund promising technology businesses to locate in the Flanders region of Belgium, the two men started L&H by raising money first from local farmers, and then from wealthy Flemish carpet and beverage industrialists. They went on to describe Jo Lernout as a marketing wizard and Pol Hauspie as a financial magician who planned to turn Flanders into a speech-technology hub. I learned that — symbolic of their cleverness — during the early 1990s Lernout and Hauspie placed advertisements in a San Jose, California newspaper seeking business plans to fund. It was one of those plans that prompted them to choose the promising though labor-intensive field of speech recognition software for their core business. Compliments of a California entrepreneur's plan, L&H launched into this business. It was able to grow quickly by acquiring other small firms, further aided by millions of dollars in capital that it received in a 1996 public offering in the U.S.

At 7:00 a.m. on Friday morning I received a call from Gerry Calabrese, L&H's vice president of sales, inviting me for breakfast in a
half hour. During our breakfast meeting, I learned that Gerry was an
American and an accomplished veteran of the U.S. consumer electronics industry and that, like Gaston, he was excited about Cellport's
potential use of L&H's speech-recognition technology. Gerry assured
me that if our companies could strike a licensing deal, he would help
us generate exposure in the media and that L&H would feature Cellport's Universal Hands-Free products at trade shows. This, I thought,
was fine marketing pep talk, but there would be no such opportunities unless I made real progress with the fellows from FLV Fund that
day. After breakfast we shook hands and I told Gerry that as soon as
Cellport closed its funding round, I'd contact him.

At 8:50 a.m. my driver picked me up and while en route to the FLV
Fund for the day's meetings, I received a call from Gaston's assistant,
who asked me for my airline and flight number for my trip from Brussels to the states on Saturday. After I gave her the information, I asked
if Gaston wanted to meet with me. She responded unequivocally.
"No. Gaston has already given your company a green light," she said.
"Please continue working with FLV and Gerry Calabrese."

During what turned out to be an intense, all-day session of due- diligence discussions, the FLV team asked many and more-detailed
questions about Cellport's patents, design architectures, target markets, personnel and hiring plans. They seemed to have a solid understanding of the technical and engineering issues, but several of their
team members had worked in the investment banking field in the past
and asked very precise questions about our business financials and
strategic plans as well. In the mid-afternoon they let slip their perspective that the Cellport investment plan was an excellent opportunity
for them. I used the opening to brief them on Cellport's most critical
issue: We needed to close a $5 million investment by year end. The
room quickly fell silent and after a few minutes of an intra-FLV conversation in Flemish, they asked me to leave the room so they could
make a phone call. Near the end of what appeared to be a half-hour
break, I received a call on my cell phone, this time from Gerry Calabrese's assistant, who asked me for the number of my flight back to

the states on Saturday so she could confirm it with United Airlines for me. One thing appeared certain: The Belgians were very hospitable and caring people.

The FLV staff invited me back into the conference room shortly thereafter. Philip Vermeulen, the CEO of FLV, informed me that there were several challenges associated with concluding a $5 million equity investment by year end. However, he said they were enthusiastic about Cellport and believed that if we all worked hard a solution should be possible. FLV's biggest challenge, he said, was that they had already committed their fund's entire investment allocation for the fourth quarter of 1998, but he said they would raise the Cellport issue with their Board of Directors for a potential waiver. We spent the balance of the afternoon discussing the many due-diligence tasks that they needed to accomplish to meet a year-end funding goal. That evening as we all shook hands and said goodbye to one another, I was completely impressed with the FLV team's dedication and seriousness in making an investment in Cellport.

Before dinner I went back to my hotel to call Andy Quartner, along with our investment bankers Mark Connell and John Palmer to report on the promising progress with FLV and I reviewed with each of them the long list of due-diligence assignments we needed to complete. Fortunately, Andy had completed dozens of deals that were much bigger in monetary terms and in very short time frames as well, and he assured me that if all parties have "deal heat" motivation, the funding could be closed by month's end, now less than 20 days away.

That evening I had dinner alone in a local restaurant and then went to the bar to sample a few of the local Belgian beers, where I struck up a conversation with several locals. All claimed to know Jo Lernout and Pol Hauspie personally and they portrayed both men as heroes. As one man said, "They are destined to become the Bill Gates and Paul Allen of Belgium." During the walk back to my hotel that evening I remember feeling most fortunate that I had found an opportunity to pursue a business partnership with such well-regarded technology mavericks.

In reliable fashion, my driver arrived at my hotel at 8:00 a.m. the next morning for a two-hour journey to the Brussels airport. In contrast to the day I left the U.S. for Europe earlier that week, this travel day was warm and sunny, much like my attitude, which had rebounded from this productive week in France and Belgium. The plane was nearly half empty, which makes flying in coach more comfortable, especially for long flights. Shortly after lunch I heard a familiar voice say, "Do you mind if I join you for a while?" Much to my delight it was Gerry Calabrese from L&H. He was seated in business class but wanted to sit by me for a bit so we could catch up on my time in Ieper with FLV.

I happily gave Gerry an overview of the progress our two companies made and I also told him how impressed I was with the astuteness of the FLV staff. Gerry then said to me, "Let me tell you how it all can work out. You make sure Cellport issues L&H a purchase order for a $1 million pre-paid speech software license by month's end, which will help me make my quarterly sales goals, and I'll make sure you get your $5 million investment." It was the second cinematic moment of the week. Before I could utter a response, Gerry stood up from his seat and said, "Have a nice flight and a merry Christmas."

It was the last time I saw Gerry during the flight. Now I understood why the executive assistants at L&H had been so interested in my air travel details during my stay in Ieper!

Upon arriving back home, I called Andy and told him he had a new and unique challenge. The opportunity to close the funding by month's end came with a quid pro quo. As our general counsel it was Andy's job to keep Cellport's end of the deal clean. Andy asked me only one question: Would Cellport use L&H speech software in our new product even if L&H were not going to fund us? "Yes," I answered, "if we are still in business."

Andy assured me that as long as we're sincere about planning to use L&H speech software, a legal deal structure could be developed to enable all parties to meet their objectives. During the next two weeks, nearly everyone at Cellport helped out in the work to meet FLV's due-diligence questions that focused, primarily, on our distributors, market demand, employees, patent ownership and numerous product design issues. Again we had to assign a valuation to Cellport, which we calculated at $38 million. Andy and I also had many meetings with L&H's staff from its Boston office to negotiate the terms and conditions of a license for Cellport to use L&H speech software in our new Universal Hands-Free system design.

The week after Christmas we had addressed all of the due-diligence questions to the satisfaction of the FLV investment team and both companies had completed the terms of the L&H speech software license for Cellport. On December 29, 1998 we received the very welcome news that the FLV Board had approved an investment for $5 million in Cellport. Yet the commitment came with a potentially devastating condition that could unwind the entire funding transaction: FLV still did not want the investment to close until 1999. Yet, on that same day, L&H pushed us to sign a purchase order for a $1 million license. We told them we couldn't sign the purchase order without the investment. We were stuck, and the stress of non-stop phone discussions that day tested everyone's diplomatic skills.

At 6:00 a.m. on December 30 our investment banker, Mark Connell, called me at home with what appeared to be a most creative solution, one that would meet the needs of all parties, at least in theory. Since FLV couldn't fund Cellport until January 1999, and since both L&H and Cellport needed their respective deals closed in 1998, Mark proposed a time-zone arbitrage. He suggested that FLV sign the investment-closing documents at 12:01 a.m., January 1, 1999, Belgium time, which would meet the FLV Board's mandate. FLV would then fax this funding commitment document to Cellport in Colorado, where it would be 4:01 p.m. Mountain Standard Time on December 31, 1998.

Then, immediately after receiving the signed FLV funding contract, Cellport would fax the purchase order and licensing agreement to use L&H's speech software to L&H's office in Boston, where it would be just after 6:00 p.m., Eastern Standard Time on December 31, enabling Gerry Calabrese and L&H to meet their fourth-quarter sales objectives.

After discussing the triangular time arbitrage scenario with Andy, I called Mark and told him, "It works for us, so now you must sell it to the FLV team." Within a few hours he called back to say the Belgians were on board with the signing plan. We just had to make sure that Cellport's fax machine was in good working order!

A few minutes after 4:00 p.m. on December 31, I was in my office looking at the fax machine when it began printing a contract with Philip Vermeulen's signature and the date of January 1, 1999, to close a $5 million investment in Cellport. Wearing an ear-to-ear grin, I in turn signed a license contract for $1 million in favor of L&H, dated December 31, 1998, and faxed it to L&H's Boston office. Mark's time arbitrage theory had worked beautifully. As I drove home that evening I called Andy at his home in Maryland, asking him to conference in Mark and John at their respective homes in New York. I congratulated everyone for completing the mission and wished them all a happy and successful new year. That evening I hosted a New Year's Eve party at my home, wearing that $5 million smile on my face the entire time. I basked in the festivities until I fell asleep on January 1, 1999, Colorado time.

As 1999 got underway, auditors reviewed Cellport's financial statements and found it to be a sound company, giving it a thumbs-up to continue operations. With the FLV investment funds in hand at Cellport, we would not have to auction our patents and we began designing our second-generation system that would use L&H's speech-recognition software to produce what we believed would be the safest hands-free product in the world. Soon into the New Year FLV's Philippe Vercruyssen moved to the U.S. He joined the Cellport Board and became a most helpful supporter.

Unfortunately, a year later, in mid-2000, the wheels came off L&H. The firm, at its zenith, had a $9 billion market value. Yet on August 8, 2000, an article in *The Wall Street Journal* reported highly suspicious accounting between L&H and a variety of affiliated companies in Asia, with a particular focus on L&H's operations in Korea [1]. Fourteen months after that article appeared, in what was one of the first Internet-bubble implosions, L&H filed for bankruptcy. L&H's founders Jo Lernout and Pol Hauspie, as well as their president, Gaston Bastiaens, were all charged with perpetrating corporate fraud. As a result of the L&H bankruptcy, thousands of people lost their jobs and investors lost billions of dollars. The collateral damage was extensive, negatively affecting the voice-recognition business for years.

After the L&H implosion, I learned that Jo Lernout and Pol Hauspie never did fund that California entrepreneur's business plan for a speech-recognition company in the early 1990s. They IdeaJacked the plan for themselves.

What a difference $5 million makes. For our small crew of 12 employees, the comfort of knowing that the investment money was successfully wired from FLV to Cellport's bank account catalyzed a shift in our collective mindset from "want-to-do" to "let's make it happen!" Cellport had the vision for a second-generation Universal Hands-Free design, funding and plans to hire enough engineers to develop our idea into an actual commercial product.

In reality, we had less than $4 million left in the bank because we had paid Gerry Calabrese's company, L&H, $1 million to license its speech-technology software. Plus we paid our investment bankers a hundred thousand dollars in deal closure commissions. Nevertheless, our bank account balance was $3.9 million, a record amount for our company.

The energy in the Cellport office on the first Monday in 1999 was effervescent. To help keep our employees grounded I espoused the importance of understanding the difference between dreams and visions. I made sure to recognize the importance of the free-flowing and abstract nature of dreams and the wonderful impetus such thoughts can have on one's insights and ambitions. But it takes a refined vision, project plans, as well as proper execution to convert a dream into reality. We would use the cash from FLV to convert our dreams into visions, with tangible schedules and delivery dates, which we would need to meet to fulfill our dreams. I am most productive myself when I follow this type of process. Essentially, that is what I had done just 18 months earlier while flying home from the spring 1997 trade show after realizing Cellport's business was threatened. My anxiety during that time sparked visions of the strategic changes we needed at Cellport, and I had since put these changes in place, which helped bring us to this more secure and comfortable time.

During the next several months, Ralph and I interviewed nearly 100 candidates to fill more than a dozen openings we had for engineers. Finding candidates in Boulder, Colorado who had the combination of talent and work ethic we required was always challenging, even before the hot employment market created by the Internet and telecom bubble depleted the field of available candidates and made top engineering talent hard to come by. Boulder is a university town blessed with a picturesque environment, wonderfully sunny days, hundreds of miles of scenic trails and an endless amount of outdoor activities. The idyllic environment is a magnet for people — even highly talented professionals — who place a higher value on lifestyle than career.

Through the tedious process of reference checking we did manage to find many gifted and hardworking people to augment our talent base and we brought in several consulting engineering firms to take on non-critical aspects of our design work as well. Ralph needed all the help he could get, for he was working 60-hour weeks and had less than 18 months to introduce the first of our second-generation Universal Hands-Free products to the market. And on top of all the mechanical, electrical and software design work required for the new system, we still needed to nail down some specific and challenging details of the architecture, especially if we expected to file worthy patent applications.

Just a few months earlier our high-level architecture work was convincing enough to give FLV the confidence that the second-generation system would be a hit and worthy of an investment. But as all experienced product developers and patent holders know, the devil really is in the details. We needed to add at least 20 more people to the company during the next six months to fulfill all of our engineering and business commitments. We had positions available across the company, though the vast majority of the openings were for engineers.

I had learned two key lessons in hiring over the years. First, gifted and highly productive people tend to cost more money than those who are not so fortunate. Yet the most talented people often contribute two to five times more, from both productivity and value-added standpoints, which often easily justifies their salaries. As we recruited to fill new staff openings, I insisted that we work hard to find those gifted and motivated individuals who would help Cellport maintain its unparalleled leadership in the design of cutting-edge telematics products.

The second key hiring lesson I had learned was that although the kernel of an epiphany that leads to a great invention may come from one person, the stimulation that leads to that "ah-ha" moment often comes out of a group dynamic, where a team of diverse individuals, through spirited discussions and a challenging atmosphere of give-and-take, create the thought processes that trigger the invention. Yet discerning if a person is really a good team player may be the greatest hiring challenge of all. All five of Cellport's issued patents and many of our pending patents at this time had been developed by contributors who were motivated by the founders' success, team spirit and stock in the company, and as we grew it was critical to keep our prolific invention machine stoked. Certainly we planned to offer stock options to important new hires, but these new employees would have to contribute in a way that would continue the wonderful alchemy that had led to so many significant innovations over the previous eight years. This was clearly a new challenge.

One way I've helped make the seriousness of the company's work and commitments more palatable to new employees is to promise everyone the opportunity to participate in a personally empowering environment and the freedom to contribute without overzealous or nagging supervision. In fact, I am always excited to make this promise to key hires, for truly gifted people and those who want to make something happen on their own generally desire and need this type of work environment. A workplace that is not sensitive to this — or a too-bureaucratic work environment — would stifle their creativity. Thus while Ralph and I had created the high-level architectural designs for the second-generation Universal Hands-Free product, the architecture would serve as merely a guidepost for our new engineers who would then turn it into highly detailed engineering designs, patent applications and products.

We made many good hiring decisions during this critical period in early 1999: Doug Daniels as vice president of marketing; Kathy Delianides and Mike Durian as lead engineers; and two more vice president-level talents, Paul Heller in business development and Steve Parrish in finance. It proved to be a great crop of new hires and all of these individuals made exceptional contributions to our later success.

Cellport experienced an uptick in marketing talent when we hired Doug Daniels. I expected much from Doug, for I knew him well; I had hired him fresh out of college in 1990 at my old company, Cellular Solutions, where he quickly bubbled-up in the ranks with star capabilities. When we sold Cellular Solutions in 1992, I helped Doug get a job at McCaw Cellular where he became a successful salesman. He outperformed his peers in creating new sales campaigns and he broke through sales goals one quarter after another. Doug was also gifted with an ability to come up with keen marketing insights that he could quickly transform into ideas for creative technology applications.

Doug studiously reviewed all the customer comments from our first-generation product, Michael's and Ralph's experiences from the CTIA hands-free standards committee meetings and the market research we conducted in Japan with Nissho Iwai. He and I also spent a lot of time together discussing product and market goals, and we both agreed that mobile phone power and performance capabilities were likely to at least triple in the next five years. For example, computing chips had already become much more powerful and cheaper by 1999 compared to the components that were available when we built our first-generation design in 1994. I insisted that our second-generation system use these newer and better components as a way to make the design scalable; that is, the design needed to be able to add improved computing power, applications that would likely find their way into mobile handsets and even technologies we might develop ourselves at Cellport. The design had to be both versatile and "future-proof."

The mantra Doug continually repeated in our weekly engineering design review meetings was that the product design must be smaller, easy to use and agile enough, technically, to accommodate new and as yet unknown mobile phone and telematics applications that were sure still to be discovered. While his insistence on these design goals ultimately became a most helpful source of pressure on our engineering staff during the second-generation design effort, his manner was initially abrasive. He was an astute people-reader, however, and recognized quickly not to push the already ambitious team too far. For one thing, it wasn't necessary; for another, it wouldn't have worked with this group. Doug's insights and insistence on these design goals were well timed, however, because Cellport's expansion was taking more of my time away from marketing guidance, which had been one of my traditional roles.

By now I had already spent years thinking about solving the data communications incompatibility caused by the fact that each automobile manufacturer had its own set of in-vehicle network protocols that were not shared with other manufacturers and that each handset maker used its own connector design and protocols that it also would not share with its competitors. A Universal Hands-Free system that could solve these incompatibilities would encourage the safe use of cellular phones in cars and open up a new world of application possibilities. When I had first begun understanding the magnitude of this challenge some years earlier, I had hoped to develop a standard software interface in and out of the bottom connector of all mobile handsets that would solve this problem — at least on the handset side of the envisioned system. But even this approach was not likely to succeed because the mobile handset market was constantly changing and growing more diverse, which would make this approach obsolete in no time.

This subject had seriously captivated me six years earlier, and at that time I started a project folder on the topic. I named the file "Phone-

Tail Spec," which referred to specifications for the software communications and electrical connectors that were built into the tail end of mobile phones. But by now I was concerned less about the connector itself and more about the software-based logic capabilities our new system would need to have to allow the cellular phone and vehicle systems to exchange data with one another. I filled the file 5-inches thick with my random notes on relevant market trends and technologies as well as hundreds of published articles that, in some fashion, pertained to our goals of enhancing communications between portable handsets and vehicle electronic systems to ultimately support voice-activated dialing and other data applications, such as interfacing to our MobileWeb products for vehicle network communications.

Armed with the "Phone-Tail Spec" project file, I assembled our brightest electronic systems designers in our main conference room for what I called an art-of-the-possible discussion of this problem. This was an all-star design team. The participants included Chuck, our sage network-solutions architect, Ralph, our hands-free systems expert, plus Mike Durian, our new software engineering hire who brought bright fresh eyes to the group. I always felt like I was making a sacred visit to an inventor's temple when I came to these discussions because there was so much brainpower and camaraderie in one conference room. I loved the energy in these meetings, and because of this I liked to schedule the phone-tail spec design sessions for three hours or even longer.

We had certain ground rules at Cellport to keep everyone motivated and in top form for these lengthy and intense art-of-the-possible discussions. We did not allow email, telephone calls or any other interruptions that would compromise our concentration on the subject at hand. We expected everyone to comment and contribute and to be polite and considerate of others' perspectives. We always kept a good supply of healthy and energy-friendly snacks such as nuts and grapes, and basic drinks such as water and coffee, so that no one felt too hungry or too full to focus.

To get everyone on the same proverbial page for the first phone-tail spec design meeting, I gave a tutorial on the challenges with data communications between mobile handsets and vehicle network technologies and my concern that lack of an innovative design solution would deprive consumers of many wonderful potential applications. As a homework assignment for everyone, I distributed copies of my years and years worth of notes from my file along with the most germane articles, and told everyone that we would regroup in two weeks in a serious drilldown session to discuss how to pursue the phone-tail spec design ambition.

**

By April 1999, Cellport was on a roll. We had made some excellent hires and there was a sense that the new Universal Hands-Free design was on track to surprise and delight all the Cellport shareholders as well as the market. When it rains it pours, and during an atypical rainy day drive to my office, I received a call out of the blue from Ray Sokola, a vice president at Motorola who had just been transferred into Motorola's telematics business unit, which the company had recently beefed-up with new funding, personnel, and a mission to become the global leader in this industry. This call proved to become the start of a long friendship between Ray and me and between the telematics pioneer Cellport and the potentially powerful telematics partner, Motorola. Ray said that though he was new to the Motorola telematics business unit, he noticed that Cellport's name seemed to pop up at least once a day. Curiosity drove him to request a meeting with Cellport in Boulder. I was ecstatic to receive this call; maybe Les Hatcher was wrong about how much longer Cellport would have to survive before we saw a liquidity event for the shareholders. Motorola was actively buying companies in an effort to regain the cellular phone market leadership it had lost to Nokia, and Cellport seemed a logical extension to Motorola's ambitions to build a larger and more influential telematics franchise that would boost consumer interest in its cellular phones. With nearly 50 million automobiles produced annually, dominance in this global market would definitely improve Motorola's cellular phone sales. Sure enough, within a few weeks, Ray Sokola visited Cellport. I scheduled a three-hour meeting but, to make sure I did not distract the design teams from their work, kept the participant list limited to just the two of us.

Ray Sokola was a completely likeable, gifted engineer with an alert and collaborative team mindset that had become second nature to him during college when he played soccer at the University of Delaware. Although Ray was naturally modest, I learned over the years that he was a middle-class American success story, a born engineer whose curiosity and intellect were honed in college with the aid of soccer scholarships. Ray's career at Motorola was legendary; he was a gold badge inventor with more than 10 patents to his credit. Still young, in his early 40s, Ray had been promoted to the rank of vice president after one of his patents used in cellular phone audio technologies in the 1980s and 1990s became a blockbuster, helping to advance the cellular phone industry and making Motorola hundreds of millions of dollars in royalties.

During our first meeting, the discussion flowed as easily as if we were two old college friends enjoying a long-awaited reunion. There was too much to cover in three short hours. Ray and I shared our perspectives on the challenges and opportunities in the young telematics market. He was fascinated that Cellport had contributed its first core inventions in the wireless-to-vehicle connectivity field in the mid-1990s before the Germans had even named the market "telematics." Although I fully expected Ray's interest in our work to focus on our new Universal Hands-Free system, I was delighted to find that he was most interested in our two mobile network technology patents, the Dynamic Digital Bus and Vehicle Server designs that led to our MobileWeb product. Ray did not need a lot of explanation about the importance of either, especially the Vehicle Server patent. His jaw dropped when he read the abstract of the Vehicle Server patent noting that it awarded Cellport 21 claims, of which 8 were independent [1]. Ray's comments were music to my ears: "Cellport invented an Internet-connected vehicle and you have eight independent claims? Wow, that's big."

Ray was anxious to meet Chuck Spaur, the primary inventor of the Vehicle Server patent, to hear firsthand how he came up with such a blockbuster invention. Acting like he had found a treasure trove of design goodies, Ray proposed that within weeks our two companies should sign a non-disclosure agreement and he asked if he could schedule a follow-up meeting with Cellport and the new leaders of Motorola's telematics business unit. Anxious to advance a relationship with my new best friend, I agreed that a non-disclosure agreement was in order and promised that at the next meeting I would invite our two design vice presidents, Chuck Spaur and Ralph Poplawsky, to attend as well.

**

As excited as I was about the prospects of building a relationship with Motorola, Cellport's engineers and marketers needed to focus on our current design challenges. The fourth gathering of the phone-tail spec team was another half-day meeting and it yielded several major advancements that would help make it possible to establish data communications between any mobile handset and any automobile electronic system.

Typically during these architectural-design meetings, I would play the role of asking "what-if" questions for discussion, and since I had already spent hundreds of hours on this problem, I pushed this study team hard. About halfway through the meeting, while Mike Durian and Chuck were engaged in a debate about an obscure data communications structure, the optimal solution hit my brain and my entire body tingled for what seemed like minutes. The physical sensation must have been comparable to the condition Hiro experienced that day at NTT in Tokyo when he came up with the Universal Port idea.

Sensing that I had just come upon a big-bang idea that could make a major design contribution I said, "Guys, here is my proposed solution for a completely new paradigm. Take your best shot at it."

I then proceeded to draw, on the white board, a data communication design, which we later named the Dual-Processor Multi-Bus invention, and which eventually led to a core Cellport patent. I suggested that we put a microcomputer processor in a phone-specific adaptor — similar to the adaptor we had already designed in our first hands-free system — and that we put another processor in a vehicle-mounted docking station that would connect to the adaptor and phone in the vehicle and provide power supply and other car-kit functions as well. I suggested we design the devices so that, when a phone and its adaptor are connected to the docking station, the processors would be positioned between the mobile phone and the vehicle's networking hub, and that we design a software language and middleware the two processors can use, in common, to communicate with one another. In addition, the microprocessor located in the adaptor would have the capability to translate data communications between the mobile phone and the processor in the docking station, and the processor in the docking station would have the capability to communicate with the vehicle's electronics as well as various mobile phone adaptors. Chuck knew immediately that I had hit pay dirt. Mike Durian and Ralph did a good job of challenging my proposition, but they too became quick converts to my Dual-Processor Multi-Bus epiphany. Upon the conclusion of the meeting they all agreed this idea was indeed the ideal solution for improved data communications between the rapidly changing world of mobile handsets and the conservative world of vehicle electronic networks (see Fig. 7).

The Dual-Processor Multi-Bus design was also valuable because it created a bridge between our Universal Hands-Free design and MNT technologies (see p323 and p325 for a diagram of the HCS and MNT Portfolios). While I attribute substantial credit for this epiphany to my tenure in telematics and work with very bright engineers, I give most of the credit to my project folder and file system, which allowed me to diligently organize, for many years, a comprehensive assembly of thoughts and published material on this topic.

With the general system challenge resolved, we now needed to conduct months of detailed engineering work to choose the right silicon chips for the Dual-Processor Multi-Bus and, most importantly, to write a software code that would elegantly translate data communications between a mobile handset and a vehicle electronics system connected via the Dual-Processor Multi-Bus. Writing this code was a substantial challenge. It forced us to pool our collective experiences because we expected that mobile phones would become the center of people's communication and entertainment resources in the future and we needed to develop and design for a "wish list" of services that the customers might use in years to come. I used to say to our design team that this challenge was the equivalent of newlyweds defining the dos and don'ts of their relationship for the first few years of their marriage before they even start their honeymoon. You want to avoid a future scenario that is full of complaints such as, "You never said that!"

**

If the Dual-Processor Multi-Bus invention wasn't providing enough excitement, Ralph's mechanical engineering team was reporting significant breakthroughs with a new cordless latching interface between the phone adaptor and Universal Hands-Free docking stations. It would be a major improvement over the first-generation devices, which connected the adaptor to the docking station via a coil cord. I knew the mechanical design team had made significant progress when they invited the respected critic, Doug Daniels, and me to a design review meeting in early June. During their short four-month tenure at Cellport, Kathy Delianides and Jim Wilkinson gained reputations as gifted designers who worked at lightning speed. Kathy's and Jim's complementary skills were exactly what Ralph needed on his mechanical team. Since we had solved the fundamental data communications challenge with the Dual-Processor Multi-Bus design, Ralph wanted balanced innovation on the mechanical side too, especially to satisfy Doug Daniels. Ralph cleverly asked Kathy and Jim to lead the design team's presentation, and he decided to sit between the demanding Doug Daniels and his crew.

Cellport staff affectionately called Kathy "the gazelle." A svelte runner, she was wired with a passionate, kinetic energy that, combined with an in-your-face engagement style and booming voice, delivered an air of authoritative confidence. Kathy and Jim were the mechanical leads on Ralph's design team and both were bright and confident enough to respond to Doug's demanding product specifications.

Kathy began the team's presentation by reviewing Doug's very own product requirement list and then went on to explain the challenges mechanical engineers and industrial designers have in the real world when trying to create designs to meet highly theoretical marketing ambitions. This was either to condition Doug and me for the reality of design constraints or to tone down our expectations for a knockout punch.

Kathy then pulled our first-generation unit out of a brown box and said, "This is what we need to improve on for delivery in less than nine months, not a lot of time." By this stage of her show I knew she was extracting revengeful torture against Doug for all of his design demands. And by the looks of Doug's body language, Kathy was about to score an Oscar. Doug, a typical "my-agenda-first" salesman personality, was now butter in Kathy hands. He was red-faced and fidgety, anticipating a kill in which he would be the victim. With a stroke of humanitarian compassion, and with a move that recalled Mori-san's unveiling of NTT's revolutionary phones in Tokyo eight years before, Kathy opened up the brown box and carefully pulled out a foam prototype — a design marvel.

The proposed design, which the mechanical and industrial design teams called an Adaptor Latching System, was not only aesthetically appealing and easy to use, but it also looked every bit as compact in size as the demanding Doug Daniels had requested.

It was small enough to fit in a car under the dashboard or in the console between seats, easy to install, and it could hold a microprocessor to store speech-technology software for voice-activated dialing and speech-to-text features that could eventually facilitate the reading of email to the user, among other functions. Also importantly, the design met government regulations that it would be able to withstand impact forces in the event of an automobile accident. As a matter of safety, the phone had to stay firmly in its docking station during an accident; otherwise it could fly loosely around the car and potentially injure passengers (see Fig. 8).

The atmosphere in the room shifted from a somber mood, like one would encounter in a steam room, to the type of party mood that would take over a locker room after a team wins a championship game. We spent hours playing with and discussing the prototypes, which included one docking station and three adaptors. Everyone seemed satisfied that our second-generation Universal Hands-Free design, with its new Adaptor Latching System, would impress design critics and users alike.

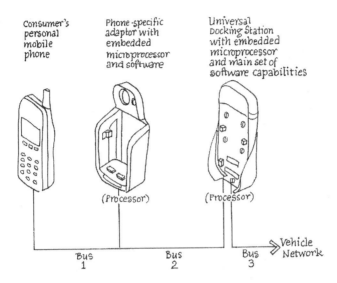

Consumer's personal mobile phone

Phone-specific adaptor with embedded microprocessor and software

Universal Docking Station with embedded microprocessor and main set of software capabilities

(Processor)   (Processor)

Bus 1   Bus 2   Bus 3   Vehicle Network

Figure 7: Dual-Processor Multi-Bus

Cellport's Dual-Processor Multi-Bus invention made it possible for a mobile phone and vehicle to communicate with each other in a way that bridged the protocols that automobile and handset manufacturers employed in their products. Microprocessors built into the phone-specific adaptor and the docking station, along with specially designed software, provided a software bridge the two systems could use to communicate with each other.

I had learned in an economic history course that war times have often led to some of the world's greatest historical inventions, and after experiencing the recent wave of inventions at Cellport, I better understood why this is so. The mood at Cellport was clearly war-like. We were passionately driven in our war challenge to design a new generation of our technologies that would improve the safety of mobile phone use in automobiles and that would be so widely accepted that they would create a de facto industry standard. We were further driven by self-imposed tight design schedules to leapfrog the IdeaJackers who theoretically stole our first generation designs. Our industrial designers, mechanical and electrical engineers needed to prototype multiple designs if they were to continue to improve upon available and emerging technologies. For the project, Cellport had already invested more than $500,000 in prototypes for concept designs alone. Without reservation, I made additional funds available for the war cause.

For the next six months, our lead patent attorney, Dave Zinger, spent a tremendous amount of time at Cellport working with our lead design engineers to capture the essence of our two new major initiatives, the Dual-Processor Multi-Bus and the Adaptor Latching System, for patent application filings.

Filing patent applications on new inventions is a hotly debated issue at many companies, but it never was at Cellport. In addition to the many economic benefits patents have delivered for society over the centuries, I had seen firsthand that the prospect of eventual ownership of patents helps stoke the creative fire inventors have and attracts investments.

This motivation has helped launch many great companies in the past and should certainly continue to do so in the future. While the preparation of quality patent applications is both time-consuming and costly, in Cellport's case patents yielded three additional strata of benefits: On one level, the patent application allowed us to prove first invention leadership at a particular point in time. Patent ownership enabled us to push for a standard interface between mobile phones and vehicle electronic networks as well as open architectures based on our designs. On another level, we benefited from the internal design discipline created by the application process, which requires that a multidisciplinary team frequently review the invention art from concept to product reality. The constant questioning and evaluation of our work and ideas through multiple reviews strengthened the quality of our designs, inventions and our patents.

Figure 8: Adaptor Latching System

The Adaptor Latching System used new mechanical and industrial design techniques to reduce the physical size of the adaptors and to firmly latch the phone in place in the car. The design is able to adapt to steadily-shrinking modern phone designs and to make it possible to install the hands-free products into space-constrained car areas, such as under the dashboard or in the console between seats. The system can securely hold any mobile phone in place regardless of shape, and it can be installed directly to a car's interior surface without disassembling the surface area involved.

That June, Ray Sokola was scheduled to come to Cellport along with an entourage from Motorola's telematics business unit. In preparation for the meeting, I decided that only our senior technical vice presidents should make presentations. Chuck Spaur would brief Motorola on our MobileWeb product innovation and Ralph Poplawsky would give a presentation on our second-generation Universal Hands-Free design project.

I also had a strong hunch that Motorola would either want to buy Cellport or make an investment in the company. Michael Braitberg had actually predicted, back in 1993 before we had incorporated the company, that Motorola would be the most likely of any potential buyers of the company. Therefore I asked Steve Parrish and Paul Heller to participate in listen-mode only, armed with their astute economic antennas. Steve and Paul both were highly enthusiastic vice presidents and they both possessed solid economic IQs. If Motorola was indeed interested in consummating a deal, an investment of

Steve's and Paul's time and attention would be well spent.

Much to my delight, Ray brought several colleagues to our meeting, including Marios Zenios, the vice president and the new general manager of Motorola's telematics business unit; Helena Stelnicki, a specialist in finance and transactions; and Mike Bordelon, a gifted system architect. Based on the organization chart for the telematics business unit, I could see that our visitors were core to the senior leadership team. And they seemed very interested in Cellport. Right after Ray and I signed a non-disclosure agreement, I told the Cellport presentation teams that we should be completely forthcoming with Motorola about our wireless-to-vehicle network technologies. But because they were our guests, I asked the Motorola executives to brief us first on their new organization and their near- and long-term business objectives.

Marios Zenios took the lead and explained that over the past few quarters, Motorola had increased funding to build a much larger telematics business than it had previously operated and that the company, eyeing this fast-growing market, had infused the team with the company's top engineering and business talents. Given Motorola's history of supplying product to both the automotive and wireless industries, the company appeared to have the perfect internal competencies to address this new market. When it came to sharing their current and future product offerings, however, it became clear that Marios' new team had yet to gain much traction from the product offerings it inherited from Motorola's previous intelligent vehicle initiatives. Motorola's current product line clearly lacked excitement. About an hour after he concluded his remarks, Marios was honest enough to say that part of the reason Ray wanted the team to visit Cellport was to hear about new technologies and product ideas with the intention of finding a way for Cellport and Motorola to work together. In good candor, Marios expressed frustration that the car makers treated telematics as a vehicle system and that they were slow to recognize that it represented a convergence of both wireless and vehicle electronic network technologies. At this point Chuck couldn't hold back and said, "Do not forget the warp speed growth of Internet applications as well," which was his way of establishing the importance of Cellport's expertise in bringing Internet applications to telematics systems. This was a perfect way to transition the meeting from Motorola's honest and open representation of itself as having oars in the water but lacking a rudder, to our presentations about Cellport, whose entire history was steeped in pursuing its telematics strategies.

Knowing that Ray was keen on our MobileWeb product line, I decided a little humorous teasing was in order. I mentioned to our guests that Ralph would deliver a presentation about our new Universal Hands-Free design vision and that Chuck had developed a tantalizing presentation on his brilliant Internet-ization of vehicle telematics applications via the MobileWeb product. But before they would have an opportunity to hear from Ralph and Chuck, I spent some time giving them a presentation on Cellport's history, explaining to our guests how Cellport came to spend eight years and in excess of $10 million conducting research that allowed us to accomplish our two avant-garde telematics product design families with accompanying patent portfolios. I emphasized that Cellport was the first of the telematics industry's pioneers to conduct extensive concentrated research in this field and that Cellport was unique in the industry for focusing solely on developing wireless-to-vehicle connectivity solutions and for proclaiming a commitment, as part of its original business charter, to openly license its technologies to promote the adoption of telematics innovations by all. By 1999 the boom in the most sensational open system of all — the Internet — had started convincing even traditional technology companies that had closed-system approaches, such as Motorola, to start thinking about sharing more technologies and adopting the open licensing model as a commercial optimizer. All of our visiting Motorola executives were youngish and more liberal-thinking technologists than the majority making up the Motorola old guard, who often reflected the attitude, "It's the Motorola way or the highway." There is little doubt in my mind that Motorola loaded its new slate of telematics executives with Grade A players.

After my hour-long briefing, Ralph gave his presentation on our first generation Universal Hands Free system as well as our development plans for our second generation system. He gave overviews of the Dual-Processor Multi-Bus and the Adaptor Latching System advancements, explaining that the designs his team was developing would make it possible to connect emerging and more powerful mobile devices to vehicle electronic networks in a future-proof manner. These developments received a thumbs-up from our Motorola guests. Unfortunately, the Motorola "A-Team" believed the universal aspect of our hands-free product would cause certain tribes within Motorola some angst. While our guests completely understood the openness that the Internet would bring to the world of applications, they expected that accommodating other brands of mobile handsets with a standard vehicle interface would become a major issue of internal debate at Motorola, and it did, for years to come. Plus Ralph's second-generation product was nearly a year away from market viability.

Next on deck was the main event: Chuck Spaur and our MobileWeb invention that taught the world how to connect the vast resources of the Internet to closed-vehicle electronic networks. For nearly two hours Chuck stood at the white board, explaining the telematics advancements we achieved through our work that led to both our Dynamic Digital Bus and Vehicle Server inventions (see p325 for a diagram of the MNT Portfolio). He methodically described how we leveraged arcane insights from one technology development experience to another to propel our innovation leadership into new areas. Ray and the others asked dozens of questions, but the questions addressed broad process or topical matters such as, "How did this lead to that?" They often made favorable comments, such as "Oh, that makes great sense." The friendly probes and compliments from the Motorola telematics team created an opening for much early camaraderie at the most senior levels of our two companies

For flight departure reasons the Motorola group had to leave Boulder by 4 p.m., so a little after 3 p.m. they asked our Cellport team to give them 15 minutes for an internal huddle. Thirty minutes later, Ray asked us to rejoin them in the conference room. There we were, four of Cellport's vice presidents and me, face to face with the new executive muscle from a monster-sized company, Motorola, who wanted to become the global leader in telematics. We were about to receive a briefing on what might come next between our companies. As the senior voice for the Motorola team, Marios opened the conversation with warm compliments for Cellport's two separate families of innovation. On the economic front, he said, "Motorola is in check-writing mode, and we think Cellport is an important ally for Motorola to partner with. If Cellport is open to an investment from Motorola, I think an investment strategy should be negotiated and signed by the end of October."

With little time left and everyone looking at their watches, I responded by saying Cellport welcomed a deeper strategic relationship with Motorola's new telematics leadership and that a financial investment would prime the pump for significant collaborations. I told them we were hoping for this type of interest from Motorola. Hence, I would assign Steve Parrish and Paul Heller from our economic team to work with Helena, who Marios said would lead Motorola's work on the investment project. Ray Sokola, who continued to lead Motorola's positive energy throughout the meeting, offered strong compliments to both Ralph and Chuck for their inventive engineering work. Sitting alongside Marios, Ray expressed delight and pride that his entire team was interested in advancing a strategic partnership with Cellport. Aside from the business benefits, it now appeared that I would have the opportunity to pursue a more progressive friendship with Ray, whose combination of integrity, gifted intellectual agility and inventiveness was a great cultural fit with our invention team. Considering the Motorola executives' fondness of Cellport and the fact that Helena had an MBA from The Wharton School, we assumed that getting an investment document finished and signed in four months would be a cakewalk.

The October funding date that Motorola proposed was fortuitous as well because at Cellport's current spending rate, we projected that we would have spent our way through the $3.9 million from FLV by January 2000, only six months away. Our staff had ballooned in the recent six short months to more than 35 people, and expenses for developing prototypes that Ralph's second-generation Universal Hands-Free system design efforts required had us burning nearly $200,000 a month of our precious funds. The investment we expected to receive from Motorola, about $5 million or more in cash, would arrive about three months before we expected to hit the proverbial "wall," which is entrepreneur-speak for running out of money. I was confident that Steve, Paul and Andy, our economic deal team, could produce the data and a contract outline that Helena would need to secure approval of her investment proposal. We were told that once this investment proposal was drafted, the Motorola telematics vice presidents would need to bless the document, and then it would go to Motorola's Senior Investment Board for final approval. Andy, of course, would be responsible for all document exchanges with Motorola's attorneys to close the final funding contract.

As the deal-team leader, Helena made several visits to Boulder that summer to conduct technical and business due-diligence sessions and she requested a seemingly endless number of documents that caused Steve and Paul to put in long hours. In contrast to the streamlined FLV funding experience, Motorola assigned two very bright engineers to help Helena with her work, and they seemingly left nothing to speculation, not even our cash burn rate. After attending one of Helena's meetings, I realized that through this strategic investment process Motorola had learned all the idiosyncrasies of Cellport's market research and product designs. Andy kept saying that Motorola's informational requests point to either a very big investment or a desire to buy the entire company. Either way, Andy said he was ready for a few all-nighters. This was Andy's way of out-working the other attorneys during the final few days of contract draft exchanges before closing a deal.

We knew Helena had three steps to get a deal done. She had to 1) complete the due diligence and draft an investment proposal that would describe Motorola's and Cellport's collaborative projects and strategy as well as Motorola's cash investment in Cellport; 2) get the Motorola telematics vice presidents to make comments on the contract and then sign-off on it; and finally 3) get the strategy proposal and investment document approved by a senior investment committee in the automotive business group, which had authority over Motorola's telematics initiatives.

We also learned that Helena's investment proposal document had become the subject of active debate between the Motorola telematics vice presidents, who were considering whether it would be better to invest in Cellport or just buy the company. I was beginning to feel some concern over the process and reached out to Ray for his opinion. Ray assured me that the due diligence was progressing well and that the Motorola executives were now in consensus that a strategic investment made the most sense. Ray and Helena felt that if Motorola bought Cellport outright, Motorola's bureaucracy would ruin Cellport's open and inventive culture.

**

That September, as the Cellport and Motorola investment teams were wrapping up their work, Philippe Vercruyssen invited me to attend a FLV meeting in Belgium and, immediately after, to travel with him to Germany to attend the Frankfurt International Motor Show. This was a much-welcomed invitation. The FLV investment team was very supportive of Cellport's business model and I wanted to show them the progress their funding support had yielded. Plus, going to the large auto show with Philippe would surely be educational and open doors for me in Germany, the automotive capital of Europe.

By this time in late 1999 I had heard numerous rumors that all reminded me of that hauntingly familiar call with Allan Batts in the spring of 1995. We were now certain that Hello Direct's sales of our first-generation product to German customers allowed several automotive systems and components manufacturers to "borrow" Cellport's Universal Hands-Free system concept. The rumors indicated that these German companies had really flattered Cellport's design work; they all used a phone-specific adaptor that was identical to ours and that connected to a universal docking station, which is exactly what Cellport's pioneering patents and products addressed in the early 1990s. I welcomed this visit to the Frankfurt auto show because it would give me an opportunity, in a neutral and public venue, to see if these companies were indeed IdeaJackers or if they had solved the universal connectivity problem for mobile handsets independent of Cellport's inventions.

Within an hour of walking into the show, I made my way over to the Audi booth to admire several new Audi car designs. I was particularly curious to view the 2000 A6 because I had just purchased the very same model for myself at home. There in the Audi booth I discovered the day's first IdeaJacker. The proof was staring boldly at me from the A6, which incorporated both Cellport's Universal Port and adaptor inventions, though these devices were slightly repackaged and called Cullmann, whatever that meant. Sitting in the driver's seat of the A6, I played with the Cullmann system like it was an old puzzle that I had worked a dozen times. I was amazed; Cullmann liked our design so much that their engineers copied our system design down to the finest details.

During my fixated analysis of the A6 system I felt rushes of so many emotional crosscurrents that after less than 15 minutes, I had seen enough. I told Philippe that I wanted to get a drink and think about what I had just seen before asking the Audi people product-specific questions about the Cullmann solution. I topped off my already adrenaline-racy body and mind with a soda and then felt ready to drill the Audi sales engineers for detailed information.

I spoke with two Audi engineers who were somewhat helpful. They knew that at the present time there were four phone adaptor cradles approved by Audi engineering and several more undergoing testing. They proudly pointed out that Cullmann, which was a company, was gearing up for some very large orders because Audi's customers were showing a very positive response to the Cullmann-manufactured efficient Universal Hands-Free system. I went into a daze, thinking that this IdeaJacker has sweet orders flowing in from Audi, using Cellport's design! The only significant change Cullmann made was to substitute the type of universal connector Cellport used in favor of theirs. It was evident that Mr. Cullmann had his own distinct business ambitions. Right after lunch, Philippe went to an FLV-related meeting and I proceeded to walk the trade show floor, looking at some of the world's most impressive vehicles while scouting for more IdeaJackers. By 2:00 p.m. I stumbled across an electronic distributor's booth, and there I discovered the second IdeaJacker of the day. This one was called the ESMO Universal Hands-Free design. The ESMO unit, much like the Cullmann system in the Audi booth, was an obvious knock-off of Cellport's first-generation product design, circa 1995.

Edgar Schumacher, the president of ESMO, was a jolly old peddler, who along with his stepson, Clemens Lucke, was testing the market for this new Universal Hands-Free concept. They happily confessed that ESMO was marketing the system on behalf of a German industrialist by the name of Stefan Voit. ESMO had signed a special distribution agreement with Voit's company to conduct market tests to determine how best to sell this new Universal Hands-Free system idea to the German automotive community.

The ESMO gentlemen were very friendly. Our conversation fluidly jumped from one subject to another, all related to our common interest, the success of Universal Hands-Free designs. During our closing words the effervescent Edgar made me two offers. He wanted Cellport to consider hiring ESMO as our technology representative in Europe and he also said he would be happy to introduce me to Mr. Voit and his company, Votronic. I thanked Edgar and Clemens for their sincere openness and promised to stay in contact. As I turned to walk away from the ESMO booth, Clemens said one more thing: "There is a company called Funkwerk Dabendorf, from the Old East Germany, and they too have a Universal Hands-Free design at the show."

"Oh, I see. Yet another company. Please, where would I find the fellows from Funkwerk Dabendorf?" I asked. Edgar and Clemens said the Dabendorf company had a broker helping them in a pavilion, sponsored by the European Bank for Reconstruction and Development, on the second floor of this mega-sized Frankfurt International Motor Show. With only about an hour until the show closed for the day, Dabendorf from the Old East would have to wait until tomorrow. My head was already spinning from the day's events and I was truly emotionally exhausted.

While waiting to rendezvous with Philippe at a small restaurant, I ordered a local German beer and sat in a comfortable chair at a curbside table trying to absorb the shocking events of the day. As I sat there taking in the scenery and watching locals enjoying themselves in the city, the reality started to sink in: two, and likely three, fresh IdeaJackers in one day at one trade show. Hello Direct's sales into Germany just four years ago had inspired a lot of small German companies to

IdeaJack us [2].

My entire business model and my market perspective were jolted, not only by the counterfeiting of Cellport's products, but from market intelligence I had gathered. Edgar and Clemens had talked with me for nearly three hours. They spoke extensively about the growing number of regulations in Europe that allowed the police to ticket any automobile driver who is using a cellular phone without a hands-free system. I learned from them that the leading German carmakers produce more than 5 million new vehicles each year. Given that a single Universal Hands-Free system can sell for several hundred dollars, this market alone gave our technology a potential market of more than $1 billion per year. In the U.S., which for the most part still resisted such regulations, our market would be far smaller for a long time to come. But here in Europe the stars were already aligned nicely. Automobile makers actually embraced the notion of embedding our Universal Hands-Free solution in new cars and the practice was becoming popular. These were all major developments.

When Philippe finally joined me I was pretty dazed by the whole experience and I had difficulty synthesizing my lengthy discussions with the men from ESMO. Luckily, English was Philippe's second language, so he was accustomed to the many various ways in which English is used. My stupor-generated inability to articulate was thus just another interpretation challenge for Philippe. After talking about ESMO for only 10 minutes, it became clear that I was drained. It was now best to let Philippe do the talking. Philippe had a slightly less crazy afternoon, but did manage to arrange a meeting for us with Nokia's telematics leadership team the next afternoon, which I welcomed. That would leave me with only the morning to meet the fellows from Dabendorf, but I knew of the booth that sponsored their show presentations and was confident that tracking them down in the morning, when I would feel fresh again, would be no big deal. That evening, after a very German entrée of pork ribs in horseradish-mustard sauce, asparagus and sauerkraut, along with yet another beer, I was ready to unwind. My goal was to crash into a sound sleep by 9 p.m. and I succeeded.

The next morning the motor show doors promptly opened at 10 a.m., and I was there to head directly to the booth sponsored by the European Bank for Reconstruction and Development (EBRD), which was located on the second floor. It took me a half-hour to trek across the vast show floor complex to find the booth that housed the fellows from Dabendorf. During an anxious walk through the agency's massively sized booth, which looked like an engineering product bazaar, I must have seen representatives and samples from at least 50 small companies from the Old East, but no sign of Dabendorf. All of these Old East companies were eager to find any opportunity to participate in the enormously successful West Germany automotive industry.

Eight years into the reunified German political structure, Easterners were anxious to share in the West's capitalistic wealth that the Soviets had denied them. With only an hour left before having to rendezvous with Philippe, I needed a Plan B. I had to find these Dabendorf fellows quickly. My eyes locked onto an obvious booth diva, a tall blonde-haired woman who seemed very much in-the-know about everything the EBRD booth had to offer, as evidenced by the six people asking her questions. When my turn came to ask Frau Booth Diva about the Dabendorf company, she knew its status exactly. "Oh, yes. Those Dabendorf gentlemen," she proudly bellowed, "are meeting with car executives all day today and tomorrow. They were very popular yesterday!"

Shit! Yesterday I should not have talked to the affable ESMO guys so long, nor been so lazy when I still had an hour left to see the Dabendorf products. I blew it. The best I could do was to pick up a Dabendorf system brochure from the booth diva. I looked through it as if I were taking a quick look at a familiar family photo. Dabendorf's Universal Hands-Free kit was directly IdeaJacked from Cellport's first-generation design. I now needed to start my hike to meet Philippe to attend our 1 p.m. meeting with Nokia.

The Nokia meeting was similar to my initial discussions with Motorola a few months earlier. Nokia was anxious to bust into the booming telematics market, but the carmakers were calling all the design shots and their draconian control stifled dynamic design progress. Unlike

Motorola, which had a history of selling chips and products to car-makers, Nokia saw the telematics market as just another side bet for its cellular phone business, which was even more flush with cash than Motorola's. Like Motorola, Nokia also wanted to invest in growth markets that used wireless phones.

Nokia assigned a dynamic Finn by the name of Kalevi Kaartinen to run its telematics business. Kalevi understood well the Nokia corporate mandate: To sell one Nokia phone per vehicle was not sufficient. He expressed an interest in exploring use of Cellport's technologies and promised to visit Cellport during his next trip to the states for technology and partnership discussions. Unfortunately for Cellport, the bright and independent Kalevi left his Nokia telematics assignment before he could visit us. He apparently considered his work in telematics for Nokia to be the equivalent of being sent to Siberia. He left Nokia to run Samsung's cellular business in Europe, compounding the loss for Nokia. A Finn leaving Finland's most beloved company, Nokia, to work for a competitor from another country was truly walking the line of treason. Subsequently, while Motorola's Ray Sokola would give the Cellport technology a lot of visibility to help drive Motorola's next telematics technology push, Nokia's relationship with Cellport floundered for years after Kalevi's departure.

During my flight back to the states, I thought deeply about all three German IdeaJackers; they were all terribly real, their existence was no longer a theory. I was amazed at how closely they copied our first-generation design. Their IdeaJacking design philosophy appeared to be simple: Follow Cellport's lead closely and don't get too creative with risky design deviations. Happily, I knew Cellport's second-generation system would leave their current designs in the dust. We would finally be in the position to take complete leadership in the Universal Hands-Free business and to drive a global standard, compliments of our growing patent portfolio.

During vulnerable times like these, I become very analytical and reflective. I was certain of one thing: Having Michael Braitberg and Dave Zinger as my patent mentors and investing a lot of resources to build a portfolio of patents in an area of unique competency was a wise strategy. Without the strength of Cellport's granted telematics patent portfolio, along with the Dual-Processor Multi-Bus and the Adaptor Latching System ideas now headed toward patent application filings, we would find it very difficult to assert market leadership or to raise money to continue the research perpetuating our pioneering technology solutions.

Back in Boulder, I was delighted to see Ralph's second-generation design teams making substantial progress. But it was less than exciting when I heard from Andy that, after talking to Steve Parrish and Paul Heller, it appeared that Helena's work was taking more time then any of us anticipated because of the newness of their business unit within Motorola as well as the size of the Motorola bureaucracy circa 1999. We had just learned that the timetable to invest in Cellport had slipped until December. Andy's sense was that the company was in check-writing mode but that the check-signers were not acting like Cellport Labs was a priority investment. Having drafted and negotiated hundreds of major investment and acquisition contracts, Andy had developed a good sense about whether a deal was on a track toward consummation or looking like it would fail, and his read of Helena's status reports was not good.

To gain another perspective, I called Ray. I learned from him that indeed, the senior investment committee members — who were drawn primarily from the old guard that ran the automotive business group — wanted more information on the strategic investment proposal in Cellport and that they would review the information when they met again in December. I pressed Ray for his confidence that the Cellport investment deal would close with a funding agreement; he said that he was reviewing Helena's work and he was pleased with her progress, which he thought should produce an approval during the next meeting. I relayed this reasonably good news to Andy, Paul and Steve, yet each of these members of the Cellport economic team cited back to me three different examples in which Motorola's due diligence team had signaled inconsistent stories. Andy finished our discussion on Motorola by saying, "The deal has a death stench. Let's examine our Plan B option now."

Steve reported that we could stretch Cellport's cash to late January, but that would leave us too highly leveraged with our vendors and put us at risk of losing our intellectual property assets if we went out of business for lack of funding. My first thought was to go back to Philippe Vercruyssen for assistance, for he was a helpful Cellport Board member and his FLV Fund owned nearly 14 percent of Cellport. Paul said that if I took on the role of approaching FLV for a short-term bridge loan, he would pursue some new interests in Cellport that he thought might be brewing with other strategic investors. While Paul and I rallied to bring in funds to keep us from hitting the wall, Steve and Andy would watch our spending closely and work to keep the ship financially stable.

To help ease the anxiety of our funding slippage with Motorola, I started to spend more time with Tim Jones, a key member of our MobileWeb design team, and Chuck on a very clever new architecture that Tim was leading called Managing Disparate Protocols. Having shipped MobileWeb solutions to dozens of customers by late 1999, the MobileWeb design team realized that we needed to find ways to make it possible for applications to flow through network systems that were innately incompatible, such as a cellular phone network, a GPS system, the in-vehicle network that communicates with electronic components, a speech-recognition technology, Web browser, and the Internet, to name a few examples. The inventive work that Tim oversaw led to a complex yet elegant communications module that would be located in a vehicle, and which would use software applications to make it possible to transfer information and data between or among these various disparate types of networks. The design effort that led to the filing of a patent application for Managing Disparate Protocols, which we later dubbed CP-Jazz, culminated the most inventive year in our history. Now we just needed to be able to survive to see Tim's and Chuck's most clever architectural work become a reality.

**

The brief yet brilliantly attended-to friendship that Bernard Joseph and I had created at the InCarTech conference in Paris in late 1998 continued to grow throughout the next year as Bernard introduced

Cellport to members of the telematics team at Peugeot and I opened doors for Bernard in the U.S. technology community. Bernard and I enjoyed an easy exchange of stimulating conversations on a breadth of subjects, from earthly business issues to abstract philosophical topics. For the Second Annual Telematics conference in Paris, scheduled for December 1999, Bernard was again selected to recruit speakers for the event. He graciously invited me to speak once again to update the audience on Cellport's latest technologies as well as to work on potential business opportunities together in France. Prior to arriving in Paris I would follow up on my commitment to our economic team and visit Cellport's most recent and second-largest shareholder, the FLV Fund, to warn them of a potential Motorola funding setback. While in Brussels I met with FLV's President Philip Vermeulen over dinner to explain Cellport's current bind: that we were less than two months away from hitting the wall and that Cellport's economic team thought the wheels were falling off the Motorola funding. Our hope was that FLV would provide us a bridge loan to protect their investment until we found a replacement for Motorola.

A veteran banker, Philip said these setbacks happen. He expressed happiness about the progress of Cellport's designs and said he was delighted that we were successfully using L&H's speech-recognition software engine and vocabulary words in our second-generation Universal Hands-Free system prototypes. As we departed that evening Philip looked me in the eyes and said, "Let's all work together on this problem. We'll find a way."

The words were encouraging, but it was clear to me that Cellport would need to be a week from collapse before FLV would step in to help. The next day I traveled south to Paris on the TGV train. Ironically, I traveled on those very same tracks almost exactly a year earlier heading north to Belgium to seek the $5 million that FLV subsequently invested, which gave us the year of fabulous progress at Cellport. My hunch was that FLV would provide enough bridge funding for only two to three months but that after that period we had better find a way for either Motorola to invest or for another strategic company to fall in love with Cellport's technology and visions.

The Paris telematics show was helpful, albeit at this event I would not find an eager investor as I had the previous year. What I had hoped for was that I would be able to develop a relationship between the Paris-based Peugeot and Cellport that would yield us a well-funded design project. During a lunch with senior members of Peugeot's telematics team in the executive dining room at Peugeot's headquarters, however, I learned shocking new telematics market intelligence. Peugeot did not need to write checks to fund telematics design developments with Cellport because these clever Parisians had talked Microsoft into giving them tens of millions of dollars for design integration and a press announcement describing Microsoft's telematics platform, which Microsoft called "Auto PC."

The Peugeot team had figured out that Bill Gates desperately needed a design win and a product launch date announcement from an important vehicle producer as a competitive move against Palm Computing, which dominated the market for hand-held computers and which was then in the process of staging an initial public offering. Microsoft's Auto PC used Microsoft's less popular operating system for hand held computers, Windows CE; a substantial win for Microsoft in the automotive industry could help Microsoft deflect attention away from Palm in the handheld market and give Microsoft an advantage in the potential but high-volume market for small computing platforms in the automotive industry.

The early relationship exchange was simple: Peugeot would receive tens of millions of dollars to launch the Auto PC in Europe and in turn it would draw attention to Microsoft's planned product line from the international media by employing colorful French theatrics at their press conference. Microsoft certainly had the money and ambitions to buy their way into the now hotly coveted telematics market, however, its strategy emphasized using GSM mobile phone networks, which weren't well-suited for data. The positive takeaway for us from this lunch was that Microsoft was obviously inexperienced in this industry and making some fundamental mistakes. These savvy Parisians had cleverly seduced Bill Gates and team into a dandy of a deal. That night I decided to brief Paul Heller on Microsoft's naiveté in the hands of Peugeot and to suggest that he put Microsoft on his short list of strategic funding prospects. Paul said he would do that. He then explained that he had determined that there was a very strong need for network equipment companies, like Sun Microsystems or Cisco Systems, to play a role in the bourgeoning telematics market and he was becoming very excited by the prospects this represented. In typical Heller fashion, to substantiate his case for pursuing partnerships in this industry, he talked me through the nitty-gritty details of his analysis of the numerous market and technology factors that he had considered. Paul was feeling somewhat vengeful that Motorola had approached us, telling us they were in check-writing mode, and now, six months later, couldn't even give us the date for the December meeting of their "senior investment committee," whose decision-makers were still anonymous to us.

Paul was an academic scholar through graduate school and was blessed with smarts and a passionate drive for success, but he had grown up in Colorado and deep inside he was a hardy Western mountain man. His propensity for both intellectual analytics and athletic competitiveness made him a highly focused and effective senior contributor at Cellport. In addition to Paul, two of the other new vice president-level talents Cellport had hired earlier that year, Steve Parrish and Doug Daniels, were athletes. They had little fear of competition and they were well-matched additions to Andy, Chuck, Ralph and me. I was pleased with our hires and product design direction. Despite going broke fast, I was still feeling perky. After all, I knew that FLV would help us financially when we would need them in January.

**

Immediately upon returning to Boulder, I sensed an emotional setback at Cellport. In small companies there are no secrets, and everyone on the staff knew of the economic team's consensus, that Motorola was off track and that we had less than two months of cash in the bank. I tried to counter the fears with the encouraging news: On the design front, Ralph's team was making huge progress building the engineering prototypes of the second-generation Universal Hands-Free products, and we had just filed the CP-Jazz patent. On the market front, Doug had been getting some very encouraging news from prospective customers. I did some cheerleading on the importance of keeping one's chin up when the chips are down. My review of Motorola investment team's due-diligence process with my economic team did not give a pretty picture; I started to pick up signals that it was indeed a very bad situation. Initially, I was reluctant to address the negative evidence, but I needed to flesh out my theory with this leadership group. "Guys, would it be fair to say that Helena and the new "A-Team" that Motorola brought in to turbo-charge the growth of the telematics business unit is experiencing discrimination by the old guard?" I asked.

No one dissented. Steve Parrish said he was impressed with the Motorola group, based on his dealings with their due-diligence teams that visited Cellport that summer. But Steve's sense was that this was their first major project together and although they were excited, they were clearly cutting their teeth, both on our technology and as a team. Now I better understood the degree of pessimism our economic team felt toward ever closing the Motorola funding. The Christmas holiday was a very eerie period, energy-wise. It was cold and cloudy but there was no more than a dusting of snow outside. The ground was dry and, somehow, symbolic of Cellport's circumstances.

On Tuesday, December 21, with no word out of Motorola on our deal, I decided to call Helena's cell phone. It was 6:30 a.m. in Chicago and I foolishly assumed that because of the early hour, I would get her voice mail and I could leave her a message to call me. Much to my angst, she answered my call, sounding very alert.

"So, no need to apologize for waking you up?" I asked.

"No, that's OK. I've been up for hours," she said.

"Helena, that's a bad sign. Is some of your sleeplessness due to troubles on the Cellport deal?" I asked.

"Yes, I am afraid all of my sleeplessness is due to Cellport!" she acknowledged.
She went on to explain that Motorola's "senior investment commit-

tee" had held a very short meeting due to the holiday season, and the only feedback she got on Cellport was a cryptic request for more information on the deal. This was one of those moments where I needed to completely take the high road with Helena, for there was much to sort out. My compassionate feelings went out to her and the entire Motorola telematics team, which had worked closely with us, as partners. Strangely, I felt worse for Helena than I felt for Cellport. I had recently experienced the shock of getting IdeaJacked, but this well-educated, bright and hard-working executive was now experiencing the pain of a corporate political system that was working against her new team, their hard work, and their exciting and well-funded charter. The rest of our conversation had the tone of an amicable break-up of a relationship. We complimented each other's efforts, and in a final shot at tenacity, Helena said she was committed to get back in front of Motorola's senior investment committee in early 2000. "Right," I said. But I knew our Motorola funding prospects were dead. Holy shit!

When I finished this historic call with Helena I was in the parking lot of my health club. I quickly made my way into the steam room. My head was spinning, and I felt a strange combination of energetic compassion as well as rage toward my new best friends at Motorola. In stark contrast to ecstasy moments that success brings, these conflicting emotions made me feel like I was watching a gut-wrenching film. In this dramatically imagined film, Motorola's old guard foolishly and unjustly employed subversive corporate politics that badly bruised its well-intentioned partner, Cellport, and, worse, cut deep into the hearts of its own company's younger and more energetic talents.

Oftentimes, I have wondered if my life would have been more stable and sane if I worked inside the comfort of a large corporation like Motorola. After witnessing the personal pain and wasted resources that bureaucratic companies can wield, I'm happier with my life on the outside, on the bleeding-edge of technology. It is more risky in this environment, to be sure, but at least I have my autonomy and, when situations such as the failed Motorola partnership occur, I know I will figure out a way to move on.

8 | The Bubble

1991
1992
1993
1994
1995
1996
1997
1998
1999
2000
2001
2002
2003
2004
2005
2006
2007
2008
2009

January 2000 began in stark contrast to the ebullient beginning of January 1999, when Cellport was flush with new and substantial funding. This New Year we were perilously low on cash. While we had certainly faced financial difficulties before, our needs by now were much greater. We were burning more than $300,000 a month. If that and the feeling that we had been left at the altar by Motorola were not bad enough, Chuck Spaur gave me notice that he needed to take a sabbatical to attend to some family matters. Chuck astutely assessed that with the cellular industry's plans to build a nationwide CDPD wireless data network stalled, it would be years before his team's work to commercialize MobileWeb Internet connected vehicles would yield actual deployments in real-world settings and meaningful revenues for Cellport. Until then, Cellport would likely be able to support only a small architectural design team, and its designers would have little more to do than custom projects for specialty applications.

Yet some of the adrenaline highs in an entrepreneur's life come from rebounding off the lows. I knew that if we could survive this very scary low period, then any good news of even moderate impact should provide one hell of a major bounce. To stabilize the business I assigned our senior staff to attend to issues critical to our survival. I instructed Ralph to ensure that his engineering team would meet all project milestones on time, Paul to accelerate his fundraising efforts with another strategic investor to replace Motorola, and Steve Parrish to keep our creditors happy. Andy and I would articulate our survival plan to FLV.

Paul had a breakthrough right away and it looked like it had the potential to provide a real ray of sunshine to our gloomy group. Paul had just begun working on an opportunity that fit perfectly into his new strategy of pursuing relationships with network equipment companies, and he already had a very big prospect: Cisco Systems. Some of Cisco's executives, who had learned about Cellport's advanced telematics design work at a conference, were seriously interested in both our Dynamic Digital Bus and Vehicle Server inventions as well as our MobileWeb application platforms based on those two inventions. At this point in 2000 the telecommunications and Internet markets were still booming, and Cisco, whose routers and switches had helped build and fuel the growth of the Internet, was at its high point in terms of market value. Because Cellport played a similar role connecting Internet applications to vehicle networks, it appeared to be a natural partner and even an acquisition target for the cash-rich and growth-hungry Cisco. Paul rallied our MobileWeb design team, now without Chuck, to help him put together a presentation of more than 50 slides about the Dynamic Digital Bus and Vehicle Server architectures and the MobileWeb applications platform for an upcoming visit by Cisco executives.

To make sure Cisco's executives completely loved Cellport's telematics connectivity story, Paul had Doug Daniels contribute, for good measure, another 20 slides on our new Universal Hands-Free design. The guests we were expecting from Cisco represented the company's advanced engineering team, so I suggested to Paul that he keep Andy, Steve and me out of the discussions until he could determine how enthusiastic the visitors were toward our technologies. In preparation for the meeting, Paul rehearsed the slide presentation at least six times before an audience of a few Cellport engineers, who played the roles of the expected Cisco visitors. When I learned of Paul's intensive preparations for what promised to be a six-hour-plus meeting, I suggested to him that he plan to feed our guests a good, catered lunch and plenty of strong coffee. Paul agreed that having the lunch catered would be a good idea, but he said that his real ambition was to get them eating Cellport's technology right out of his hands. Paul's determination illustrated, for me, one great benefit of empowering motivated and take-charge people to handle critical and challenging assignments: the luxury of being able to watch them work and wait for their efforts to yield fruit because you have confidence in their abilities to perform and deliver.

With Cisco on the horizon as a logical strategic funding partner, I approached FLV's Philippe Vercruyssen again about a bridge loan to help Cellport meet its operating expenses until we could consummate another major investment. The value of the numerous trips I made to Belgium over the past year to show Philippe's boss, Philip Vermeulen, and other FLV Fund members Cellport's significant progress, and to build goodwill with FLV, was about to be tested.

The FLV Fund was truly the lender of last resort. Both Andy Quartner and John Thompson had said that Cellport's short-term cash needs were too sizeable for their community of angel investors to be able to help, and Steve Parrish reported that we had only enough cash for one more payroll. Cellport was again in war mode and I might as well have been a commander trying to stave off the loss of his supply line by appealing to FLV. Yet I was the head of a young development company in the high-risk technology business and had a critical need of cash to avoid hitting the proverbial wall.

During my discussions with Philippe, I offered to fly to Belgium if necessary, but he assured me that I had conducted my relationship with his partners well enough over the past year that a personal gesture was not needed. Philippe said the fund members would meet the following week to discuss the Cellport issue and he would let us know immediately of any decision. Philippe appeared to cast an optimistic light on the prospective outcome. He said it should bode well for Cellport that, since it had received FLV's initial support a year earlier, Cellport had developed three new architectural advancements and filed respective patent applications for what were now the Dual-Processor Multi-Bus, Adaptor Latching System and Managing Disparate

Protocols technologies. Plus, it had attracted Cisco's interest.

The next week, Philippe called me as soon as he finished a telephone conference call with his FLV Fund partners. Philippe had a dry sense of humor and he conjured it up for this call, telling me that FLV agreed to "move the wall out" for Cellport a few months. It would loan Cellport $500,000. He said he would work with Andy to draft a note that had favorable terms and as soon as Cellport signed the note, FLV would wire transfer the money to our bank account. I thanked Philippe profusely and sent an email to Philip Vermeulen expressing my deep gratitude for FLV's spirit of partnership and support. Andy wasted no time. He drafted the loan documents that evening, signed them, and faxed the papers to Belgium so that by the time the gentlemen at FLV arrived at work the next day they could wire the funds to Cellport.

I was naturally very happy to have secured FLV's support, and an exciting voicemail I received from Doug Daniels stoked these good feelings. Doug had been working to pursue a partnership with a venture-funded company in California, called @Road, whose business plan was to use wireless technologies to provide vehicle fleet-management services to large corporate customers, an approach that came right down Cellport's Main Street. Doug's efforts were showing great promise. For one thing, the company was in strong shape; it had just hired Kirish Panu, a bright and energetic CEO, and it had recently raised around $30 million from several west coast venture capital firms. Secondly, Doug said that @Road understood Cellport's long history in the field of establishing connectivity between wireless and vehicle networks and that it wanted to quickly develop a meaningful strategic relationship with us in order to accelerate its own schedule for bringing handset-based telematics solutions to business fleet operators.

Doug said Kirish Panu and @Road's chief engineer wanted to visit Cellport within a few weeks to pursue a number of strategic initiatives, and he needed to know if I could be available for a meeting. I cleared my calendar for a welcomed strategic discussion on what sounded like an ideal opportunity: As a fleet vehicle management firm, it was obvious that @Road would find both of our patent portfolios and product lines of great interest. We held the meetings at our offices. Doug gave the @Road leadership team a presentation on Cellport's two primary markets and consumer-centric applications. I gave an overview of our history and vision and went into more detail about our two core technology families. Cellport's message resonated with our guests, who were quintessential Type A personalities from Silicon Valley. They wasted no time in getting to the point of their visit and right after lunch made a proposal that sounded like music from heaven: @Road wanted Cellport to extend the design of our Universal Hands-Free system so that it would enable a portable wireless data device to communicate with @Road's in-vehicle computer, a project that would cost $150,000. Plus, @Road offered to help Cellport's fundraising efforts. It proposed investing $1 million immediately into the company.

During the early part of 2000, a frenzy of investments in telecommunications and Internet related businesses was taking place in the U.S. economy. Financial news analysts such as CNN's Lou Dobbs, and reporters and analysts from throughout the print and broadcast media paid rapt attention to the era's rising stock market and the business expansion and personal wealth it created. The telecommunications and Internet sectors created not only two growth engines in the economy, but also widespread predictions that these sensational technologies would transform the way economies and civilization function. And of course, the predictions from that time have been borne out. Today we cannot imagine life without broadband services, wireless phones, Wi-Fi and, most importantly, the Internet. We can barely remember how we managed our lives before this digital communications revolution, when society moved at a much slower "analog" pace.

The thousands of U.S. and international companies created and built during this telecommunications and Internet technology bonanza can trace their roots back to the 1950s when the transistor was invented, effectively launching the modern technology era. The business growth that was well under way by 2000 was further fueled by hundreds of 30-something technology bankers on Wall Street who extolled the idea that new valuation and funding rules needed to be applied to our nascent technology-based economy. The concept of "increasing returns" (a belief that technology advancements enable buyers to pay less tomorrow yet obtain greater performance than was available yesterday) and classical price-per-earnings ratios and return-on-investment valuation matrices were set on the shelf.

This period is often referred to as The Bubble, and with good reason. @Road was a classic example: Here was a small and young venture-funded company that had $30 million in fresh capital and now they were investing $1 million in a similar-sized company, Cellport, for strategic reasons. The excess capital The Bubble generated led to an investing environment akin to a situation in which gamblers place their bets on the possible outcome of other gamblers' hunches.

Because @Road wanted to waste no time moving forward with its investment in Cellport, I asked Andy to start work on a funding document, and in classic fashion, an extensive funding document was done in a matter of days. The @Road investment thus started our fourth round of funding. Although the company agreed to fund us quickly, with an early spring closing, the valuation of its investment could not be determined until a large investor, such as a company like Cisco, invested and set the price. Yet @Road's timing was ideal for us, because its investment and project funding would likely influence other prospective partners to believe that Cellport's telematics connectivity technologies provided a golden key for opening up the wireless device to vehicle network challenges. Having just crawled out of a financial abyss, we wanted as much interest in Cellport as we could get. We were enjoying the effects of easy Bubble money.

To build on this momentum of this exceptional time, Paul booked another session with a now eager Cisco to follow-up on our very positive initial meeting with its executives. This meeting would be attended by a Cisco senior executive, Dr. Michael Frendo, who had a say in the company's investments decisions. Given Michael Frendo's expected participation, Steve Parrish and I planned to attend the meeting to help Paul convince Cisco to make a major investment in Cellport.

Michael Frendo was a bright, high-energy engineer who, as a leader in Cisco's advanced technology organization, was indeed the person authorized to give a Cellport investment a thumbs-up or thumbs-down. Michael liked Cellport's early architectural work to connect wireless and vehicle networks and he loved the fact that Cellport had developed the world's first Internet-connected automobile. When Michael heard that @Road was anxious to invest, independent of a valuation price, to help Cellport, he commented that deal heat is a good sign of technological prowess.

During this period, Cisco's visionary CEO, John Chambers, often gave speeches in which he described all types of things, including automobiles, connecting to the Internet. We learned that he had recently spent time with the CEOs of the "big three" automotive companies in Detroit at the time, Ford, General Motors, and the Chrysler Corporation, and promised each of these companies that Cisco would help lead the development of technology innovations that would connect their future automobiles to the Internet. The system Cisco wanted to develop was one in which each vehicle automatically reported any maintenance or safety problems to the car dealership; the envisioned system also provided traffic updates, news and entertainment to the vehicle's occupants. Chambers' promise to the automotive community was a big one and Cisco needed Cellport's MobileWeb technology to fulfill that commitment. Michael Frendo said he knew his boss, Mr. Chambers, would appreciate our progress.

Paul ran a well-orchestrated and eventful meeting. Afterward, Michael Frendo told us that Cellport was exactly the kind of company Cisco wanted to invest in. Plus, he said it would give him personal pleasure to beat Motorola to the altar of strategic-funding with Cellport. When the meeting wrapped up, Michael and I shook hands and agreed to expedite the due diligence process for a $10 million investment. After Michael left, I congratulated Paul on his excellent work to create a partnership with Cisco — not only the Bubble period's number-one prized strategic investment partner but also the leading firm in the network equipment sector he was now targeting in search of partners to help build the telematics industry. I called Andy with the news and told him how easy an investment closing from Cisco appeared to be. Andy replied, "From your lips to God's ears!"

Andy said he would call Paul and Steve Parrish the following day to begin preparing the Cisco investment documents. I decided to spend more time with Ralph and his team to ensure that progress on our second-generation Universal Hands-Free system was on track. During our first major project briefing in weeks, Ralph and his team reported a slippage in schedule and said that with the new @Road project commitment, we would fall even further behind. With Cellport holding plenty of money in the bank and Cisco's money coming in right around the corner, my advice to Ralph was, "Let's accelerate our hiring." Ralph looked at me and laughed, "Pat when was the last time I asked you to interview a senior candidate for final approval?"

It was a good question. It had been maybe two to three weeks. "That's about right," Ralph said. "And please remember that you said that fellow was too marginal, so I passed on him."

Ralph emphasized to me that the world had changed. In 1999 we had hired more than a dozen exceptional people, but the last good hire for a senior position was Mike Lewellen, whom we brought on to lead our quality control operations, and that was more than five months earlier. In the months between that hire and the time of this discussion, Cellport had interviewed dozens of engineers, but more than 90 percent of the candidates could not meet our minimum hiring requirements. The excess capital that the Bubble brought to corporate and venture-funded technology companies created an enormous scarcity of human capital, particularly talented engineers and technology business managers in sectors that served the wireless and Internet industries. Competition for employees became tough, as firms offered employees from competing organizations 20-percent salary increases, hiring bonuses, stock options, and other perks, such as company-leased luxury cars.

This human capital shortage had begun in mid-1999 and would last through 2001. It was a completely new challenge for Cellport, whose struggles historically came from a lack of financial capital. Now money flowed easily but desirable talent was in scarce supply. I explained our hiring dilemma to Andy and John Thompson. They both believed that talented people were available but that our workloads limited the time we had available for recruiting. Andy then proposed that I hire an operations executive who could manage the company's hiring. That was a good idea, particularly with Cisco leaning toward investing around $10 million and other investors sure to join them, all of which would create new and substantial personnel needs. Furthermore, after years of development, Cellport's products were closer then ever to market, and product demand would put added pressure on our staff. For the sake of the company, Andy and John said that I should divide up my duties to make sure I could give my responsibilities of advancing Cellport's technologies and strategic relationships all the focus they deserved. The next day Andy called to introduce me to an executive recruiter who he thought would be ideal to help us find a capable candidate for the operations role.

That weekend, I was preoccupied with a conundrum that kept me from sleeping: Doug Daniels was reporting wonderful response to our product marketing efforts. He had hand-carried a suitcase containing a Universal Hands-Free demonstration unit to numerous meetings with car companies. All ordered test units and proceeded to expedite testing, and many had their tier-one suppliers buy units from us as well. Yet, I wondered, how could a small company like Cellport ever supply the global automotive market of 55 million new vehicles per year? [1] Plus, how could we ever design and build enough phone-specific adaptors for all the new phones that the cellular phone industry was producing? The cellular phone market was enormous and growing at an exorbitant rate; its global sales were more than 284 million units in 1999 and on the way to exceed 412 million units in 2000 [2] [3].

Modeling business and technical scenarios is one of my favorite intellectual exercises, and this conundrum presented a most interesting set of variables and metrics. I first needed to create an economic model of the Universal Hands-Free business that Cellport created. I assumed that one-third of the world's new vehicles, around 18 million automobiles, would need the docking station electronics and adaptors to provide hands-free capabilities. Plus, we knew that the global wireless industry could be expected to introduce more than 200 individual handset models each year; I assumed that we would need to build adaptors for at least half of these models, that tens of millions of current customers would purchase replacement adaptor units, and that we'd bring in nearly twenty million new customers per year. If the 18 million vehicle units sold for $300 per system and we were able to sell 25 to 40 million phone adaptors in the market for a $75 price, Cellport was looking at some absolutely astounding numbers. With this model, our product line sales revenues would exceed $8 billion a year. We would need several thousand employees.

There was no way that tiny Cellport could scale up fast enough to take advantage of the product category we had created. We obviously needed another business model. That Sunday night I had dedicated a few hours to reading the draft of a technology white paper, yet I could not stop my mind from wandering from the highly technical and detailed text. Less then 15 minutes into my reading, I hit on a major idea: We should take advantage of Cellport's charter of open-licensing its technologies and our hot new second-generation design to create a community of licensed product development companies around the world that would build products according to our exact designs in exchange for a cut of this $8 billion-plus market. It was a big idea but it needed serious vetting before I could introduce it to the Board of Directors. I jumped off the couch and sprinted out the door with our family golden retriever, Liz, figuring that a walk in the fresh evening air would help me think clearly enough to noodle the details of this epiphany. I was out for nearly two hours and when I returned home I had even greater enthusiasm for my new licensing strategy.

The next morning I awoke at 4:00 a.m., still thinking about the licensing idea for our second-generation product. I was certain that if we handled this idea well, our technology could become standard equipment in many of the world's automobiles. I was so anxious to start designing the core aspects of this new business paradigm for Cellport that, by 5:00 a.m., I was staring at the large white board in Cellport's main conference room, taking my first sip of coffee, and thinking: Where shall I start developing a vision for this wonderful kernel of an idea?

I kicked-off this pre-sunrise business planning exercise by giving my idea a name: Cellport Global Partners, or CGP. But before I could disclose this grand idea to my fellow Cellporters, I needed to identify the key business components that would make up a successful technology sharing and licensing program for our future Cellport Global Partners. That's where the hard work began. Over the course of the next several days the CGP business model components began to grow in number and detail. I identified the following as key components of this program:

•   A formal set of specifications to explain, to our partners, how to build adaptors and docking stations to comply with Cellport's connectors, electronics and software. This would require that we prepare volumes of technology-design guidelines and establish quality-control inspection criteria.

•   A specific Web site that would give all CGP participants a forum for sharing ideas. CGP partners could also buy and sell products via this site.

•   An investment of Cellport personnel committed to the program. We needed someone to lead the program as well as an engineer to oversee the process of transferring our technology know-how to CGP partners and a technology compliance testing program.

•   A short list of early CGP prospects.

•   Terms and conditions that Andy would need to weave into a formal contract.

•   A list of the CGP's key objectives and the benefits it would bring to the market, to its licensees and to Cellport.

As the week progressed, so did my work on the project and my confidence that the CGP idea was truly significant. I was convinced, from my analyses, that the CGP would generate several hundred million dollars a year in licensing royalties and establish our design as a de facto worldwide standard. This was hot, and I was now ready to roll it out to selective members of the Cellport leadership team.

I drafted a four-page document, with diagrams, that included a summary of the CGP's key program components. Toward the end of my business day, when the document was ready for our vice chairman's critique, I emailed it to Andy with a note asking him to call me when he had time to discuss it. That evening, shortly after the kids were in bed, I received a call from Andy, who was anxious to talk about the CGP program. Andy's first words were music to my ears. "I love this CGP idea," he said. "Let's talk about turning it into a reality."

As a quintessential nocturnal worker, some of Andy's best work happens late at night and that evening we talked about the CGP program for three hours, extending the conversation until it was well after 2:00 a.m. at Andy's home in Maryland. Andy had numerous good ideas, particularly with regard to two critical matters: how to establish the CGP licensing contract and how to structure the business. By the time we hung up, I was numb from a combination of joy and exhaustion, but with Andy's support of the CGP program I had gained a feeling of restfulness that I had not enjoyed since the previous Sunday.

That night I slept eight hours straight. When I woke up the next morning, I was ready to share the CGP program idea with other members of Cellport's leadership staff. That afternoon, I had our vice presidents assemble in the conference room for a briefing on the proposed CGP program. I also solicited their thoughts about it. The feedback was mostly positive, with the exception of some comments from Ralph. As a design architect and the lead engineer for the second-generation Universal Hands-Free system, Ralph was understandably protective of his work. He feared that the concept of sharing our design breakthroughs with other companies would create competition we might not otherwise have. He was also concerned, and rightly so, that the "cat was too far out of the bag" with companies like Cullmann, Dabendorf, and THBury, which were already experiencing better success than Cellport in the safety and gadget-centric German automotive market with products that were knock-offs of our designs. There was another German company, Peiker, that had mock-ups of products based on our designs that it was marketing to car companies as well. On an emotional level Ralph's resistance was understandable, but I reminded him that we were having troubling scaling up our design staff to meet our current obligations, and our marketing efforts were just getting off the ground. If we generated even a small proportion of the orders we expected, we would not be able to handle the work. The CGP program was the best solution to date.

**

The months of April and May of 2000 were intensely busy. In addition to creating a formal business plan for CGP and drafting the CGP contract terms and conditions, we were making good progress on our second-generation Universal Hands-Free design and Paul's work on our fourth round of financing was more spectacularly successful than any of us had anticipated.

Cisco had come through on its plan to invest $10 million in Cellport, and as soon as we shook hands on the deal, Paul was flooded with requests from other firms who were clamoring to invest side-by-side with the mighty Cisco. One day that spring, Steve Parrish and I were in New York for an investors' conference where we delivered a presentation on Cellport's product designs and business model. After we concluded our presentation we were corralled by several principals from a small Florida-based specialty investment fund, called Rock Creek Partners, who were seeking to initiate a conversation with us. The Rock Creek partners informed us that they were keen to follow Cisco's interest in Cellport. They were interested in participating in this investment round and had a few questions for us.

Steve and I agreed to meet with the fellows from Rock Creek that evening. Much to our surprise, they informed us that they had wanted to invest $3 million in Cellport, and that they had already approached Paul Heller about this, but after hearing our presentation they wanted us to consider allowing them to double that amount. In keeping with the Cellport spirit of respecting the roles of executives back home who were empowered to make these decisions, I told the Rock Creek principals that we welcomed their interest but that Paul and Andy were making the final determinations on the investors for our fourth round.

That evening I called Paul to tell him about Rock Creek's strong interest. He told me he was inclined to say yes to their proposal. He added that if investor interest in Cellport's fourth funding round continued on its current course, we would easily raise more than $20 million. Andy was concerned when he heard the news about Rock Creek's heightened interest. He said to me, "That's great. But do you realize how crazy the market is for hot private technology companies like Cellport?"

I admitted that it all appeared feverish. "No, Pat," he said. "This is beyond feverish. Do you realize we have not even picked a valuation price and people are lining up to give us millions just to participate with Cisco?"

Andy asked me to pick a price within the next few days. "Then we will see how many people still love Cellport," he said.

Whenever I need to make a big decision, like assigning a valuation to Cellport, I like to have several days to consider the numerous key variables involved. This was a very big decision that I needed to weigh carefully. Because Cellport's annual sales were under a few million dollars and our burn rate now exceeded $10 million annually, it was impossible to do a classic calculation based on multiples of sales or earnings. My gut told me that we made enormous progress since the FLV Fund invested $5 million at a $38 million valuation. In order to recognize FLV's support, we should show them a substantial markup in asset value. I decided that a $100 million valuation would speak volumes about our progress.

"Let's price the company's valuation at $100 million dollars for all those who still want to participate," I told Andy when I called him a few days later. The next week, Paul announced the valuation price. Not one investor stepped away from the negotiation table. During the course of the next several weeks, Andy finalized the investment contract and the funding agreements that were specific to each investor. As the lead investor, Cisco was given a seat on Cellport's Board of Directors, a role that Michael Frendo would assume [4]. Paul tallied up the investment totals. Much to our surprise and delight, Cellport raised more than $24 million dollars in fresh capital.

**

During the late spring months, Doug Daniels continued to attract encouraging interest in the market for our second-generation design, which gave me added motivation to formalize the establishment of the Cellport Global Partners program. I spent several hours each day and evening on the phone with Andy to help refine the business plan and contract drafts. By June 2000 I was ready to test market the CGP concept. Initially, I asked my old friend and partner, Hiro Sakurai, to study the CGP program for marketability in Japan. Concurrently, we sent letters to four European companies that seemed to have a strong interest in the Universal Hands-Free market. We sent the first CGP introduction letters to companies we knew were using our first-generation Universal Hands-Free system design — Cullmann, ESMO, and Dabendorf — and to another small German company we had learned of, called ALAC, that also provided hands-free technologies to the automotive market. In this letter, I informed the companies that Cellport had designed a second-generation Universal Hands-Free system that we intended to license to certain companies. Within two weeks we heard from ESMO, Cullmann and ALAC, all requesting to meet with us in Boulder in early July. This was a far more enthusiastic and encouraging response then I had expected from these relatively small German companies.

The ESMO fellows, whom I had met the previous fall at the Frankfurt International Motor Show, were our first CGP visitors, and, as I expected, they loved Cellport's new second-generation design. They were eager to sell their customer, Mr. Voit, on a cooperative CGP license program.

Our second guest from Germany was an exceptionally bright marketer by the name of Alf Naber, who was the founder of ALAC. Alf understood well how difficult it would be to build enough phone adaptors to serve the many types of mobile phones being introduced to the market. He also grasped the challenges that small companies in our line of business would face if we suddenly needed to supply tens of millions of docking station units to automotive companies. Alf was very enthusiastic to pursue an agreement that would give his company an opportunity to serve the large market that a new, de facto standard would create. As the principal of ALAC, he was able to commit directly to the contract.

The last guests to visit Boulder to learn about the CGP initiative were from Cullmann, the company that supplied hands-free technologies to Audi. The owner of the company, Wolfgang Cullmann, came accompanied by his lead engineer, Thomas Schlegel. The meeting with Wolfgang and Thomas lasted all afternoon and it was the most colorful and challenging of our CGP meetings to date. Clearly, they were the largest and most established of the European companies that had pirated our designs, thanks to their growing sales to Audi and, now, to Volkswagen as well. While Cullmann had clearly appropriated our technologies, these executives, oddly enough, had the attitude that Cellport was the smaller company and that they were interviewing us for a prospective partnership. When I briefed Wolfgang and Thomas on our second-generation design they were visibly shocked by how much smaller Ralph's team had been able to make the docking station as well as the agility and powerful application capabilities of our Dual-Processor Multi-Bus design.

After several hours of discussions, I could see on Wolfgang's and Thomas's faces that they were quite stressed about our second-generation design, so I suggested we break for a few hours until dinner that evening. Wolfgang jumped at the opportunity to have time to confer with Thomas on both the new Cellport design and our CGP business model.

I picked up our two Cullmann guests at their hotel at 7:30 p.m. As Wolfgang got into my car, his first words were, "What a coincidence. We both have nearly identical Audi A6 models, except I have the bigger engine. As Thomas can tell you, I love the power."

This was not an encouraging sign. Unlike the warm, cooperative spirit the ESMO and ALAC gentlemen had put forth, Wolfgang was asserting a distinctly competitive spirit. During our drive to the restaurant, we engaged in plenty of small talk about how lovely Boulder is and Wolfgang and Thomas both expressed how much they enjoyed their accommodations at the 100-year-old and elegant Hotel Boulderado. In my mind, however, I was preparing for a conflict of business styles. I thought to myself that Wolfgang was not a team player like Hiro, Steve Parrish, Andy and other senior people at Cellport. Even his name symbolized the individualistic personality of a lone wolf, I thought. There was no doubt in my mind that Wolfgang was a significantly smart businessman, but would he be a good citizen in the CGP community that we intended to establish? The restaurant we were heading toward was the Flagstaff House Restaurant, which offered fabulous cuisine and breathtaking views of the entire Boulder Valley. If the conversation went sideways during dinner, I thought, at least the meal and view would be memorable.

Our table did afford us great scenic views and Wolfgang seemed impressed with the restaurant and appreciative that I had selected it. His first goal was to order a bottle of red wine to toast our new relationship and the day's work. He seemed to have a much better spirit than I expected just 20 minutes previously. After our toast I sat silently, an approach that I learned long ago from my Japanese friends as a strategy for prompting a nervous aggressor to make the first move in a delicate situation. Within a few minutes, Wolfgang could not stand my silence.

He opened the conversation with a recap of the day's events. He said he appreciated getting to meet me and seeing Cellport's future Universal Hands-Free designs. Wolfgang then went on an interesting tangent. He stated that although Cellport's designs were visionary, the U.S. was definitely the wrong country in which to launch such a great product. I asked him to elaborate.

With exemplary logic, Wolfgang said Cellport had three big challenges in the U.S. First off, there were no hands-free laws to speak of, so people did not give a damn about driving with a Universal Hands-Free solution. Second, U.S. automakers are known for not partnering well with their suppliers, while German automakers do make good partners. I interrupted him to ask him to explain this point.

"Simple," he said. "In Germany, my automotive customers tell me what phones I should build adaptors for and then they pay me all the expenses for designing a phone-specific adaptor. This level of cooperation is one of the primary reasons German cars have the best technology and quality; we work together to build great cars. This would never happen in the U.S."

Wolfgang then made his third point. "Americans," he said, "Do not think 'safety first' like Europeans do, so the market for a truly full-featured system that holds the mobile phone in secure position for hands-free safety, provides an outside antenna for better reception and charges the battery at the same time is just not a priority for Americans."

Wolfgang's observations were most interesting to me and I used this opening in the conversation to assert my understanding of these circumstances. "That is why I called the licensing effort to launch our second-generation product Cellport Global Partners, because I deeply believe that the market is global."

"Yes, yes. You are right, Pat," he said. "As Thomas and I discussed during our break, the Cellport product design is brilliant and we are completely confident that this is the way of the future. It is your business model that is wrong."

I asked Wolfgang to please critique the business model. I told him that I was open to learning how we could improve the CGP program.

"OK, I'll do my best. But please don't be insulted," he said. "With the CGP program the only assured winners are Cellport and the consumer. The losers are your licensees, who are left to fight like dogs over standard designs that will create a commodity market, and the automakers, who want unique products so they can have higher profits. Your program does not address the profit needs of those two groups."

"I hear you, Wolfgang," I said. "Let me noodle your points, and, in the meantime, let's order dinner and another bottle of wine."

Over the next hour, we ate and drank while Thomas asked many good, technical questions. He was particularly curious about how we came up with the Dual-Processor Multi-Bus design. Wolfgang and Thomas were a highly partitioned tag team, I realized. Wolfgang handled all the business matters and avoided technical discussions; Thomas, in turn, handled all the technical questions and communicated my answers back to Wolfgang in German.

As we wrapped up our dinner, I steered the conversation back to the objections Wolfgang had with the CGP program and asked him how we could work together. By now, having enjoyed more than a bottle of red wine, Wolfgang had become a little more relaxed and friendlier.

In his now free-flowing state of mind, he made a profound comment that explained the core of his philosophy.

"The CGP program would turn Cellport into the Intel of the telematics world and all your licensees into low-profit drones," he said. "Frankly, the world does not need another American company dominating a market like they do with almost every technology area. As a European, I cannot support any more American economic dominance."

I shot back with a very American answer. "But Wolfgang, it is a U.S. company that has invested more than $10 million dollars and taken all the risks in advancing this Universal Hands-Free business. Why shouldn't Cellport harvest the benefits for our shareholders and employees who took all the risks to do this inventive work?"

Wolfgang volleyed back: "You should have done your marketing homework before you invested so much money and time," he said. "As I said to you before, Pat, you live in the wrong country to launch such a great automotive technology."

"Well, Wolfgang," I replied. "I think you missed my point."

After dinner, as we drove back to the Boulderado Hotel, Wolfgang said we should keep our communication channels open. "As you pointed out earlier today, the worldwide market for this Universal Hands-Free solution will be in the billions of dollars and we should find some opportunity for cooperation." As one to never burn a bridge, I welcomed his offer and told him that Cellport would continue to move its research efforts and the CGP licensing program forward, and if he changed his mind, I would welcome his company into the family of CGP licensees.

Just before I bade Wolfgang and Thomas goodbye, I thought it was important to draw a line in the sand establishing my position on the invention ownership that our patents and pending applications already affirmed. I said, as one of my last comments, that given Cellport's invention leadership and growing telematics patent portfolio, I was certain we would find the opportunity to cooperate at some level.

By this time, Wolfgang's accumulated feelings of jet lag, exhaustion from the eye-opening day and drinks over dinner imbued him with a friendly tone. "Ya ya," he said. "Men as determined as you and me will find a way. Let's keep in touch. I like you as a fellow business leader. Good night for now."

9 | A Death in the Cellport Family

1991
1992
1993
1994
1995
1996
1997
1998
1999
2000
2001
2002
2003
2004
2005
2006
2007
2008
2009

The dinner discussion with Wolfgang Cullmann reverberated in my head all night and it was still affecting me the next morning when Doug Daniels and I met to discuss a variety of marketing issues. When I told Doug about Wolfgang's stance on our technologies and the Cellport Global Partners program, he laughed. "I need to send him flowers for conditioning you for my proposal," he said.

"Great," I said. "Are you in cahoots with Wolfgang? Is this round two of Pat-jolting?"

"You know I am a committed, pro-Cellport team player," Doug said. "But you need to hear my proposals and take these ideas to heart. Pat, do you realize there are only four employees who are focused on marketing and sales out of the 65 people you employ? With what is assured to be a white-hot Cellport product launch announcement this winter, we must increase our budget to position Cellport as a consumer brand, and we need to hire at least a half dozen people ASAP to prepare for the product launch.

"You were a great product marketer, Pat, but now you're concentrated on finance and more geek-like innovations. You need to refocus, and that is what I'm here to help you do."

"OK, boy genius," I said. "Please proceed. I'm all ears."

Doug launched into a long presentation. He listed more than a dozen initiatives he said were necessary to reposition Cellport in the market and prepare us for a commercial launch of our second-generation product in November 2000, just four months away. At the top of the list was a recommendation that we drop the word Labs from our corporate moniker, rename the company Cellport Systems and create a new consumer-friendly logo. This was a spot-on idea; Doug had picked up a victory on his first initiative. As our meeting progressed, Doug convinced me that we needed to invest in new strategic communications counsel, update our Web site, build several dozen demonstration kits for important prospective customers, hire three more sales people and open a Detroit office to help respond to the dozens of product inquiries we expected to receive. Finally, Doug urged me to accelerate the hiring of an operations executive. He was convinced, despite Wolfgang Cullmann's anti-Detroit attitude, that Cellport would have an order from a U.S. automaker by year-end. Yet the manufacture of our Universal Hand-Free products, which had been delayed while we awaited the availability of the powerful new processor chips that were the heart of the system's new feature-rich design, was months behind schedule. I gave Doug the green light on his proposal to beef up marketing and sales capabilities, regardless of the outcome of the CGP licensing program that was now threatened by Wolfgang Cullmann's abstention.

Cellport needed senior management not only to lead our operations, however, but to lead the MobileWeb team as well. Unlike our previous two strategic funding partners, AT&T Wireless and L&H's FLV Fund, which had left Cellport alone to pursue the product design work they funded for us, Cisco had become very demanding of our MobileWeb designers soon after its investment closed. It quickly became clear to me that without Chuck Spaur's design leadership skills, our MobileWeb design team had been swayed by Cisco's engineers to take our designs in directions that seemed very biased toward Cisco's view of the market, which entailed putting a new Cisco Internet router chip in our MobileWeb servers. Although there certainly were some merits to adding a sophisticated Cisco chip to our MobileWeb equipment, in my gut I did not believe that the consumer automotive market would tolerate Cisco's pricing ambitions. I thought to myself that following Cisco's advice might indeed be a good idea, but I needed stronger leadership on our MobileWeb team to determine if Cisco's approaches were as good for Cellport as they were for Cisco.

By the fall of 2000, opportunities were so abundant and our cash position was so strong that it was obvious Cellport's two core technologies had become extremely popular telematics connectivity solutions for dozens of important customers and prospective customers as well. I reflected back on how utterly destitute we were just two years earlier and how the telecom-Internet bubble had now brought us a seemingly endless amount of money and opportunities. But all periods in history have certain downsides, and this bubble period was saddled with at least two: the extreme shortage of engineering talent and the challenge of determining which of the many business opportunities before us were truly great and sustainable and which had only temporary value and would eventually become nothing more than artifacts of these crazy times.

One certainty I did have was that I could always count on my dear old friend and fellow founder, Hiro Sakurai, when I needed help and insight. Hiro visited Cellport that September. He proposed that Cellport open an office in Japan, which would bolster our ability to develop our business internationally. Plus, hiring engineers in Japan could ease our U.S. talent shortage. Hiro brought with him a significant amount of data that characterized a very favorable Japanese telematics market and he made a very compelling business case that Cellport's advanced connectivity technologies and licensing model would be well accepted by mobile phone and automotive companies there.

On one hand, it was easy to be seduced by Hiro's arguments; a Cellport office in Japan would give us a presence in the world's fastest growing wireless market. But I also knew that Hiro was as talented as Doug Daniels in bringing new opportunities to the table, and that, oddly enough, was a downside for me. Frankly, I was concerned that if we invited too much demand for our products and technology expertise, we might end up drinking out of two fire hoses simultaneously.

Over the course of the next several days, I asked Hiro to spend time with our senior leadership team while I concentrated on several interviews with the final candidates for our operations leadership position. By the end of the week I had received emails from many of the members of our management team saying what a great idea it was to establish a Cellport-Japan office. Frankly, I should have known not to let Mr. Personality have so much time with the Cellport management. I had intended for our team members to brief Hiro on their respective programs and progress; but Hiro took advantage of these meeting opportunities to pitch everyone in Boulder, and even Andy by phone, on the wisdom of opening an office in Japan. I knew I was in trouble when Hiro sauntered into my office with our chief financial officer, Steve Parrish, in tow to schedule a time to review the budget for "our new Cellport-Japan office." Luckily for Hiro, I had just finished a very encouraging third interview with our lead candidate for the operations position and I was beginning to feel that help with our operational challenges was on the way. Perhaps Cellport would have enough organizational capacity to support an office in Japan. I agreed to Hiro's request and he committed to give 50 percent of his time to the new Cellport-Japan business; in the remainder of his time he worked selling a suite of software to Japanese wireless carriers for some U.S. and European companies.

Cellport was about to achieve three major milestones that would each have a profound effect on our history: hiring an operations executive, launching into a volume production contract from an automaker and signing CGP licensees. I was busier than I ever imagined possible. I was excited to recommend to our Board of Directors that we hire James Mayhew to oversee our business operations.

James had enjoyed a career in operations and finance — with progressively increasing responsibilities — at a highly respected global telecommunications firm; his credentials ideally complemented our needs. He could start in two weeks. He would oversee more than 80 percent of Cellport's staff in the departments of production, design engineering, accounting, sales and marketing. This would leave me with more time to devote to advanced technology development, finance, the Cellport Global Partners program and, most importantly, mapping out our future strategy. James Mayhew's incorporation into the company was well timed, because the design and tooling of the plastics parts for our second-generation Universal Hands-Free product were now finished and our prototype crew had made dozens of samples for our early customers to evaluate. With these key product objectives accomplished, Mike Lewellen, our vice president of production, planned to start transitioning the product to our contract manufacturer, Elcoteq, for volume production runs in early November. Doug prepared to spend a week hand-delivering the final design products and demonstration kits to numerous domestic and foreign automakers in Detroit. I was glad that James would be on board to take over the time-intensive jobs of overseeing production and managing key account sales. There was no doubt he was about to experience a baptism by fire during his first few weeks at Cellport.

Doug reported that he had hit pay dirt in Detroit, where he enjoyed successful sales meetings with General Motors, Nissan, Honda, BMW and, most impressively, with Ford Motor Company. Doug told James that he had never participated in so many customer prospect meetings where he was asked for price quotes and samples and, in the Ford case, where he had received a request for an immediate quote for 8,000 units to be delivered in the second quarter of 2001. That was a radically fast timetable. Upon his return from Detroit, Doug said it was critical that we have the senior leadership gather for an automotive planning meeting; his trip had been so successful we were on track to far exceed our aggressive sales goals for 2001 and 2002. James scheduled a meeting and invited me to participate. I agreed, on the condition that I would take a very passive role out of respect for his new leadership role.

Doug kicked off the session by listing the names of the five companies he had met with and their degrees of interest, requests for samples and needs for engineering support. Ford's immediate need for 8,000 units was the big story. Ford would supply the units to one of its largest fleet customers, Hewlett Packard (HP), and it planned to expand its use of the Cellport product to other market segments shortly thereafter. The HP angle was a direct contrast to Wolfgang's opinion about Americans' lack of interest in hands-free safety; HP had a corporate policy mandating that its field sales and service personnel could talk on cellular phones while driving company cars only if their phones were secured in the cars and operating in hands-free mode.

James helped organize our management team, including the fledgling engineering liaison team we had by now established in Detroit, and he helped them agree on the resources needed to respond to Ford's request. Ford's anxiousness to use Cellport's second-generation system was obvious. It had already tested the sample unit Doug had left with its executives and demonstrated its effective use in Ford vehicles. And to really capture our attention, Ford offered to issue Cellport a purchase order for almost $3 million within a few days.

Delighted with Cellport's ability to attract the interest of so many automotive companies, I shifted my attention to the CGP program and to pursuing strategic initiatives with cellular phone vendors such as Motorola and Nokia, which were now swiftly moving into the telematics market. To move the CGP program forward, I would need plenty of face time with executives from the leading European prospects such as ALAC; ESMO's supplier, Votronics; Dabendorf; and a Swedish company we had recently learned about that had IdeaJacked our designs, called Smarteq. Planning for the CGP tour of Europe turned out to be easier then I had imagined. By the fall of 2000, Cellport's second-generation Universal Hands-Free design had become the buzz of the European telematics industry, as was our proposed licensing program. My trip to Europe was set to span 10-days in November, but first I wanted to make a quick trip to Motorola's campus in suburban Chicago to explore business opportunities with that company and to advance my friendship with Ray Sokola.

The news out of Motorola was highly encouraging; in the year following our initial attempts to form a relationship with Motorola, Ray reported that he and his team had recently won the OnStar product business from General Motors, beating out Delphi, which had designed OnStar's early generations of the emergency cell phone and airbag notification service. In the short time since Ray's team at

Motorola had taken over the OnStar account, GM and a few German companies had expressed a strong interest in the next-generation universal wireless technologies that Motorola promulgated. Fortunately, these technologies centered on Cellport's vehicle network platforms, in particular our Dynamic Digital Bus and Vehicle Server technologies, which GM had learned about during our work with IDB Forum demonstrations dating back to 1998. I pushed Ray for specific insights, but all he said was, "Stay tuned for some good news in 2001." I pushed Ray as well for some encouragement that Motorola might have possible interest in joining the Cellport Global Partner program, but this effort had less promise. Ray said he thought any deal with Motorola to sell a Universal Hands-Free solution would take years to develop.

I briefed Ray on Cellport's hiring of James Mayhew, Doug's early win with Ford on the Hewlett Packard fleet program and Ford's talk of a much bigger expansion of business over the next few years. Ray looked at me with skepticism and said, "I am not sure if I should give you my congratulations or condolences."

While trying to be as diplomatic as possible, Ray described Ford as a company that is both confused about its priorities and difficult to do business with, especially in telematics. "As an example, one group in Ford is anxious to give you an order for 8,000 units while another group in Ford is investing tens of millions of dollars into a telematics business called Wingcast that is sure to cross Cellport's Dynamic Digital Bus and Vehicle Server technologies," he said. Although Ray noted he had no extensive dealings with Ford directly, his cohorts in Motorola's automotive business unit considered Ford the most difficult of the U.S. automakers to work with.

"Make sure you get purchase orders for all the work you do. These guys are not the genteel types that Cellport is used to doing business with in the telecom space," Ray cautioned.

Upon my return to Boulder, I briefed both James and Doug on Ray's warning that Ford would be a challenging customer. James assured me he would be careful and would not commit to building products for Ford without a purchase order. Doug, noting the strong reception Cellport was receiving from domestic and foreign automakers, proposed that we expand our small office in the Detroit area and hire an office manager who had a strong automotive engineering background. I turned to James and said, "This is your call. Why don't you work up an office budget for expanded presence in Detroit, and we can review its cost-benefits next week?"

While we were flush with cash from the $24 million Cisco-led investment round, we did have to be cautious with our funds. We now had an office in Tokyo and more than 70 people on our staff. Our cash burn rate was more than $1 million a month and we expected that the costs to prepare for shipping products to Ford and other carmakers and to open up after-market retail sales channels would require an inventory budget of $4 to $5 million.

**

During the morning of October 31, James walked into my office and said, "I don't want to alarm you, but Jeff Platz may have been on a flight out of Taiwan that reportedly crashed."

"What was Jeff doing in Taiwan and how did you learn this frightful news?" I asked.

James told me that Jeff, our purchasing manager, had gone to Taiwan to pick up parts that were critically important for our Universal Hands-Free product from an electronics components vendor that was slow with deliveries. By picking up the components personally, Jeff would have been able to verify that the product met our quality standards and he would have been able to ensure delivery of enough units for our production run, which was scheduled to take place the next week. In fact, Jeff was going to fly from Taiwan to San Francisco and then directly on to Mexico to hand-deliver the components to our manufacturer. I accompanied James into a conference room where he had set up a TV to track the news reports that were now streaming out of Taiwan. A Singapore Airlines jumbo jet had mysteriously crashed within a minute after taking off from the Chiang Kai-Shek

International Airport in Taipei. I saw Mike Lewellen, Jeff's boss and close friend, in the conference room, staring at the TV. Mike was one of Cellport's strongest individuals and most reliable leaders, but when I saw him I knew we were in the midst of a very serious issue. He was as red as a beet and visibly shaken.

"Mike, are you confident that Jeff was on that flight?" I asked.

"Fairly confident, but not 100 percent sure," he replied. "I have a call into our travel agent to verify Jeff's itinerary."

There were more than a dozen Cellporters in the conference room, transfixed by the TV, watching live footage of the jet's flaming wreckage. The aircraft had broken into several pieces. The news reporter said that Taiwan had been experiencing a monsoon rainstorm that afternoon but that dozens of planes had departed safely and that the cause of this accident was unknown. The only encouraging news we heard was a report that there were dozens of survivors and that emergency crews were still looking for more, although they were hampered by darkness and severe rains.

As we all sat dazed and hoping for the best, Mike Lewellen announced that our travel agent had confirmed that Jeff was indeed scheduled to take that flight. Mike was particularly affected by the news. He and Jeff had actually flipped a coin, days earlier, to decide who should go on the trip, and Jeff had won the toss. Both Mike and Jeff had been frustrated that the manufacturer had seemed uninterested in expediting delivery of a key component. They had decided that it was necessary to travel to Taiwan to take charge of the situation. Mike said that Jeff had been enthusiastic about taking the trip; he enjoyed the idea that it is possible to get to any place in the world so quickly to help the Cellport cause.

The balance of that day at Cellport was unforgettably difficult, especially for Mike and Ralph, for both were close with Jeff and both knew his girlfriend, Sherry, and his ex-wife and children. Yet there were survivors on Singapore Flight 006, and we all quietly prayed for Jeff to be one of them.

Throughout the day, most of the senior management team watched various news channels for what appeared to be growing insights into this now-complex tragedy. The accident might not have been caused solely by the intense monsoon rains. Reports were starting to indicate that human error may have played a role in Flight 006's crash and fiery break-up moments after takeoff.

The small conference room became command central, and James gave Mike authority to make whatever decisions were necessary to help us determine Jeff's fate, which was still unknown. It was obvious from all reports that the emergency rescue work was difficult. It was in the wee hours of the morning in Taiwan, with rain pounding down monsoon-style on a runway full of chaos and disaster.

Mike dispatched Bill Weakley, a production engineer, to leave the next day for Taiwan. By 3:00 p.m. in Boulder, Mike had booked an airplane ticket for Bill, whose mission was straightforward: Get us better data on Jeff's status. Bill had good instincts and he was resourceful, exactly the type of skills one would need to navigate through the chaos of a large disaster in a foreign country.

Late that afternoon, newly available film footage showed emergency crews carrying dozens of survivors out of the wreck on stretchers, injured but alive. The accident had happened more than eight hours earlier, yet we had received no "I'm OK" call from Jeff. We intensely studied the faces of the survivors shown on TV and saw a very dazed 30-something Caucasian male who seemed to have Jeff's side profile. Maybe Jeff was alive but injured. Mike was also following news sites on the Web, where he found a photo that he thought showed Jeff being carried on a stretcher. He printed several color copies of what we all hoped would prove to be a photo of one Jeff Platz.

Early evening arrived in Boulder as daytime was beginning in Taiwan. Reports started to surface that the death count was high and that the plane may have hit a piece of construction equipment on takeoff. This accident was looking worse and worse. As we left work, everyone agreed to take all news updates first to Mike, and he would then disseminate the latest news to me and all of Cellport's vice presidents.

But the evening came and went with no news from Mike.

The next morning the story we did hear was unsettling. Jeff's girl-friend, Sherry, told Mike that she had spoken to Jeff right before he boarded the plane. He told her that the heavy rain pelting the roof of the airport made him nervous about the flight. Yet he was anxious to return to the states that evening, she said. He was pleased to have se-cured the critically important components Cellport needed to produce early sample products, especially on behalf of the pending sale of products to Ford.

The Cellport office was hauntingly quiet the day after the crash. Bill Weakley was en route to Taiwan, and Mike was in frequent touch with Sherry and with Jeff's ex-wife, Zena, and now Jeff's mom and dad. The silence in the office reflected our increasing understanding that it was more and more unlikely that we would receive good news.

After several days of physically and emotionally exhausting travel, Jeff's father, who had joined Bill in Asia, was able to identify Jeff's body, and DNA testing further confirmed what was by then fully un-derstood. Not long after that, Jeff's remains were flown to Colorado Springs for a memorial service.

The week of Jeff's death went by in a panorama of sadness and grief. By the time of the memorial service, we knew that the Singapore Air-lines disaster was caused by a series of mistakes. After receiving clear-ance from the control tower to take off, despite the torrential mon-soon rains, the pilot tragically turned his plane, loaded with hundreds of travelers, onto a runway that was closed for construction. Just as the plane was lifting off, it hit a large piece of construction equipment that was parked in the middle of the closed runway.

Jeff's memorial service was surreal. Jeff and his ex-wife, Zena, had just recently started to find more peace with their post-divorce rela-tionship and now, tragically, she was left as the sole parent of two chil-dren, who were in a state of shock and sure to miss their father dearly. Jeff's mother and father were both crushed by this radically sudden loss of their high-tech, successful son. To complicate the human tragedy, Sherry had been too new in her relationship with Jeff to feel that she was a full-fledged member of the family, and that exacerbated her grief. Many, many people were hurt and saddened by the loss of this terrific man, who lost his life in support of our company's goal to be a good supplier to Ford. The dozens and dozens of Cellporters who attended the day-long memorial events in Colorado Springs expressed their deep personal condolences to the Platz family. Saying goodbye afterward to the family was especially hard for Mike and Ralph. They had both met Jeff years back, when they all worked together at a tech company in Colorado Springs. It was Mike and Ralph who had recruited Jeff to Cellport as our purchasing manager of strategic components for Cellport's second-generation Universal Hands-Free product. Mike, James, Andy and I discussed ways Cellport could aid Zena's and Jeff's children. We agreed to pick up certain expenses and to continue to pay his salary until the insurance company financial settlements arrived. We also converted his stock options to longer-lasting stock warrants.

After Jeff's death, everyone at Cellport fell into a state of mourning that lasted for weeks. I made a personal vow to myself to always remember Jeff and to honor his contributions and commitment to Cellport. I kept this in mind as I got back into the work of promoting our second-generation Universal Hands-Free designs and the CGP licensing program. I continue to draw inspiration from his memory today.

Others at Cellport exhibited similar passions. Doug's progress toward solidifying a deal with Ford, for example, began moving at breakneck speed and Ford began talking about potential production numbers that were astounding. Ford wanted to know how quickly we could ramp up to deliver tens of thousands of units a month. That would give us more than $40 million in revenue from just this one account. Doug and his small team in Detroit were making other promising inroads at Nissan, BMW and with GM as well.

Ford had reason to be motivated. By 2000, its market research had found that more than 90 percent of new Ford vehicle buyers preferred owning and using their personal portable handsets for use in both mobile and in-car usage scenarios, rather than having to own separate mobile phones for in-car and non-car use. This market intelligence was not lost on many leaders in Ford's purchasing and marketing departments. Cellport's Universal Hands-Free design had anticipated this consumer trend and would give end-users this type of choice and flexibility, while the design that Ford's own Wingcast venture was proposing was initially limited to work with a car-embedded phone.

Mike pushed back their first production start by a few weeks, but they, too, were eager to deliver products to customers. Both Ralph and Mike were personally motivated; they both hoped that early and substantial sales would potentially help improve the value of the stock warrant certificate that Andy had drafted for the Jeff Platz estate.

I was also now ready to make my trip to Europe to advance the marketing of our CGP licensing program, and I was determined to deliver a strategic win for Cellport. As my flight departed for Germany, I thought about Jeff's death and the scenes at his memorial. I felt very sad for a long time after takeoff and could not get out of my mind the brutal reality of just how fragile life is.

As my plane passed over eastern Canada and the Atlantic Ocean, I made myself steer my thoughts to work. I was on my way to Frankfurt, Germany, where I would be greeted by Edgar Schumacher of ESMO, who would drive me to meet Stefan Voit, the owner of Votronics, the company that built the Universal Hands-Free products that ESMO distributed. In less than 12 hours I would be face-to-face with someone who had pirated my technologies, someone I would try to convert to become a contributor to my envisioned community of CGP partners. This would be my first pro-active launch in Germany and my first big initiative, since we had contacted the various German companies about CGP in the summer months, to seek support for my vision of creating a standard worldwide Universal Hands-Free platform based on Cellport's technologies and to ask companies to adopt our physical design, which would provide economic advantages to us all. Having spent the previous 10 years developing bleeding-edge technology solutions, I was confident I could lead the technical discussions. But what would these German entrepreneurs have in mind for their own economic interests? I wouldn't know until the next day.

Meeting Stefan Voit was like meeting a sane version of the billionaire industrialist Howard Hughes. He had an absolute facility with American English that was instantly impressive and he articulated stories about his life that were full of industry-building invention work. Stefan told me that years ago, for his honeymoon, he had piloted his young bride on a small airplane from Virginia Beach, Virginia, to the west coast of the U.S. That story sealed the Hughes comparison for me.

During an introductory tour of Voit's facility, I learned that Stefan's primary work was managing his family's machine tool factory as well as an aluminum die casting foundry. Both of these family operations were amazingly sophisticated and somewhat like one would expect to find tucked away in a small German village. The Voit family's tooling and foundry operations employed hundreds of skilled German tradesmen and engineers, who built mostly ultra-lightweight engine and transmission castings for Germany's four premium automotive companies: Audi, BMW, Daimler-Benz and Porsche. Votronics was a side business for Stefan to build ESMO's Universal Hands-Free system. Stefan appeared to treat Votronics as a hobby venture set up primarily to engage his renaissance-man intellect.

Back in Stefan's office, I gave Stefan a briefing on the CGP business model and licensing program. About halfway through my slide show I sensed he was losing interest. A wonderfully honest guy with a brilliantly high IQ and charisma as well, Stefan stated that in creating his Universal Hands-Free system for ESMO, he had simply modified the Cellport design that ESMO had provided him. He did not realize how committed Cellport was in leading the market. His real interest in the product was that it gave him an entry into either the BMW or Daimler-Benz electronics design departments, where he hoped for a new business challenge in an area other than machine tooling and castings.

Stefan professed that he thought Cellport's ambition to establish a global standard would be great, if Votronics owned the technology. He did not want to become a mere licensee. Edgar began showing signs of stress as he sat there, watching Stefan. I was observing this as I worked to efficiently sort out our respective economic ambitions, and I modeled some alternative potential business scenarios, but it was obvious that the partnership between Edgar and Stefan appeared to be crumbling on the spot. Based on Stefan's early read of the business opportunity, he said he would most likely prefer to exit the business and find a new product to occupy his hyper-energetic mind.

The drive back to Frankfurt the next day with Edgar was clearly an uncomfortable one for him, so I decided not to mention Stefan's slip-up about his source for the Cellport Universal Hands-Free kit he had copied. But the circumstances were obvious: Edgar had tried to IdeaJack a Cellport product line. Appropriating our existing designs eliminated, for him, the need to invest years of product development time and enabled him to immediately benefit, financially, from over $10 million in research and development that Cellport had by now invested.

IdeaJacking is highly efficient, particularly from a capital standpoint. Companies that get away with it can sometimes yield a better return on their investment than the actual inventor! The scenario that played out in Stefan Voit's office in Germany is exactly why Michael Braitberg, from the very beginning of Cellport's history, preached to me that an investment of time and money to protect our inventions with sound patents would prove to become critically important in our company's survival strategy. Although we were unsuccessful in developing a partnership with Stefan Voit, this European industrialist realized that he was violating our company's patents, and therefore he would discontinue that line of business.

**

My next visit was with ALAC's Alf Naber, who picked me up outside Frankfurt for a three-hour drive into the beautiful Sauerland region of northern Germany. Alf hosted a dinner in a fabulous restaurant fitted into a centuries-old castle overlooking a quaint German village. We talked at length about the economies of scale in the production process that the Cellport CGP program would offer, which was critical for our stated goal of supplying docking stations to a third of new automobiles produced each year and the need to build adaptors for dozens of different portable handsets per year. Alf understood the CGP model.

If adopted, the model would grow the market more quickly and at less cost for all suppliers, and it would make hands-free capabilities more affordable for customers. Alf had a Ph.D. in marketing and a well-schooled fluency when discussing economics, which were refreshing to an old econo-head like me. After dinner, Alf and I made plans to meet at his business office the next morning for more CGP business modeling as well as contract discussions.

Alf's business employed several dozen local people working in sales, engineering and final assembly of products for shipments throughout Europe. Alf gave me a tour of his business, which was strikingly orderly and clean. His conference room was beautifully illuminated by the natural morning sun and furnished with the lovely wood grains and clean lines of high-end Danish style designs. In true German tradition, a plate full of delicious cookies was centered on the conference table and coffee was soon served. This business welcoming ceremony is a wonderfully warm tradition that is commonly practiced by German companies, especially the small- to medium-sized businesses. I briefed Alf and his engineers on the details and the elegantly smaller and improved performance attributes that Cellport's second-generation Universal Hands-Free architecture was able to achieve with the Dual-Processor Multi-Bus design. Alf and his lead engineers immediately understood the significant improvements this invention provided compared to the first-generation Cellport design that many German companies had copied. I explained that my goal was to sign up enough German companies to adopt Cellport's second-generation system design so that we would together effectively create a single universal platform instead of the six versions, including Cellport's, that existed at the time.

During a working lunch we all discussed the types of training the CGP would need to provide to successfully transfer the second-generation technology know-how from Cellport to ALAC. After lunch, Alf dismissed his staff and together we shared our respective thoughts on what the CGP license would need to cover as well as various aspects of the CGP business model. This was exactly the type of discussion Andy was craving notes on because he had been creating the CGP contract completely out of whole cloth and wanted market feedback about it. He wanted the CGP contract to address business issues that real, prospective licensees like Alf would have, not just theoretical concepts that we developed internally at Cellport. Alf's desires and concerns for a CGP contract were fair and constructive. I took copious notes as this very smart and worldly guy established the parameters he would expect us to consider when framing a relationship within the context of my CGP vision, which was now just six months old.

In the spirit of building the CGP licensing cooperative, Alf offered to introduce me to the Funkwerk Dabendorf company from Old East Germany. Alf wanted to recruit Dabendorf into the CGP community. He would help explain that the approach that ALAC, Cullmann, Dabendorf, Votronics and the Swedish producer, Smarteq, were currently using, in which each created a different "Universal Hands-Free" product platform based on Cellport's design, was not sustainable. None of the companies, individually, would be able to scale their businesses to produce an adequate variety of adaptors that the many new types of wireless handset designs flooding the market would require. These five European IdeaJackers represented both a challenge and an opportunity to me in my work to establish a standard interface for mobile handset connectivity in vehicles. I was grateful that Alf, one of the five that I needed to convert to join CGP, understood this and supported me.

Before we would be able to visit Dabendorf, however, I had to travel to southern Germany to visit the supplier of a particular speech technology software we were interested in. Afterward, I flew into Berlin, where I once again met up with Alf Naber, who had generously driven for four to five hours from his home in the Sauerland region to pick me up at the airport. From there we drove to the small village of Dabendorf to visit the Dabendorf company. We arrived well into evening and checked into a modest hotel-guest haus on a country road just outside of the village. Alf and I had dinner and wine to culminate what had been a very stimulating day.

"Not too bad," I later thought. I was batting 50 percent. ALAC looked like a great partner and although Stefan Voit was an unlikely participant, I considered that he, too, would have been a fascinating person to build a business ecosystem with. In the morning I would meet a new IdeaJacker. Would that company follow Alf's lead and join our CGP community? Or would it, like Votronics, consider leaving the business altogether?

**

At 6:00 a.m. I gave up on a restless night of little sleep and put on my jogging clothes for a brisk, crack-of-dawn run in Northern Germany, my first real exercise in several days. As I found my pace, I started studying the homes, which were grouped in small neighborhoods of 5 to 20 units. Stretches of shabby farm acreage separated these small housing clusters. My mind flashed back to a time in the mid 1970s, when I had a research internship, facilitated by the University of Buffalo's Department of Economics, at the Department of Commerce in Washington, D.C. This internship was part of a five-year multi-university study program in international economics that I was grateful to experience, compliments of the types of generous scholarships and stipends that many students at American universities are fortunate to receive. The Washington, D.C. internship was a wonderful experience and a major eye-opener for this middle class, public university student from blue-collar Buffalo, New York. As the internship was structured, I spent three days a week at the Commerce Department conducting hands-on economic research and two days attending classes in economics at the Johns Hopkins School for Advanced International Study, also in D.C.

At the Department of Commerce, I was assigned to help investigate and analyze the impact that new industries and technologies had on the Hungarian economy from 1960 to 1975. This research became forever helpful to me. I learned that at the time, Hungary was experiencing a strong, four- to six-percent economic growth rate. But

I discovered that the numbers that the Commerce Department was reporting on Soviet bloc countries, such as Hungary, Poland and East Germany, were most likely the result of double and triple counting of data. The Department of Commerce was reporting these statistics to the White House and Department of Defense, which in turn relied on the data for policy-making purposes. Once I learned how to ask the right questions about the economic growth numbers, it became obvious these were political numbers rather than factual data. These growth numbers were modeled based on capitalistic assumptions, not socialistic and communistic realities.

During the final week of my internship, I was invited to have lunch with my research supervisor, Dr. Ellias, a Hungarian-trained economist who left that country in the 1950s and never returned. During our lunch over sandwiches his wife had packed for us, Dr. Ellias reminded me that I was still an undergraduate and should wait until finishing graduate studies before suggesting that the Commerce Department's economic modeling of the Soviet sphere was erroneous. Recognizing that he was putting me in my place, so to speak, and warning me not to meddle in his assignment objectives, I thanked him for his advice and agreed that more study would be helpful. During this same lunch, Dr. Ellias asked me if I would consider taking on work with someone he knew at the Central Intelligence Agency during the forthcoming year, when I would be pursuing economic and cultural studies in Colombia. "No thanks, Dr. Ellias," I replied. "After the last five months experiencing government work, I am more inclined to toil in the business community."

My internship experience, however, gave me a window into the Soviet-controlled economy of Eastern Europe. I became convinced that the region had only spotty episodes of real growth, that most of the region was poor, that the people worked in a quasi-slavery economy that favored communistic oligarchs, and that the countries were frail and vulnerable to shortages of goods in all sectors. I theorized that Dr. Ellias and others at the Department of Commerce knew the White House and Department of Defense wanted to hear these inflated economic growth numbers to fan the perceived threat of the Soviets as a superpower, which in turn helped justify bigger defense budgets during those Cold War days. So my run along the streets of Dabendorf in the Old East in the winter of 2000 was my first real-life view of this region.

I immediately understood the economic poverty left by the Soviets after their ungraceful abandonment of Eastern Europe following the fall of the Berlin Wall in 1989. Few homes had cars and if they did, most were dated. The backyards were devoid of any signs of consumer wealth, such as children's swings, family barbecues or general landscaping that was abundant just 30 miles to the west, in the former West Germany. In short, the people in the town of Dabendorf lived poorly.

I thought back to my internship at the Department of Commerce and realized that I had quite possibly been far more accurate with my undergraduate-level analysis of near economic stagnation for Soviet-controlled Eastern Europe than I had been led to believe at the time. I considered my new, direct observations an affirmation of the analytical and extrapolative skills I had begun developing in college and, more importantly, of the gut feelings about the Eastern European economy that I had held for 25 years.

**

Alf and I enjoyed a traditional German buffet breakfast and afterwards headed off to see the mysterious Dabendorf company, a manufacturer we knew to have pirated Cellport's Universal Hands-Free technology. The Dabendorf factory was located at the end of a long country road, and as we drove there I thought deeply about the vast cultural and economic differences between the Germans of the capitalistic West and the East's Soviet-schooled peoples. I had just recently read about the depth and breadth of the contrasts between these formally separated Germans in *The Economist* [1] magazine. And now I found myself suddenly immersed in the Old East that I had once studied and on my way to meeting with three businessmen and IdeaJackers of Cellport's technologies who grew-up under Soviet ways. The many nuances and implications these circumstances represented for me pushed my thoughts into many directions at once, stimulating my brain into overdrive.

We pulled up to the Dabendorf factory, which was spruced up and freshly painted, in great contrast to a nearby, abandoned old brick factory building from the era of Nazi Germany. Called the Hirschfield Milling Factory, the deserted building sat directly in our view from where Alf parked his Mercedes. The symbolism represented by the juxtaposition of these two facilities was enormous, suggesting that perhaps reconstruction and healing were at work, yet the ghosts of the Nazi period still lingered. Alf and I walked into the Dabendorf factory lobby and were pleased to see our names posted on the welcome guest board. Just off the main lobby area was a large room, full of balloons and streamers. We looked in, and I privately wondered if this might be a greeting party for Alf and me. An administrative assistant escorted us away from the party room and into a large conference room on the second floor where I met Lutz Pfister, Dabendorf's general manager, Volkmar Reidlich, vice president of marketing, and Frank Heyder, chief engineer.

What I soon learned from the Dabendorf fellows could make for a book unto itself. In its early years, the Dabendorf factory built radio communication gear for the Soviet military and, I suspect, in earlier times for the German army as well. After the Berlin Wall fell, the Soviets came in, took all of the high value equipment from the factory, and convoyed it in their fleet of trucks back home to Mother Russia.

In the early 1990s, Dabendorf had a skeleton crew that worked with the new German government's unification program to find a buyer for the abandoned company and to employ its team of radio engineers and production staff. Fairly quickly, the Hoermann Group of Munich bought the company for an amount that is broadly rumored to have been around $1. It pledged to find work for the company with ongoing assistance from German unification program subsidies.

To the credit of the Hoermann and Dabendorf teams, the company quickly pulled in large orders from the automotive industry for a cellular phone power amplifier used in vehicles that they claimed credit for designing. They also shyly showed me their version of Cellport's first-generation Universal Hands-Free design that they had IdeaJacked, which used a coil cord containing the universal connector to attach to a phone-specific adaptor. This shocking sight of another IdeaJacked product made me feel like I was watching a scene from an old movie. They told us that during the previous year, Dabendorf had successfully secured BMW and Mercedes-Benz Truck as customers for the hands-free system. I was pleased with how genuine and open these Dabendorf fellows were. They seemed very different than their West German brethren — they were more humble, to be sure, but I perceived other dissimilarities in the two cultures' levels of business sophistication, assertiveness and agility, which I needed time to decode. I briefed our hosts on the design milestones Cellport had accomplished with its second-generation Universal Hands-Free system and explained the CGP program as they politely took notes. Unfortunately, except for countless technical questions, they did not ask many business questions. This meant that we either had a language issue or that they were not in complete control of their operation and that the Hoermann executives were making many of the big business decisions in Munich.

As we got up for a lunch break at a local restaurant, I asked Frank Heyder if Dabendorf was celebrating an early Christmas event in the room off the lobby area. "No," he replied. "Dabendorf is having a celebration party this afternoon. Today our company went public on the big Neuer Markt exchange in Frankfurt. With all the excitement over our Universal Hands-Free product, we got a super value and a price jump on day one, today" [2].

What a cinematic moment. Here was a straight-talking engineer who had been raised in a socialist system telling an entrepreneur from the West that the engineer's company, which had pirated the Westerner's technology, had just celebrated a better-than-expected initial public offering, thanks to the immense popularity of the Western company's innovative product design. Having received this surreal shot of economic perspective and intelligence, I could not help but insert some humor into the moment: "We should toast at lunch to celebrate your new wealth," I said.

When everyone nervously said yes, I suspected they understood Frank's faux pas. For sure, Alf understood. Lunch was a clumsy time for all of us. It was clear that Lutz and Volkmar had told Frank of his egregious mistake while they were on their way to the restaurant. Frank was speechless during the entire lunch. He looked like someone who was about to be fired on the very day his company had achieved public market trading value. After lunch, Alf and I talked privately and agreed to limit the afternoon session to an hour or less and to let the gentlemen from Dabendorf stew on the CGP offer.

As Alf and I pulled away from the Dabendorf factory and office complex I found myself sitting quietly, partially out of emotional and physical exhaustion and partially because I needed to reflect on what was now eight hours of insane and intense cerebral stimulation in the Old East. As Alf drove me to the Berlin Airport, his business and social acuity helped me put the experience in context. He wove together a few helpful stories illustrating how people from the Old East are still adjusting to the ways of Western business. I assured my new friend that I understood Frank had not intended to be malicious, but I was shocked by his absolutely obtrusive attitude about intellectual property considerations. Alf steered the conversation back to one of my favorite subjects: his interest in joining the CGP program sooner than later. I made a commitment to him that Andy would get him a draft CGP contract by early December and that we would strive to close the contract at the Consumer Electronics Show in Las Vegas the coming January.

**

Back in Boulder, I was pleased to see early production samples of our second-generation Universal Hands-Free product from our contract production manufacturer, Elcoteq. That week Ralph promised to distribute samples to me and 10 other Cellporters so that we could each use the product in our personal automobiles. Everyone had instructions to test the units extensively, for in less than two weeks we would make production-level samples available to key customers such as Ford, BMW, Nissan, GM Parts, Circuit City and Best Buy. Ralph's design team had delivered an excellent product and our sales team was proving to have extraordinary ability to sell it.

To the lawsuit-sensitive automakers, Doug pitched the benefits of securely docking a hands-free system's portable handset in a vehicle. The auto industry was already concerned that unsecured hands-free mobile devices might fly loosely around inside a vehicle during an accident and harm passengers, exposing the industry to potential litigation. Cellport's solution eliminated this risk. Doug went on to emphasize that the Cellport docking system design for portable handsets also recharged the handset's battery, eliminating the clutter and inconvenience that desktop chargers create at the office and home — an attribute that would help sell the product to consumers. The vehicle producers also liked the external antenna that the Cellport gear used because it provided better reception than a typical handset's antenna, and this meant fewer dropped calls and safer and happier drivers.

Doug was at his finest, however, when demonstrating how easy it was to operate the voice-dialing feature that used software we licensed from L&H. He concluded his presentations with a pitch on the system's economic value to consumers. The universality of Cellport's second-generation Universal Hands-Free design meant that it could work with a variety of handsets, giving customers the freedom to upgrade to a new mobile phone and new adaptor at any time, without having to purchase or install a new docking system. As the pioneers of Universal Hands-Free connectivity solutions for telematics systems, Doug and all our vice presidents felt excited that these messages would resonate with our audiences and motivated to educate customers and our partners alike on Cellport's leadership and research and development investments in this field.

**

As December progressed, Cellport's employees were beginning to adjust to the loss of Jeff. The forthcoming Consumer Electronics Show (CES) in Las Vegas, which would open in January 2001, captured everyone's focus. The company prepared to establish a large booth presence at the show and the work was intense. We expected this convention to bring Cellport even more exposure and accompanying sales to potential CGP licensees. The Las Vegas CES event was an auspicious way to start the new year. It would be our second trade show presence, but the first since we officially started volume production capabilities. The second-generation Universal Hands-Free system was getting a lot of attention in the auto industry and with the Germans clearly leading in hands-free product sales, we needed the advantages of our new design to establish sales leadership with a high volume of U.S. vehicle producers. With big sales promised to Ford and an expectation of signing on three or four CGP licensees in 2001, we finally began feeling confident that we could drive the industry toward the adoption of a single platform to replace the splintered and economically inefficient approach the industry was then using.

I arrived in Las Vegas on day two of the show, due to commitments back in Boulder, and stayed for just two days of the five-day show. The booth and demonstrations our engineering and marketing team had developed were very well done, thanks to James Mayhew's leadership and his ability to get engineers and the marketing team to cooperate with one another on cross-department projects. James was very excited to be in Las Vegas. He gabbed at the show and flirted with the models in the adjacent booth as if he were a junior James Bond. That night he hosted a dinner at Rum Jungle for 10 Cellporters and a few spouses who had accompanied their mates to Las Vegas. As the former organizer of these types of events, I was shocked to see just how big Cellport's trade show team had grown and I was afraid to think about the size of this dinner tab. After we were seated, James took on the role of the dinner's host. He toasted the group and promised to double the booth size at next year's CES event, suggesting that Cellport was closing a new deal with Ford for tens of millions of dollars. Of course, I knew that our team in Detroit was advancing talks with Ford to bump up orders substantially, but James' composure and easy confidence about spending money made me think I missed some recent news on Ford.

I decided to bid everyone goodbye while desserts were just being served. A good night's sleep was far more important to me that night than late night team building. The next morning I made a short visit to the hotel gym and afterward felt like a completely new person, fully recharged to experience another exciting day of deal heat. I was surprised, however, to see only two other employees in the Cellport booth. Was there food poisoning in the dessert last night? What I learned was that James had taken five men to his favorite Las Vegas strip club. It appeared that his expense report from the evening likely increased greatly in amount, because he had ordered lap-dances for the engineers who partied with him. When I asked Doug for details, he replied that he had left around 1:00 a.m. He suggested, while laughing, that his companions still might be at the club. As the morning progressed the story unfolded that James and several other Cellporters got back to our hotel at 5:00 a.m. This seemed out of character for James, so I brushed the story aside.

I first saw James in our booth at around 4:00 that afternoon. He was on his mobile phone, engaged in a seemingly humorous call. I said to myself that he better be talking to Ford about the new order he spoke of last night! After his call ended, I approached James and asked how his day had gone.

"Fine. As you can see, we are making great progress at the show," he said.

This was Teflon talk at its finest. Angry that he was deflecting my question, I asked him to explain what happened the previous night. With a big laugh, he said, "I wish it was as much fun as the engineers made it out to be. I will fill you in on the silliness that took place when I get back home. I've got to get to a meeting in another booth, Pat. See you next week in Boulder."
"Fine, James," I said, as I, too, needed to hurry to make my flight back to Denver.

I made it a point to relax over the weekend. I was preparing myself for my first week back at the office after the holidays and to begin what promised to be a huge breakout year of substantial sales and the promise of our first profitable year since we founded Cellport 10 years earlier. By now Cellport had become recognized as a prolific inventor of telematics architectures and credited with building the resulting core connectivity patent portfolio. The combination of our research and development grants and our strategic investor investments had raised nearly $40 million.

By now, Cellport's unique and particularly recent history had brought us into a distinct business category: pioneering invention house and money-raising machine. I believed that the only business in the wireless community comparable to Cellport was one that I considered to be an extremely good company: Qualcomm. Both Cellport and Qualcomm focus their businesses entirely on pioneering new technologies. Qualcomm was known for its fabulously innovative work to revolutionize a new digital-wireless technology solution and products, which it began in the late 1980s and continued throughout the 1990s. The cellular phone technology it developed, known in the technology world as cellular CDMA, ultimately produced operational and performance advantages for wireless networks and phones that were beyond expectations for the time. With great interest, I studied Qualcomm's brilliant technical contributions and market strategies that essentially gave birth to today's enormous, global CDMA-based cellular industry. I followed its ingenious strategic moves and even the numerous gaffes that it, like all risk-takers, experienced. Qualcomm's founder, Irwin Jacobs, was the visionary leader and chief executive behind these accomplishments.

While at trade shows in the early 1990s, I would hear fellows from the European wireless industry representing companies such as Alcatel, Ericsson, Nokia and others mock Qualcomm's new technology innovation and disregard it as nothing more than a wacky idea, while they chose to use a more pedestrian digital cellular technology, called GSM.

In a circumstance that also mirrored the reasons Wolfgang Cullmann had given me for avoiding Cellport's technology, many of these European companies also did not want Qualcomm, an American company, to disrupt the market for new digital cellular technologies, and this fear gave them another reason to resist using CDMA.

I often warned cynical Europeans not to discount Irwin Jacobs' capabilities; with a Ph.D. in physics from MIT and better promotional skills than a car salesman, he was the real deal. Ironically, after 10 to 15 years, the European companies' main complaints against Qualcomm today are based on their need to pay Qualcomm royalties if they use its now seminal technology contributions. As pioneer and primary contributor of this vastly better digital wireless technology, Qualcomm deserves the billions of dollars it collects each year from its now-aging portfolio of breakthrough CDMA cellular patents.

Another lesson I learned from studying Qualcomm was that Irwin Jacob's greatest skill might be rooted in his highly savvy practice of surrounding himself with very bright people and skillfully stoking the inventive fires that prolifically advanced CDMA cellular technology. I tried to follow Qualcomm's example and build my company with the same tenacious focus on the art-of-the-possible.

**

It would not be long before I learned, however, that James Mayhew did not measure up to the standard of personnel I had established for my company. Around 10:30 in the morning on Tuesday, our second day back at work, Steve Parrish walked into my office, closed the door and said he needed 15 minutes to discuss a big problem with me.

"Pat, did you track the gossip that swirled around Cellport yesterday?"

"Steve, if you mean the Las Vegas strip club party, yes, I have heard stories and when I catch up with James I will get his perspective," I said. I scheduled to meet with James on budget and other general business matters on Wednesday afternoon.

"You have bigger problems than the strip club to discuss with James," Steve said. "First off, yesterday he asked me to hold back Alexis' and Stephanie's bonus checks until he gives me email approval to issue them. First thing this morning, Alexis went to see Eileen O'Donahue and broke out crying because of James. Why? According to Eileen, James told Alexis that until she goes to bed with him, he will hold her bonus check."

Shit! This was news that went completely in the wrong direction. Steve was livid. What was Cellport's policy on sexual harassment, he wanted to know. "Steve, you know if this is indeed true, this behavior is way out of bounds. Please get Eileen and return to my office at noon for a follow-up discussion," I said.

Immediately I tried to reach Andy, but to no avail. Next I placed a call to John Thompson, our longest-serving Board member, who had a law degree and had been a valued advisor to me. I told John's assistant that I had a real emergency, and John took my call. I gave John a short briefing on what had happened. John then gave me the sage advice I was seeking. He advised me, first, to find the name of a senior lawyer in the Denver-Boulder area that specialized in labor law and hire him immediately to give Cellport advice on this critical issue. Second, he said I needed to take notes of all my conversations and try to discreetly interview both Alexis and Stephanie, with the aid of a witness in each interview, about their harassment claims. When Steve returned at noon with Eileen, our personnel manager, she added more color and detail to Alexis' and Stephanie's sexual harassment charges. The information I learned made me realize that James was what my grandfather called "bad paper," and he had to go in short order.

That afternoon I spent over an hour on the phone with a labor attorney, who informed me that unless Alexis and Stephanie completely recanted their stories, Cellport would need to terminate James [3]. This was our second major personnel loss in a short period of time. The death of Jeff Platz was still painful. We were having real trouble hiring personnel in the competitive Internet-bubble employment market. And now the head of operations at Cellport would need to be fired. The loss of Jeff and now the imminent dismissal of James created a soberness at Cellport during a time that otherwise would have been gloriously successful days.

Firing James after a little more that three months on the job, while clearly necessary, would also be very inconvenient, because we were just ramping up delivery on a half-dozen important initiatives. Andy and I caught up with each other that afternoon. Predictably, he shared my disappointment that Cellport had experienced this situation but he also shared the consensus belief that it was important not to let James' style of behavior exist at Cellport. Per John's and the labor lawyer's advice, we interviewed Alexis and Stephanie. Eileen arranged for Alexis to meet us for a coffee at an obscure restaurant late that afternoon; Eileen and Steve interviewed Stephanie in a separate meeting. During the meeting with Alexis I witnessed the indignation Alexis harbored toward James. Alexis convinced me that James was experienced at this sexual harassment game. His inappropriate behavior toward her had begun a month earlier. Initially he described wild dreams he had of her. In the past few weeks, he had begun insisting that she join him after work for a drink. She politely refused his advancements, but now he had raised the stakes. He would withhold her bonus check until she went to bed with him. In keeping with the legal protocol I had been advised to follow, I asked Eileen to join me at 10:00 the next morning to confront James about these sexual harassment allegations and to witness his termination. That evening I spoke with three Board members about what I learned from the labor lawyer and Alexis. They all agreed that James had to go immediately.

At 10:00 a.m. the next morning, Eileen and I walked into James' office and closed the door to address a most serious human rights violation. James initially said that Alexis misunderstood his intentions and that he just wanted to know her better. Holding her bonus check was an office joke, he insisted. Eileen was completely the wrong person for James to play cat-and-mouse denial games with. Having grown up near New York City, she grilled him like a city-savvy district attorney. Within 10 minutes, Eileen had him squirming and sweating, and after a half hour, James had enough. He agreed to resign and leave the building that morning. I escorted this disgraced employee to Steve Parrish's office to pick-up his final check and then made sure he walked out peacefully.

In keeping with a commitment I had made to James that day to ship his personal items to him, I stopped by his former office in the afternoon to box up his belongings. As I walked into James' old office, I found Eileen there, in full detective mode. She had discovered that when we interrupted James that morning, he was engaged in a chat session with a woman he met on a dating Web site and that he was trying to arrange a rendezvous at a local hotel with her. He had been trying to assure this Web date that neither of their spouses would learn of their proposed affair. Eileen also learned that one of the lap dancers from the Las Vegas strip club had spent a night with him during the CES show. This lap dancer wanted to know if James had invented an excuse yet to return to Las Vegas for another night of entertainment.

1991
1992
1993
1994
1995
1996
1997
1998
1999
2000
2001
2002
2003
2004
2005
2006
2007
2008
2009

The James Mayhew debacle occurred at the worst possible time. I had just spent four months transitioning more than 80 percent of Cellport's operations to James and I had committed my time to building the CGP licensing program, helping Paul Heller with new financing initiatives and supporting Hiro's newly opened Cellport-Japan office. Cellport had three times the business activity it had a year earlier and we were about to take the company into several regions of uncharted territory. We were preparing to make a commitment to spend millions of dollars to manufacture our second-generation Universal Hands-Free system and we were poised to sign contracts to deliver products to customers.

James' exit meant that I needed to quickly rearrange our leadership roles in a way that would allow me to step back into operations to make sure we did not lose momentum on any of our many strategic initiatives.

My first move was to ask Steve Parrish to lead the Cellport Global Partners program and to become the primary liaison with our engineering office in Japan; I also asked him to help us find someone to take over his role in finance. My second move was to expand the budget for our Detroit office, which would make it possible for us to hire half a dozen engineers. The new personnel would be able to support the growing number of automotive projects that Cellport was landing and to help our design engineering team in Boulder, which had been struggling under considerable pressure to keep up with our escalating opportunities.

Although the Internet and telecom bubble was looking a bit deflated in early 2001, Cellport was experiencing record levels of product orders and it was drawing interest from investors, investment bankers and prospective licensees. Steve Parrish gave Alf Naber focused attention and finally consummated the agreement that made ALAC of Germany our first CGP licensee. With ALAC pledging to build its hands-free products to conform to Cellport's new second-generation Universal Hands-Free platform design, we would pick up valuable design help and market presence, which would be particularly important in the post-bubble investment market. I knew first-hand from talking with numerous investment bankers at technology conferences that these bankers were now looking for real companies with real product sales.

This of course was in stark contrast to the conventional practice during the height of the bubble, when companies could raise tens of millions of dollars in public offerings based on little more than a business plan to create a Web site to sell pet supplies or toys. Sensing a developing instability in public and private funding markets, I asked Paul Heller to consider whether Cellport should raise more private capital or eye a public offering to accelerate the demand for our technologies.

Within days, our automotive sales team laid a bombshell on us. Ford's finance department had learned that its marketing department was planning to issue purchase orders worth tens of millions of dollars to Cellport. The Ford finance department wanted warrants or an option to buy up to 10 percent of Cellport at a later date. The proposal was too "bubble-ish" for my taste, so I asked Andy to get a better understanding of the details. I particularly wanted more thorough information about Ford's intentions for securing such a large order. I learned that Ford had set up a new global e-business initiative called E-Ford, which was part of a new business group called ConsumerConnect, and that it had given this new enterprise responsibility for introducing new Internet-based services to its customers. The Ford finance department, which was helping the automaker build that effort, clearly viewed getting warrants for Cellport stock as a "heads-they-win tails-we-lose" strategy. As a student of boom-and-bust economic cycles, when I learned this, I suspected the bubble was approaching its zenith. It is very typical at the end of a bubble period for companies to reach long on the side of greed, and that's what I thought Ford was doing.

Because I needed to focus more on operations, I cut my travel back significantly. I did attend the annual cellular industry trade show in the spring, however, because it was an investment of my time that usually yielded handsomely for us. The convention that year was held in New Orleans. Upon checking into my hotel room, I received a call from my old friend at Motorola, Helena Stelnicki, who invited me to dinner to discuss what she described as "several important topics." Always interested in advancing Cellport's technology and business opportunities with Motorola, I accepted Helena's offer. During dinner I learned that Helena's contributions to Motorola had paid off and that she was now responsible for the financial profitability of a number of large telematics product programs that Ray Sokola was running. She was enjoying both her new role and working with her new boss.

Certainly this dinner was about more than catching up on our careers, so I kept the conversation light, waiting for Helena's real motivation to unfold. As we were looking at the dessert menus, I started to think that I might have expected too much out of the dinner discussion and that maybe Helena was just using this dinner as an opportunity to apologize for the aborted funding process that stunned us all two years earlier. Helena showed impressive restraint until we were midway through dessert, when she revealed the reason for the evening's dinner invitation. Helena said Marios Zenios and Ray Sokola were still very excited about Cellport and that they wanted to pursue two relationships with us.

"First off, Motorola would like to initiate discussions with Cellport about taking a license on your MobileWeb patent portfolio, especially the Dynamic Digital Bus and the Vehicle Server," Helena said.

"Great," I replied. "As you know I have always advertised that Cellport is in the business of licensing our telematics technology. I will ask Paul and Andy to negotiate a fair license with Motorola."

Helena then introduced her second objective. "Marios and Ray still feel badly about our failed investment attempt back in 1999. Because we still want to invest in Cellport, we would like to engage Motorola Ventures to make a strategic investment in Cellport."

Involving Motorola Ventures made sense. By asking the company's ventures unit to make the investment, Helena and her colleagues would be able to rely on the Ventures unit's staff for all due diligence activities and legal negotiations and to oversee the overall process. The telematics unit would not have to assume the financial risk.

I told her that I would turn this over to Paul and Andy as well. It certainly sounded like Motorola would be keeping Cellport's top two deal makers quite busy.

"Actually, Pat, two individuals have already been assigned these tasks from our side," Helena said. "Mike Kraus from the telematics unit will lead Motorola's license discussions and Jim O'Conner from Motorola Ventures will lead the investment initiative."

Helena's words were music to my ears.

**

One of the benefits of international expansion is that it brings exposure to new ideas and opportunities. Leave it up to Hiro Sakurai to develop both.

The Cellport-Japan team had just exhibited our technologies at a trade show in Tokyo and it was swamped with interest from the gadget-crazed and telematics-savvy Japanese attendees. When Hiro called to give me a report on the show, he was extremely excited about a potential opportunity to partner with a company, called Omron Corporation, which he had met at the event.

Omron was a $5 billion publicly traded technology company in Japan that developed and manufactured products for sale to numerous industrial sectors in dozens of countries. An Omron executive Hiro met was interested in expanding the company's sizable automotive business into telematics product offerings and wanted to learn more about Cellport's CGP licensing program. This was terrific news and a perfect assignment for Steve Parrish, who now had one company signed to the CGP program and was forecasting several more licensees by year-end. I asked Hiro to deal directly with Steve and let us know what additional help he needed to crack into the Japanese market.

The next day, Steve walked into my office and, in what was not a great surprise to me, said that he had made arrangements to fly to Japan that weekend to support Hiro in a meeting with Omron about the CGP program. I laughed to myself. I knew Steve was an optimist and a skilled salesman, but he was about to meet the master himself, Hiro Sakurai, right in his home court: Tokyo, Japan.

In typical fashion, as soon as Steve arrived at Tokyo's Narita Airport, Hiro greeted him with an agenda outlining five days of business that needed to be accomplished in three. After several days of green tea meetings with dozens of Omron executives and engineers, including the senior manager of Omron's new venture business, Steve and Hiro were convinced that Omron was very interested in joining the CGP program and that it would make for a terrific licensee. I asked Steve to let Hiro do his magic and close the deal. Having worked with Hiro and the Japanese for more than 20 years, I knew that Hiro would have the best understanding of how Omron would like to consummate a relationship. This of course would deny Steve the pleasure of the close, but he was a team player and he recognized that the remainder of the process would require close attention to international cultural nuances that he did not understand. He departed Japan and left the closing of the Omron deal for Hiro.

While we waited for word from Japan, Paul received a call from Motorola's Mike Kraus, who wanted to begin discussions about licensing our Dynamic Digital Bus and Vehicle Server technologies. Paul gave Andy and me a brief summary of the conversation and the handful of vagaries that came up in his discussion with Mike. I realized these talks would be complex and would go on for several months. In the first place, the license Motorola was seeking was a non-CGP license, our first of this type, so Andy would need to draft the contract almost entirely from scratch. Second, the need for this license had something to do with a large automotive customer Ray Sokola was working with, whose identity could not be disclosed. This circumstance would complicate and slow down the process of getting many types of information that we would need when crafting the contract. Helena had advised me about this, but what I could not understand was this: Why would Motorola move first on a patent license instead of softening us up first with a strategic investment, which might have yielded better licensing terms for Motorola? This made no sense to me, but since both Ray and Mike Kraus were bright guys, I assumed there was a method to their madness. And Paul and Andy seemed to prefer closing a MNT patent license with Motorola first; they believed that getting the now-worldwide sales leader in telematics to acknowledge our core innovations would help tremendously with fundraising, sales and eventually bringing visibility and recognition to our Cellport Global Partners program. The beauty of having tenured deal guys like Paul and Andy handle what would certainly be tough and detailed negotiations was that I remained free to focus on my growing list of operational issues.

**

As an idea man and a deal maker myself, however, I found many of the operational duties at Cellport fairly boring and I did not enjoy being bogged down in minute details, which operations management often requires. I found that I missed Cellport's earlier days, even the days of near poverty for the company, when I worked closely on exciting architectural design work with highly inventive designers like Chuck Spaur and Ralph Poplawsky. Chuck would not return from his sabbatical for another year. He was thoroughly engaged in a personal effort that reflected his roots on the family farm crafting innovative farm implements from old parts: He was in the process of building an experimental airplane, rivet by rivet, and loading it up with electronic instrumentation. Barrel rolls were his favorite acrobatic maneuver. And Ralph was up to his eyeballs in personnel management matters, making sure we were meeting our design and production deadlines and taking care of numerous other operational issues that our success-ful sales efforts introduced. Clearly Ralph had no time these days for our long art-of-the-possible invention sessions.

Although Cellport's Board of Directors consisted of a bright group of lawyers and business people, their responsibilities were to focus on operational reviews, budgets, and legal matters. I was craving high-voltage creative stimulation for my personal interest in strategic technology innovation that was unencumbered by business oversight duties. Thus, in the spring of 2001, I formed a Board of Advisors, made up of an all-star cast of bright technologists and marketers, who agreed to meet twice yearly to help me plan Cellport's future strategies in the exciting but turbulent technology world.

First on my list was a Cellport founder, Dale Hatfield, who was a true out-of-the-box technology thinker and who was also very well ground-ed in business. Next was Jim Caile, who had recently retired from his career as vice president for marketing at Motorola, and who had tremendous experience in strategic planning of both wireless technol-ogy development and product marketing initiatives. Other members included George Mansho of Qualcomm, who had a rich background in patent licensing and deal-making, and Jonathan Lawrence, an investment analyst based in New York with Dain Rauscher Securi-ties, who had expertise in telematics. While all of these men were generally interested in telematics and our pioneering patent portfolio, each had different motivations for participating; some joined to keep a friendly eye on Cellport, while others expected to find opportunities to engage in business with Cellport in the future. Participating had pragmatic value for all of us.

I called this group "Cellport's BoA," for Board of Advisors. When we met we did not follow a strict agenda or Robert's Rules of Order, nor did we review budgets, as would a typical Board of Directors.

This diverse group of highly creative individuals gathered simply to engage in in-depth discussions on a variety of technical and business topics that might pertain to Cellport's mission. In recent years, I have realized that my participation in this Advisory Board was one of the reasons working at Cellport stayed so stimulating for me, and I can say without exaggeration that some of the advice and ideas that its members contributed to Cellport helped us survive the crash of the Internet and telecom bubble. These advisors encouraged us to keep investing in our work to create innovative architectures — work that would lead to a third-generation portfolio of telematics technologies. They also motivated me to pursue licenses in defense of our patents. Their advice was that good patent portfolios are like red wine — they take years and years to age — and thus they warrant the extensive client engagement and the substantial work it often takes to prove to a company that it is crossing critical patent claims.

Today, whenever a young entrepreneur, new college freshman or other motivated individual asks me for business or career advice, I always suggest that they put together a formal or informal BoA. Indeed, each of my advisors, Hatfield, Caile, Mansho and Lawrence, drew on mentors from their own BoAs for help at various points in their careers. Most successful people, I find, are delighted to give back in a helpful and loving fashion and that was the spirit in which these individuals joined my BoA.

After a long and arduous negotiation with Ford's finance department, Andy agreed to offer Ford warrants that would give it the right to purchase up to 10 percent of Cellport stock at a fixed price in exchange for purchase commitments that would indeed be worth tens of millions of dollars. When Andy briefed me on the details of the final agreement, I thought the economics of the contract were interesting for both companies. Ford had invested some $100 million and counting into its own telematics program, called Wingcast, which had yet to introduce a commercial product, yet it was chiseling us for an option to buy equity in Cellport based on real orders. I realized no one at Ford was looking at the big picture of its telematics initiatives with a decent pair of glasses. Nevertheless, Doug was now free to finalize purchase commitments worth more than $50 million. We would begin delivering production-line installed products to Ford in the fall of 2001 and sales would escalate aggressively over the course of the subsequent year.

Although the Internet and telecom bubble was rapidly deflating, we were gaining tremendous traction from our large orders from Ford and a freshly signed contract with Nissan as well. During one of my frequent calls with Motorola's Ray Sokola, I told him about Ford's request for stock warrants and the subsequent order. Always a gentleman, Ray said, "Congratulations on such a large anchor order for your next-generation system. Now, as a friend, I must warn you, Ford is grasping for technology solutions and their CEO may be in trouble due to the Firestone tire debacle," he said, referring to the automaker's need to recall millions of dangerously defective tires.

Ray told me that Ford was continuing to pour real money into its Wingcast business, which was on shaky ground at best, due to poor execution and market direction. I told Ray that I hoped that when they shut it down even more business would accrue to us [1]. Shortly after this discussion with Ray, and despite his words of caution, I found myself in a state of euphoria from having won this mega order from an automaker. Did I want to prove Wolfgang Cullmann wrong or was I (unwisely) trying to deliver a booming product to our investors in the short term versus the three to eight years it could take to deliver on a high-margin royalty-based licensing business? I helped the automotive staff plan for a major press release and company party to celebrate this company-making piece of business for Cellport from Ford. A good celebration was important for several reasons. Aside from our funding and sales achievements, the staff had many reasons to be proud of the years of strenuous engineering and business development work that had finally borne fruit. At the same time, our emotions were still muted because we all felt the loss of Jeff, but we knew he would have wanted us to celebrate the launch of a key product he had helped build.

**

If the Ford news were not big enough, Steve and Hiro had some spectacular news out of Japan. Omron not only wanted to become a CGP member but it also asked if we would consider having them invest in Cellport. Omron was very impressed with and excited by the news of Ford's commitment to Cellport and it wanted a piece of the Cellport deal machine. The timing of Omron's investment interest could not have been better. Paul was making some progress with prospective investors, such as GE-Capital, that would put us on the fast track to an IPO, but these potential deals were still months away from closing. We now had orders flowing in not only from Ford and Nissan but from Circuit City and Best Buy as well. Cellport needed growth capital to finance its expanding production, engineering and now customer service operations. Our retail and automotive sales teams, combined, were forecasting sales of $4 million for 2001, $24 million for 2002 and more than $40 million for 2003. From the standpoints of our sales forecasts and our popularity among companies that wanted to make deals with us, Cellport was in the eye of the proverbial tornado.

Hiro worked closely with Omron executives to structure an engagement between our two companies and he proposed a two-part plan. The first part was for Steve Parrish to sign the CGP contract in Tokyo and the second was for me to meet Omron's executive vice president, Masuda-san, to discuss the details of an investment by the company, which had just established a new venture arm to fund outside projects that might support its strategic objectives. Omron was suggesting an investment in the amount of $10 million. Because I was trying to delegate as much of my work as possible and limit my travel, I asked Hiro to negotiate on my behalf and close the investment. Hiro fired back with an email saying that after 20 years of doing business in Japan, I should know better. He reminded me that any meaningful business in Japan is a people business; he said that I needed to meet directly with the Omron executive. Masuda-san and I were a match made in heaven, he added. Of course, Hiro copied Steve Parrish, Andy and Paul on this email and the next thing I knew, half of the executive staff at Cellport was asking me when I was leaving for Japan. Hiro orchestrated two signing ceremonies at which Steve and a senior manager from Omron consummated the CGP agreement and not long afterward, in June 2001, I was on a plane to Japan to meet Masuda-san.

I arrived in Tokyo for what would be just one night of rest before Hiro and I would take the bullet train to Omron's corporate headquarters in the historic city of museums and temples, Kyoto. In preparation for my meeting with Masuda-san, Hiro gave me a briefing on Omron's multibillion-dollar business empire and told me wonderful biographical details about Masuda-san that characterized not only his business successes but his recognition in intellectual circles as an author of several books on China, a topic that he was frequently invited to speak about in public venues, including the prestigious World Economic Forum's annual meeting at Davos, Switzerland. As usual, Hiro's assessment of the caliber of this fellow and the need to give the Omron relationship executive attention turned out to be spot-on.

The Omron headquarters building had all the appearances of a very successful corporate palace. Every piece of brass was polished and every furnishing was immaculately cared for. The receptionists were as formal and meticulously groomed as imaginable. As we were escorted up the elevator to the top floor, Hiro and I looked at each other and smiled. Exactly ten long years ago, we were coming down an elevator in NTT's headquarters with the germ of our first big idea, and now we were about to meet with one of the most influential and visionary business executives in Japan who would help us evolve the business we called Cellport into a global enterprise. This moment, by itself, was a great reward for our hard work as telematics pioneers.

Omron's executive floor made the impressive first-floor lobby look purely pedestrian. This top floor suite was opulently decorated. Beautiful vases held elegant arrangements of fresh flowers and original artwork graced the walls. Again, Hiro and I looked at each other, but this time we could not afford to reveal our amazement. We subtly winked at each other, did our best to look as sophisticated as the environment we were in, and kept our smiles to ourselves. I was shocked when our escorts guided us into a completely unique room where we would meet Masuda-san to discuss our potential investment partnership. I had expected that we would gather in a typical executive-style conference room for this meeting, yet the room we found ourselves in was more than 60-feet long and easily 25-feet wide, with five large pillowed chairs positioned along one of the long walls facing another five identically ornate chairs aligned along the opposite wall. There was not a table in sight. Beautiful wallpaper that was clearly made with hand-crafted artistry covered the walls and magnificent crystal chandeliers hung from the ceiling. Fortunately, Hiro knew that I was a jet-lagged American who was completely clueless about what to do next. He escorted me to the middle chair on the right-hand side of the room. "Let's sit, shall we, and wait for Masuda-san," he said.

I thought to myself that I was close to experiencing the life of corporate royalty. Having grown up in Buffalo, I never imagined that I would have an experience like this, but then again, I thought, this was the art-of-the-possible on the economic front. Hiro and I sat quietly. During the few minutes we waited for Masuda-san, I intensely studied the exquisite design and details of this room. It was truly museum quality. Masuda-san then walked into the room. He had an air of royalty and he was accompanied by several staff members. He was wearing a big smile. He approached me and said in perfect English, "Thank you, Pat, for traveling to see me. I am happy to finally meet you."

This warm greeting completely took the edge off the nervous tension I had been feeling. Masuda-san sat across from me in what I learned later was Omron's formal greeting room. We spent a few minutes exchanging niceties and then Masuda-san opened the conversation by providing a brief introduction to his company. He explained that Omron had a corporate philosophy, crafted more than 60 years earlier by the company's founder, to structure all of its endeavors to produce benefits for society, not just financial gain for the company. He went on to explain that this corporate value system helps to guide the company in its strategic business planning and that the strategy recognizes the importance of cooperating with young innovative companies, such as Cellport, which understand the benefits of building a business with products that have long term value and that serve the social good.

Much to my delight, at a deeply intellectual level, Omron's executives completely appreciated Cellport's charter of developing and openly licensing our core telematics technologies to provide safer and less costly methods for using cellular phones in automobiles and connecting vehicle resources to the Internet for the benefit of society.

Unlike any meeting I had ever attended during my 25 years in business, not a single note pad, PowerPoint presentation or product demonstration was used during this two hour session in the Omron greeting room. It was simply a person-to-person meeting. Masuda-san wanted to see for himself what I was all about as an individual and to hear, directly from me, what Cellport's true ambitions were for serving society as well as its shareholders. By the time we were midway through the meeting, I felt comfortable that our two companies would fit well together as partners and I was certain that Masuda-san had come to a similar understanding. During his concluding remarks, Masuda-san said that he now understood clearly why his staff was excited about investing money from Omron's strategic venture fund into Cellport. We all knew at this point that this was the green light authorizing the $10 million investment. As we were preparing to depart, Masuda-san began to talk about the next steps we would all have to take to finalize our verbal agreements. He asked if I would be available to return to Tokyo in a few weeks for an official signing and to participate in a press conference at the Japan Press Center in Tokyo. With enthusiasm I said, "Yes. We are delighted to have Omron as a partner and to support a press announcement of the new Omron-Cellport telematics partnership."

**

Back in Boulder, Cellport's business appeared to be on a fast track that led from one glorious development to another. Within days of my return, we hosted a party to celebrate the Ford purchase commitment to order more than $50 million in products from us over a 30-month period. Even in the midst of this happy occasion, good news continued to roll in. I learned during the party that *The New York Times* wanted to publish a feature article about Cellport and that the article would appear in its Sunday business section later that summer. I also learned that GE-Capital had become very excited about Cellport and was talking about making a large mezzanine-round investment to help Cellport go public. Then, later during this magical week, I learned that because of Cellport's expertise in wireless connectivity, Ford wanted us to supply additional system components, such as the external antennas, mounting brackets and vehicle wiring harnesses it would need to integrate our technology into its vehicles, and that it wanted us to provide these as a turn-key, tier-one supplier to Ford. We debated about this opportunity for days at Cellport, because while tier-one suppliers tend to receive long-term commitments from their customers, they typically have to lay out the capital to create new technologies or designs or to purchase sub-system components from other suppliers. And as a small company that generally feeds components to major system suppliers, Cellport was only the size of a typical tier-three company. I opposed taking on a role that was beyond our expertise, but we were clearly too pregnant with the Ford business relationship to resist their positioning of Cellport as a tier-one system supplier. Furthermore, we had mistakenly used the Ford award too frequently to advance relationships with Omron, GE-Capital and various suppliers and to gain media attention. We had, unfortunately, backed ourselves into this corner.

Yet Cellport was on a roll and we felt tremendous pressure to keep it going lest we become, like many other companies around us, victims of the deflating Internet and telecom bubble, which had fully burst by now. What gave me confidence that we could succeed as a tier-one supplier for Ford was the good work that Mike Lewellen's production team was doing in Boulder and that our automotive team was doing in Detroit, and the confirmation I had received from Hiro that Omron would close the $10 million investment. Omron had scheduled a large press event to take place in Tokyo on June 20, 2001 to commemorate the agreement.

**

Once again, I was flying to Japan, accompanied this time by Steve Parrish and Paul Heller. During our first few days there, Hiro, Steve, Paul and I received an in-depth tour of several of Omron's most sophisticated factories and we attended numerous meetings and dinners to refine our plans for launching Cellport's telematics architectures in Japan. I was not prepared for the significance of our third day in

Japan. It began formally in the mid-morning with a small investment signing ceremony at Omron's large Tokyo office building. Afterward, we attended a partnership lunch that was exquisitely hosted by Masuda-san and his executive staff. Then, Masuda's chauffeur drove us to the beautiful modern building that housed the Japan Press Center. We were scheduled for a 2:00 p.m. press conference where Masuda-san and I would address the media. Much to my surprise, the press conference was not a small meeting with a dozen or so local journalists, as I had expected, but a full-fledged media event in an expansive hall filled with about 100 journalists and numerous TV crews from all over Japan and about 20 reporters from foreign countries as well.

Masuda-san and I each gave a 15-minute speech on the importance of our partnership and the benefits telematics would soon bring to society by making cellular phone use in cars both safer and more economical for customers. We spent the next several hours fielding questions from the larger media audience and from individual journalists in one-on-one meetings. The reporters wanted to know which automobile manufacturers Omron would supply Universal Hands-Free products to, if we intended for the partnership to become a competitor or future supplier to OnStar and Wingcast and if we believed the enactment of hands-free laws would continue to spread around the world. Masuda-san was asked how much, in revenues, he expected Omron's telematics business to generate in five years. He cited projected revenues of $500 million, which would have given Omron a 20 percent market share of the forecasted market, something that was certainly possible for a technology powerhouse like Omron to expect. Omron's stock moved up about 10 percent after the press conference.

The next day as I waited in the United Airlines Red Carpet Club to board my flight to the states, I picked up a copy of the International Herald Tribune that I found on a coffee table. Much to my surprise and delight, the paper's business section had a very well-written article about the new partnership Omron and Cellport had formed to help advance the use of telematics in and outside of Japan. I smiled and immediately thought that my young sons would enjoy reading such a flattering article about their dad's company, but I had lectured them many times on the importance of humility and decided, instead, to save the article to share with them at another time. With that thought, I sent the article to my daughter, Erin, who was already grown up and living on her own, to file the article in the family archive. I put a note with it that read, "Please don't show this to the boys until they are much older."

**

In early July I took a much-needed two-week vacation with my teenaged sons, joining some old college friends and their families in a modest, rented beach house on Fire Island. I was astounded that word of Cellport's success had spread into this social circle. My friends jokingly called me "captain of industry" and asked me which mansion I would buy on the beach. Although I knew that money was not my prime motivator, I was concerned that my sons might become over-confident with all the attention and excitement Cellport's success brought to us.

I spent a lot of time during that vacation reminding the boys that it took me 10 long years to build Cellport, that there was still much more work to do before we could be sure our success was long-lasting, and that it was important that we all stay humble and not lose sight of our personal values.

Each night during this vacation, after the boys went to bed, I wondered what parts of my stay-humble speeches were meant for them and what parts were meant for me, reminding me to stay grounded. While these were clearly heady and happy times, deals were coming Cellport's way at increasing frequency and we found ourselves having to make business-critical decisions much too frequently. I was afraid that the pace would trip us up. Life does not generally give one many opportunities or much time to rehearse how to manage the non-stop variables that come at you when you're in the midst of a business tsunami. Getting swept up in a surging market is a numbing experience, especially when one has struggled for a decade to finally achieve acknowledgement in a burgeoning market for one's work. The reality is you don't manage a tsunami. You do the best you can to make good decisions and to keep your composure and you hope that when the swirling chaos — fed by many external variables — subsides, that you will have survived.

**

September at Cellport seemed like Motorola month. After nearly six months of negotiations, Andy and Paul reported that the patent license agreement for our Dynamic Digital Bus and the Vehicle Server technologies with Motorola was ready to sign. They said Motorola had become very pushy to sign the license and over the past few weeks had given up on several contract points that they had previously insisted on including. Knowing Andy, the more anxious Motorola became, the less likely he would let the company throw its weight around. In my gut, I sensed that Ray Sokola needed this license because he had convinced either GM's OnStar or a German company to give up on the rudimentary, analog system they then used and to pursue a new strategy of making their vehicles into digital nodes on the Internet.

The highly ethical Sokola knew, of course, exactly where he learned of such a scheme, and on a balmy fall day, Ray and I signed Cellport's first major license for our patented Dynamic Digital Bus and Vehicle Server technologies [2]. That evening I called Michael Braitberg, Dick Chandler and Chuck Spaur at their homes and told them the great news that Motorola had taken a license on the two core technologies that they had all worked so hard to develop at Cellport.

Michael's response was very telling. "Those technologies are already over five years old, and it will take Motorola and their customers at least three years to integrate them into vehicles," he said. "Thank God patents have a 20-year life."

Shortly after we signed the license, Jim O'Conner, from Motorola's venture arm, started spending more and more time with Paul conducting due diligence and trying to determine how Motorola could co-fund with GE-Capital. Andy and Paul were excited. They believed that if we raised $20 million between these two prestigious investors and started to ship tens of millions of dollars of equipment to Ford and Nissan, we should be able to take Cellport public and deliver handsome returns to its shareholders.

In October I was starting to hear disturbing news from our Detroit office. There were rumors spreading rampantly around Ford that the company would soon announce a major management and strategy change. The optimist in me thought this might bring an end to the E-Ford strategy and perhaps it might even bring about a change of direction at Wingcast, which by this time had cost Ford more than $100 million even though delivery of commercial Wingcast products was still more than a year away. At the end of the month Ford Motor Company did make an announcement, and it was much more radical than I expected. Ford Motor Company fired Jacques Nasser, its CEO, and replaced him with Bill Ford, a scion of the company's founder; Bill Ford immediately announced a "back-to-basics" strategy to restore the company's reputation and financial stature. This indeed was dramatic news for Cellport, because in the last nine months we had spent more than $3 million on engineering work to integrate our products into Ford's leading car models and we were in the process of committing even more money to build up an inventory of parts and components that we would need to support numerous new program launches at Ford in early 2002. The Cellport advocates within Ford whispered to us that Bill Ford's newly announced strategy would prove good for Cellport; they believed that once Bill Ford realized how much cash Wingcast was burning and how long it would take Wingcast to generate revenues, that their company would embrace Cellport's solution, which was already in production and popular among early users and the corporate marketing staff alike. All we could do was hope for the best and work to please Ford, especially since it represented more than 50 percent of our 2002 sales forecast.

In late November, Paul warned Andy and me that Jim O'Conner of Motorola Ventures wanted to discuss our valuation numbers with us. O'Conner thought we needed a reality check, Paul said. The next morning, Andy and I had a conference call with O'Conner that was distressing, at best. O'Conner opened up the call by saying that Cellport reminded him of a spoiled child. Cellport was telling investors what the next funding valuation would be rather than having the investors set the price, as is the common practice in the real world, he said [3]. O'Conner then gave us a lecture. He listed all of the investments that Motorola Ventures had made during the past year and he said that every investment had come down in value due to the Internet-telecom bubble crash. He said he was not about to follow Omron, Cisco and FLV by paying a high investment price just to meet Cellport's valuation ambitions. Andy and I both argued, in response, that unlike the other Motorola investments that he cited to us, all of which had suffered aggressive markdowns in value, Cellport was a real company that was shipping products to a growing list of customers. Cellport had a growing backlog of orders that was worth tens of millions of dollars [4]. Plus, I reminded O'Conner, Cellport's patent portfolio was second to none in the telematics market and Ray Sokola recently signed a license for several of our core patents. O'Conner fired back again in frustration. He said Cellport was riding on a high horse in an unrealistic dream world and that he did not buy our story. Needless to say, the tech-bubble implosion had put O'Conner in a poor mood.

Andy then pushed him for what he thought Cellport was worth. O'Conner said, "I am not 100 percent sure, but some value it at around $50 million post-money, which is after GE-Capital and Motorola each put in $10 million." This was the beginning of the end. Not only could O'Conner not give us a specific valuation number, but he wanted Motorola to own 20 percent of the company. When Motorola had first expressed interest in investing in Cellport that year, it would have come into the funding round when the company had a valuation of $150 million and it would have owned only 7.5 percent. In a last attempt to understand why O'Conner went from a friendly to a very frustrated prospective investor, Andy asked him, "Why are you positioning Cellport as damaged goods?"

"We are all experiencing a collapse in values," O'Conner shot back. "Why should Cellport be immune to the new valuation realities?"

We were ready to bring the conference call to a close. I said, "Jim, you are way too emotional. Maybe we should revisit the valuation issue in a few days after you have a chance to cool off."

"Fine," he said. "But I doubt I will change my mind."

**

The very next morning Paul walked into my office and said, "It's official. Cellport is damaged goods.

"Jim O'Conner called the guys at GE-Capital yesterday after he spoke with you and Andy and he told them what he thought about Cellport's valuation. Now the GE-Capital guys are completely spooked. They said that given Motorola Ventures' valuation perspective, they will likely back out of their investment commitment to Cellport for now. They'll take another look at it in six months."

As the words "damaged goods" reverberated in my head, I started to comprehend the magnitude of the repercussions Cellport would incur from Motorola Ventures' ungraceful move. It would impact us on every business issue imaginable. I thanked Paul for all his work and I apologized to him, for it had been my idea, in the first place, of having Motorola couple its investments with GE-Capital's. I should have known better. This was the second time Motorola left us at the strategic funding altar. The first time was in 1999. And now, two years later, they seemed determined to cause our business harm as we were trying to pair them with GE, another industrial blue-blood, for what would have been a mezzanine round to take us to an IPO.

I reflected on my dinner discussion with Helena in New Orleans earlier in the year, when she informed me that Motorola was eager to obtain a patent license and to invest in Cellport. I became very angry about the way Motorola Ventures conducted its relationship with Cellport and with me. Motorola had taken six months to negotiate a patent license that could have been consummated in half that time and then it pushed to accelerate the closing of the deal when it felt some pressure to do so from its unnamed automotive customer. The whole process of structuring the license under a veil of confidentiality to protect the identity of their customer added to the complexity of the contract and the contracting delay. Now, after having spent five months of our time in due diligence meetings in Boulder, gathering substantial information about our latest technologies, CGP partners, customers and inventory commitments for our programs with Ford, there wasn't a thing Motorola didn't know about Cellport. This behavior seemed malicious. But why?

As a dyed-in-the-wool optimist who innately believes that people in general are well intended, I was amazed at how angry I became over this. I took a few hours to gather my thoughts and then decided it was time to call Ray Sokola to get his perspective on all of this. When Ray answered the phone, I wasted no time in asking him why Jim O'Conner would tank a critical Cellport funding campaign at such a vital time in our history.

Ray responded, "What do you mean? The last I heard, Ventures' due diligence was making great progress and everyone seemed excited about closing the investment by year end."

"Ray," I responded, "You are truly fucking kidding me. Do you realize that Motorola Ventures single-handedly screwed up a five-month effort to close a mezzanine round with GE-Capital? Your 'vulture capitalist' arm completely screwed us. Please tell me why O'Conner had to call GE-Capital to give them a negative view of his post-bubble valuations? Why didn't he just walk away from the deal?"

"Pat, believe me, I am completely surprised," Ray said. "Marios and I wanted Motorola Ventures to lead the investment work because they could avoid all the foolish committee politics that tripped up Helena's effort in 1999. This should not have happened."

"You are so right," I replied. "But you and Marios let this venture capitalist, O'Conner, hose a critical funding round that we needed to make good on all our customer and strategic commitments. What is Motorola hoping to do? Buy Cellport after we file for bankruptcy?"

Ray was silent for close to a minute. I could tell that he was not only surprised, but that he was so shocked he was speechless. It was time to end the call. I said, "Ray, the biggest real disaster here is the damage this incident has done to our friendship. How in the world does our relationship recover after such carelessness over such an important engagement between the two leaders in telematics?"

"Again, Pat, I am very sorry," Ray replied. "It was not my intention to hurt you or Cellport."

"OK, Ray, I said. "I have to go and attend to a company that has been left on the rocks for dead by Motorola Ventures."

The night that Motorola Ventures torpedoed our funding efforts, Andy and I spent more than two hours on the phone discussing our options, of which there were few. Ultimately, we concluded that we should be able sell our way out of our cash crisis. Although this scenario was optimistic, we did have purchase orders from Ford to ship close to $6 million in products in the first quarter. We estimated that second quarter volumes should eclipse $8 million.

I resolved to reduce expenses on numerous advanced engineering development projects and to request help, from our friends at Omron, in the form of production assistance and additional investment dollars. I called Hiro right away to inform him about the collapse of the Motorola-GE Capital investment round and the cash crisis at hand. Hiro grasped the severity of the situation immediately and said he would arrange a meeting with Masuda-san. He said he would brief Masuda-san on the setback in order to open a discussion about the ways in which Omron might be able to help Cellport. I was grateful to have bright and courageous friends like Hiro to help Cellport battle against these types of setbacks, which are, unfortunately, inevitable in the turbulent technology business.

By January 2002, Hiro and Masuda-san had formed an agreement that would provide Cellport a slight reprieve. Omron would immediately invest close to an additional $2 million in Cellport and it would start a due diligence process that could lead to another $10 million investment in April. The additional financial support from Omron was great news and terrific support from an ally of growing strategic importance to our company. Hiro said that in February someone from Omron's finance department would come to Boulder to spend a few weeks studying the worthiness of the proposed, additional $10 million investment. In the meantime, Hiro said, the best thing we could do to impress Omron's finance department would be to generate incremental and positive sales growth from one month to the next. It was critical, he said, for Cellport to make as many sales to our customers — especially Ford — as possible.

We shared this message with all of Cellport's staff. By this time many of our employees were looking pretty fatigued. Most were working very long hours and the stress caused by the funding collapse was exacerbated by the generally poor business conditions of the time; our employees had watched hundreds of Colorado technology companies shut their doors as a result of the Internet-telecom bubble implosion and no one wanted to become another unfortunate statistic in this trend. The next major opportunity we would have to influence sales would be at the Ford-sponsored National Dealer Show in New Orleans in late January. At this show, Ford was planning to officially announce the availability of the Cellport product to all 5,000 Ford dealers in the U.S. and Canada. We now had to make sure we would be ready to perform our very best at this show in order to fully support our advocates at Ford. This became job number one at Cellport.

Ford's annual National Dealer Show was a well-run schmooze-fest. The emphasis at this particular event was on launching new products and helping stabilize the dealer community, which was concerned about any impacts the firing of Jacques Nasser and the rollout of Bill Ford's "back-to-basics" campaign might have on its businesses. Fortunately for us, Cellport's second-generation Universal Hands-Free system was not only the most popular new technology featured in the Ford vehicles displayed at the show, but we also got a super shot in the arm when Ford's vice president of sales, Jim O'Conner (no relation to Motorola's Jim O'Conner), devoted some time during his keynote speech to talk about the great innovation Cellport's system brought to Ford's automobiles and the real value it offered Ford's customers. The Cellport technology was showcased in three automobiles on display at the show, and during the next few days, Cellport staff members who were at the convention to support the product launch gave me nothing but glowing reports about its reception. They told me that some Ford dealers had even humorously suggested that Cellport would not be able to build products fast enough to meet demand. I responded to the sales staff with this message: Elcoteq, the contract manufacturer building our product, also produced more than 2 million cellular phones per month for Nokia and Ericsson. I told the staff to assure the Ford dealers that we had plenty of manufacturing capacity available to serve their needs.

We held a debriefing meeting in Boulder once the show was over. The Cellport staff members who attended the show reported, unanimously, that every Ford dealer they had talked to said that Cellport's telematics product was the best available and that it was exactly what Ford needed to help turn around its declining share of the automotive market. I asked our Detroit staff if the Ford marketing and purchasing departments appreciated the popularity of the Cellport product. I heard not only a "yes" in response, but also news that Ford purchasing executives wanted to meet with Cellport the next week. They wanted assurance that Cellport could build enough products for an accelerated launch program. I urged the Detroit staff to remind Ford that Cellport only designs products and reiterated the need to convey the message that Cellport contracts out all of its production processes to large manufacturers that have enormous capacity. I reminded the Detroit team that Ford's push for greater volumes was exactly what Omron wanted to see and told them to keep up the great work.

Fortuitously, by early February, Ford's purchasing department was pushing Cellport to build 20,000 additional units that it would use to launch a new, nationwide dealer-installed Universal Hands-Free system. This was a critical revenue opportunity for Cellport. Our previous shipments to Ford had been for factory-installed systems and the new approach would allow consumers to install the technology as an after-market accessory to their cars, which would create an additional market. As the program's tier-one supplier, we were now required to ship dealer-installed systems in quantities of one to several dozen units to some 5,000 auto dealers across the U.S. and Canada. Arranging for all this shipping infrastructure was a complex task, for we needed to establish an additional final assembly facility, build inventories of electronic cables and mounting systems for eight different car models and adaptors for more than a dozen different mobile handset models. The new dealer-installed program also required Cellport to invest $100,000 for new software that tied into Ford's purchase order system.

Despite the fact that an eager customer like Ford was exactly what we needed, these tasks, which might have been handled easily by a true tier-one company, were enormous challenges for Cellport. To gear up for such a big product launch we required Ford to make an unequivocal commitment to purchase the 20,000 units. With such a commitment, our suppliers would be more comfortable working with us, Omron would have more confidence investing in Cellport, and I would sleep better at night. We negotiated with Ford over the terms of the contract for several weeks, and in mid-February Ford agreed to the purchase commitment. It requested that we prepare to begin shipping the products to their dealers in early March, with an initial expectation that the inventory would last between 45 to 60 days. Finally, the stars appeared to be aligning once again in our favor.

**

In keeping with his commitment to Cellport, Masuda-san dispatched a man by the name of Iwakata-san, a long-time senior aide from Omron's finance department in Tokyo, to spend several weeks conducting due diligence at Cellport. Hiro told me that Iwakata-san would need to develop a full understanding of our organizational structure, operating costs, customers and prospective customers and that he would need to work closely with our finance department to forecast how much time it would take for us to break into a positive cash position. Hiro also advised me that after Iwakata-san's field work in Boulder was completed, Andy and I would need to travel to Japan to negotiate the final terms of an Omron investment that, ideally, would take Cellport to profitability. We would likely make this trip in April. The combination of Omron's superb partnership and support and Ford's anxiousness to launch the Cellport dealer-installed program raised our spirits and allowed us to believe that we could avoid the disaster that many had feared. To expedite and enhance the quality of Iwakata-san's work in Boulder, I communicated to our entire staff that we needed to communicate fully and openly with this important guest and partner.

After Iwakata-san had completed his first week of due diligence at Cellport, I invited him to my home for dinner. He had exceptional English language skills and, interestingly, he had a passion for 1950s Americana that proved to be educational for my family and me. Iwakata-san had been in his twenties during the early post-World War II era. He said most television shows shown in Japan during that time originated in the U.S. and that he had become a tremendous admirer of U.S. social freedoms and lifestyles through television and reading. I also sensed that as a young Japanese university student in the 1950s, Iwakata-san appreciated America's policy of helping to rebuild a free Japan versus the stranglehold the Soviets kept on the Eastern European countries in the post-war era. As the evening progressed, Iwakata-san let slip that he felt biased to help Cellport get through the Motorola setback and the Ford situation. He described the Ford situation as unfortunate. I queried him to be more specific about Ford.

Iwakata-san said that he did not want to insult our customer, but he thought it had been extremely strange for Ford to contract with Cellport as a tier-one supplier for a complex program when Cellport was a small, 100-plus person company. He said that virtually every tier-one supplier that he had ever heard of in Japan and the U.S. was a billion-dollar-plus company. He wondered why Ford would cast the financial burden of building a tier-one inventory onto such a small technology company like Cellport, one that had such a small Detroit operation.

Iwakata-san went on to say that with Omron's support, Cellport should be able to honor its current commitments to Ford, but for all follow-up orders, Cellport should insist on a role as a tier-two or tier-three component supplier, one that supplies its systems to a billion-dollar tier-one company that has the financial strength and experience to deal with such an enormous and pushy customer as Ford. Iwakata-san's lecture resonated with wisdom; it was an especially powerful addition to the warning Ray Sokola had given me about Ford just a year earlier.

At the start of Iwakata-san's second week of due diligence, we received some very troubling news from our staff in Detroit: Cellport was now in the middle of a growing political battle at Ford, one that could have potentially severe ramifications for Cellport. I immediately pushed for more details, and what I learned was not good at all: Bill Ford's back-to-basics initiative had begun focusing on eliminating wasteful programs, and the company's Wingcast telematics program, in which it had invested more than $100 million, was among those threatened by the new corporate policy. The likely shutdown of Wingcast would have political consequences that would extend to the company's other telematics program, the one based on our beloved Cellport products.

The staff in Ford's Research and Vehicle Technology unit, which had advocated the huge investments in Wingcast, took aim at the Cellport program because it was an alternative solution that was now favored by the company's marketing and purchasing organizations. Rumors were spreading rampantly that an internal turf battle had erupted between the Wingcast and the Cellport camps at Ford, and that this dispute had in turn pitted Ford's technologists against the marketing and purchasing departments. Yet we were unable to acquire any specific details about these very disconcerting rumors.

In keeping with our full-disclosure policy, I told Iwakata-san about the rumors at Ford. He was visibly bothered by this news. "Pat, this is exactly why I advised you not to be put in a tier-one position," he said. "Cellport does not have the management connections, nor the leverage at Ford, to fight this type of battle to protect your position.

"This is a setback that I will include in my report," he said. "But otherwise, I have had a very productive time in Boulder, and when

I return to Tokyo next week, I will submit my recommendation to Omron that it should work with Cellport to find a solution to aid your pending cash shortfall."

I thanked Iwakata-san for his hard work and support, and he thanked me for our openness, especially our candor about the recent turbulence at Ford. We agreed that it would be appropriate for Andy and me to visit Japan in the second week of April to submit business models that could be used to form the basis of a follow-on investment of $10 million dollars in Cellport by Omron's Board.

During the week after Iwakata-san left Cellport, I was able to gain more insight into what had become a very Machiavellian battle at Ford. I learned that the Research and Vehicle Technology department had indeed waged a nasty and underhanded attack on the Cellport product. We learned, in fact, that the department's engineers had installed Cellport's second-generation Universal Hands-Free units in several Ford automobiles for test-drives around their corporate campus by numerous sales executives in the company. They asked the executives specifically to use the Cellport voice-recognition system for dialing numbers and names, but they did not give the users our training literature or our expensively produced CD-ROM-based instruction guide. The results were predictably disastrous, and Ford's sales executives, fearing that consumers would complain about the product and that the company would suffer a public relations backlash from yet another failed product, panicked and told the purchasing department to put a hold on its orders for the Cellport product until more testing could be done or until the voice-recognition system could be upgraded.

Ironically, until then, our telematics solution had been immensely popular with Ford's marketing and purchasing staff and its dealers and automotive customers around the country had proven they liked the product; we had sold tens of thousands of units during the prior year to Hewlett Packard's fleet and others.

I knew this attack was very formidable, not on technical or market merits, but because I had seen numerous cases in which corporate geeks have intentionally and successfully intimidated the gestalt types in their marketing and purchasing departments by flaunting their tech-vernacular and introducing arcane idiosyncrasies of technology products. The intimidation of the Cellport supporters at Ford was a classic case of this behavior. It also illustrated the insecurities corporate decision-makers can develop when forced to make strategic technology choices for their companies, because the outcome of such decisions can directly affect one's carefully built corporate career. This was the climate at Ford since Bill Ford had announced earlier in 2002 that the company would be making massive staffing cutbacks. Ford employees were understandably nervous about their jobs. We dispatched several engineers and sales support staff to counter the attack on our product, but the technically insecure and career-nervous members of Ford's marketing and purchasing departments behaved like deer in a car's headlights: unable to make a move.

Our contract manufacturer was building nearly 500 units a day to fulfill the purchase order commitment for the Ford dealer program while Ford's purchasing manager delayed the commercial launch of the program from one week to another, saying the company wanted to conduct additional testing. Even worse, Ford had no official test specifications in place to guide the evaluation of the Cellport Universal Hands-Free product. Its personnel conducted the tests according to subjective and constantly evolving criteria and under the influence of the anti-Cellport Research and Vehicle Technology engineers.

Throughout March, Ford continued to delay the program launch. Our inventories grew by the day as our cash account dwindled. During this time, we received dozens of calls every day from Ford dealers who had fallen in love with the Cellport product at the national dealer show and had expected delivery in March, yet we could not get a consistent storyline out of Ford about when we could begin to ship the nearly $6 million of inventory we had built up to supply its eager dealers. I was very troubled by the mixed messages coming out of Ford. It was clear that the back-to-back calamities — caused first by the Motorola Ventures funding collapse and now by sabotage from within Ford's Research and Vehicle Technology department — had combined to create a full-blown disaster of enormous magnitude.

On the last Friday of March, Ralph walked into my office. "Listen to how utterly confused the Ford purchasing guys are now," he said. "They want to know how long it would take to change the chip that embeds the voice-recognition function in our universal docking station. When I told them it would take months and that scrapping the already built docking stations and engineering a new product would cost several million dollars, they said Cellport should not be too surprised if they require us to change this chip and the embedded voice recognition software as well. They also said that as the tier-one supplier, Cellport would have to eat the expense."

Two conversations continued to echo in my head that entire weekend: Ray Sokola's warning in 2001 about deep troubles at Ford and Wolfgang Cullmann's comments in 2000 that the American automakers do not partner well with their suppliers. We were down to $500,000 in the bank at the end of March. The meeting with Omron and funding from that company could not happen soon enough.

When the month of April began, the atmosphere at Cellport was one of disappointment, anxiety and fear. I knew in my gut that if we did not succeed in our efforts to raise capital from Omron, we would have to significantly change the structure of Cellport and lay off much of our staff. Responsibility for all the families that relied on Cellport weighed heavily on my shoulders. I desperately wanted to avoid the calamities that had befallen so many other companies in the wake of the Internet-telecom bubble collapse.

In preparation for our trip to Japan, as Iwakata-san had suggested, Andy and I developed a variety of business models that we believed would provide justification for additional financial support from Omron. We also intended to draw on these business models to answer any questions that Masuda-san and his team in Tokyo might ask of us. My encounters with Cellport's employees on the day prior to our departure had a very strong impact on me. In meeting after meeting, people would wish me the best of luck in my appeal to Omron. The employees' sad eyes and hopeful good wishes made me better understand how a surgeon must feel when asked, by a patient's family, to do his best to save their loved one. The body language each of our employees exhibited essentially said, "Please pull a rabbit out of the hat. I do not want to be another tech-wreck victim." I understood all too well their desires to avoid having fateful business failure conversations with their families and their fears of having to deal with sudden unemployment and the economic struggles and emotional damage that come with a job loss.

I didn't want to have to face those circumstances either. I did my best to assure them all that we would succeed. I told them that Hiro and I had a close relationship with Masuda-san, who was a visionary who saw the growth prospects of the telematics market. Plus, I said, Andy and Hiro were skilled negotiators and that all of us would work tirelessly to structure a win-win deal. These conversations were certainly well intended, but the truth was, there were a lot of variables at play and Ford was still pushing out our product launch day. The challenge before us seemed almost insurmountable.

I met up with Andy at the San Francisco International Airport. We prepared ourselves for the flight to Tokyo as if we were two well-trained Special Forces soldiers leaving on a mission that would literally affect many careers and families. Throughout the flight, we talked extensively about all the variables Omron would likely want to discuss and what kind of deal structure would be optimal for both companies. One of my favorite scenarios was to transfer the Ford business to our partners at Omron. It was already a tier-one supplier and it had the balance sheet to withstand program launch delays caused by the internal turf wars at Ford. When we exited the customs area at Tokyo's Narita Airport, we saw our smiling field commander, Samurai Hiro Sakurai, ready to take us, his two American partners, to the front lines.

**

In contrast to my typical visits to Japan, the agenda Hiro developed for this trip involved just one company: Omron. Hiro understood perfectly that securing funding was the only thing on our minds.

During dinner that evening, Andy and I briefed Hiro on the spreadsheets and business models we developed. Hiro's fluency in economics as well as his innate street savvy allowed him to easily grasp the seemingly endless variables that we had considered and the scenarios we had developed. We arrived at Omron's main office building in Tokyo on Monday morning. Iwakata-san and numerous others from Omron's engineering and finance departments greeted us warmly. Even as critical as time was during our planned five-day stay in Tokyo, we did, of course, sit for an hour-long conversation over green tea before launching into the briefing and discussions of our proposed business scenarios. Because there were several new faces in the room, Hiro advised us to build up to the business discussions very slowly. He wanted the new participants to get a sense of who Andy and I were, as people, before they would be getting to know us as businessmen.

At this point, Hiro and Iwakata-san took control of the meeting and proposed that we list the meeting's agenda items on the white board. This process alone took over an hour, because everyone, it seemed, politely lobbied to add new issues to the list. One thing that can be clearly said about the Japanese is that their attention to detail and consideration for others is both unique and impressive. During the final review of agenda topics, one of the young men from Omron's finance department asked to put a challenging topic on the board for discussion: Ford's back-to-basics campaign. By then, the morning hours had come and gone. Hiro asked, "Shall we all go to a local noodle shop for a quick lunch?" He had timed this lunch break perfectly, for it would have been hard for me to address this last agenda item with any degree of certainty. I needed time at the noodle shop to noodle my answer.

We spent the balance of the day bringing the Omron team up-to-speed on how Cellport's dire straits had come about, introducing the business options we had drafted for consideration and briefing the group on the Ford back-to-basics campaign. Because all discussions were in English and the Japanese have a propensity for literal details, I was very careful not to overstate what the back-to-basics program was about, yet I did not want to ignore the request for greater understanding of it. Knowing that the Japanese like to use metaphors when trying to help bridge language and cultural gaps, I decided to compare the environment at Ford to a change of government in which a liberal party gets thrown out in favor of a conservative party. I went on to explain that the party of Jacques Nasser wanted to dynamically expand Ford's business model and that it invested in programs like E-Ford and Wingcast and other experimental initiatives. Now, the party led by scion Bill Ford had decided to cut back on the experimental initiatives and to concentrate on the basics of its business, which was building automobiles for today's market.

The next logical question from our audience was, "How does Bill Ford view the Cellport program?" In full candor, I admitted that I was unsure about this, but I did note, on the positive side, that Ford's most important constituency, its auto dealers, loved the Cellport program. I also acknowledged that we were clearly under attack from the engineers who ran the Research and Vehicle Technology department at Ford. I tried my best to explain that the back-to-basics charter mandated by Bill Ford would most likely not support the company's vision — and now its $100 million-plus investment — in Wingcast. I believed this could be positive for Cellport because our alternative was not only less expensive than the embedded technology Wingcast used but it was also more consumer friendly as customers could use it with a potentially unlimited variety of mobile phones.

We used the first half of the Tuesday meetings answering questions from the day-one orientation and by early afternoon we were finally able to present, to the group, the numerous business models that we hoped would prove useful for structuring an investment. The investment discussion was now scheduled to begin the next day, on Wednesday. That evening Andy and I called the Cellport operational staff in Boulder. We sensed a high degree of panic in the office. The staff was worried about our dwindling cash reserves, continued uncertainty from Ford about a shipping date and the lack, so far, of an investment commitment from Omron. That evening, we briefed our Board on the status of the Omron discussions as well as the panic that was developing in Boulder. We agreed to brief the Board again each night until we had an outcome: either a resolution in Japan or a need to start developing specifics to reshape Cellport.

Finally, on Wednesday, we began to get good traction on an investment structure that everyone could agree on. Omron would invest another $10 million in Cellport at the same valuation we had given it before, but this time we would include warrants allowing Omron to very inexpensively buy up to 10 percent of Cellport. Iwakata-san agreed to deliver this company-saving funding proposal to Masuda-san for discussion by Omron's Board of Directors that evening. While the Omron Board met, Hiro, Andy and I went out for a celebratory dinner and we ordered a nice bottle of wine to toast what we thought was a high probability of funding success. After dinner, Andy and I once again called Cellport's Board members and briefed them on the funding package we had proposed to the Omron Board. We also began to discuss options we would need to consider if our funding attempts failed. The Plan B options differed greatly from one another. The options ranged from a massive layoff program to a proposal, which had been submitted by an investor, to loan the company $10 million for six months. This particular proposal had a catch, however; the investor wanted to hold the entire company as collateral and if we defaulted on repaying the loan, he would own Cellport.

On Thursday morning, as we entered the Omron office, I sensed a problem. Iwakata-san opened the meeting by saying we had more work to do; the Omron Board had criticized Cellport for getting itself into its very difficult position and rejected our proposal. The Board arranged to meet again that evening in a special session. It wanted Masuda-san to explain what could be done to ensure a safer and better investment structure. Hiro, Andy and I looked at each other. Each of us was thinking, "How foolish were we, celebrating before we got final approval?"

We spent the balance of the day struggling to find a way to improve the funding package. We decided to give Omron ownership of the company jewels, our patents, if we failed at our turn-around strategy. This time, Iwakata-san asked me to deliver the investment proposal to Masuda-san personally. I was escorted to his more modest Tokyo office, and when I saw him I could tell he had lost sleep over the troubles at Cellport. We sat across from each other at his small meeting table and I could see that he was tired and even upset. Masuda-san

234 | Chapter 11

said he needed to have a very personal conversation with me before I presented the overview of our proposal and the funding document to him. He said that the Board's criticism of Cellport caused him to have a sleepless night. He was very frustrated that we had let our business get in such tough shape. He went on to criticize me for accepting a tier-one role with Ford. He said that only huge companies can take on such roles because they have counter-leverage they can use against large automotive customers. Masuda-san explained that Omron itself had tier-one relationships with both Toyota and Honda for numerous programs, and because it had multiple programs, Omron had leverage. But as a small company with a single program, Cellport had little to no leverage. "They can crush your company along with my investment," he stated.

Masuda-san added that Omron had no interest in picking up our supply business with Ford because Omron lacked tier-one leverage with Ford and because the carmaker was known to be difficult and unstable.

Essentially, Masuda-san was scolding me for letting Cellport get suckered into a tier-one role as a small supplier, without any leverage, with a tough and troubled customer. I took the criticism to heart and again apologized for causing him embarrassment with his Board. Masuda-san said he would work hard to get the investment approved that evening but he wanted me to assure him that we would find a tier-one buyer, one who had leverage over Ford, to purchase Cellport's existing supply contracts. I apologized again for my mistakes and told him we would work diligently to sell off the program. I fully expected our various programs with Ford could be sold; it had product deliveries remaining that had revenue value in excess of $50 million.

That night Hiro, Andy and I had dinner in a small Italian restaurant. Our mood was much more subdued than it had been during dinner the previous evening. Using humor for therapy, we exchanged stories about our college days as we drank a bottle of house Chianti wine. We did not share in a single toast. During our Board call later that evening, Andy informed everyone that Omron's Board had rejected our proposal and he gave them details of the new offer. The call was short and somber. In fact, we could provide no confidence that the new offer would be approved. We agreed to conduct another call during the weekend to discuss whatever measures we would need to take to save the Ford program and dramatically reduce our expenses. Feeling completely exhausted from the week's 14-hour days of up-and-down emotions and the very real prospect of having to reorganize Cellport, if not sell the company, I slept solidly for nine hours that night.

Early Friday morning, Andy took a train to the Narita Airport for a flight back to the states, leaving Hiro and me to meet with Iwakata-san at Omron to hear the news. Andy promised to call Hiro as soon as he got to the airport to learn of Omron's decision. In our meeting, Iwakata-san told us that Masuda-san had slept better that night because he had received Board approval for an additional $10 million investment into Cellport. Both Hiro and I thanked Iwakata-san profusely and asked him to share our appreciation with Masuda-san. Iwakata-san said Omron's attorneys would start working with Andy on an investment document. He expected Omron to wire the $10 million to Cellport within a week.

We walked out of the Omron building, beaming with smiles, as if we had been magically transformed. Andy called and we shared the good news with him. I told Andy that I would call him after arriving in the states; we would need to discuss how to fulfill the commitment I made to Masuda-san to divest our supply contracts with Ford and exit that business. I also told Andy to expect a call from Omron's U.S.-based legal staff to discuss the terms and conditions of the $10 million funding agreement. I insisted to Hiro that I would take a noon bus to Tokyo's Narita Airport. I knew he had to catch up on work at his office because he had spent the entire week helping us negotiate the successful close of the Omron investment. As we waved goodbye, I could see in my good friend's eyes that he had aged a few years over the past week and I suspected that I had aged, too. The words Iwakata-san had used when he told us that Omron's Board had approved our request played over and over again, happily, in my memory. I was truly grateful to have such a wonderful partnership with Omron, and especially for the visionary efforts Masuda-san had made, during two grueling Board meetings, to advocate on our behalf. As I boarded my plane to San Francisco, however, I began to feel the physical effects of the exhausting week. I planned to sleep as we crossed the Pacific and I expected that I would need several days and nights to recover from a long week of entrepreneurial rallying that, thankfully, had ended in success.

When I landed in San Francisco, I was very frustrated to realize that I had been so preoccupied in Japan that I had forgotten to recharge my cell phone's battery. As I left the international terminal I made a promise to myself that I would take a long weekend and not report back to work until Tuesday, or maybe even Wednesday. Desperately, I looked for a United Airlines Red Carpet Club where I could recharge my phone and check in with Andy. When I finally reached him, I asked if he had heard from Omron's U.S. attorneys.

"Yes, I did. The deal is dead!" he said.

"What do you mean the deal is dead?" I exclaimed.

"It is dead! They refuse to talk about their mistaken reasoning for killing the funding deal," Andy replied.

My entire body and mind went numb. I just could not believe all the emotional highs and lows I was going through. They seemed unstoppable. It was like a bad dream that just would not end.
"Please," I implored Andy, "give me more details. I am in shock. This makes absolutely no sense."

"You're right. It makes no sense," he said. "Their attorneys admitted that the Omron Board did approve the investment. But their general counsel killed the deal. He told their chairman that holding the patents as collateral was not valid because if Cellport goes bankrupt, Omron would be stripped of the patents in the bankruptcy proceedings," Andy said.

"Is this true?" I asked.

"No, it is not true," he replied. "But the Omron attorneys refused to debate the issue. I even offered to put a bankruptcy attorney on the call to disabuse them of their mistake, but it was to no avail. They said, 'Japan said no deal, so it is dead.'"

12 | A Heart to Heart with My Son

There would be no rest that weekend or for a long time thereafter. Cellport had hit the wall and it was now in a full-blown tech-wreck crisis. Fortunately, or perhaps unfortunately, I had been conditioned, by 11 years of constantly navigating the turbulent waters of the high-tech industry, to take this sudden paradigm change head-on. I abandoned my fantasy of relaxing over the weekend and scheduled a critically important Board meeting for Sunday evening. I worked with Andy throughout Saturday to develop checklists of the issues before us and decision trees that would help us resolve the huge number of complex and critical matters we had to deal with, and to identify other things we needed to accomplish to prepare for the Board meeting. We needed to have our homework done and our thoughts in order for the Board call.

Andy and I quickly agreed that we had to make the Ford program our primary focus and that we needed to figure out who, among our staff, was indispensable to the program, which had consumed millions of dollars in engineering investments over the past year and now tied up more than $6 million of our cash. Yet putting all of our focus on Ford meant that we would have to lay off virtually all of our MobileWeb engineering and business development teams as well as most of our administrative and non-automotive sales support personnel. I began counting the people who would be let go. The number eclipsed 50, yet we needed even more trimming to make our new budget work.

On Saturday afternoon, I called Ralph and asked him if he could join me for Sunday breakfast at my home to discuss the next chapter in Cellport's evolution. During our breakfast, Ralph said that Cellport's employees had gone through a series of conflicting emotions on Friday. The rumors of a successful funding with Omron created an air of excitement, only to become overshadowed by more and more confusion, coming out of Detroit, about Ford's intentions to cancel the dealer program. I informed Ralph that not only were the messages from Ford scrambled but so was our time in Japan, that in the end we had failed to get a funding commitment. Now we must make some tough decisions, I told him, and shift our discussion to evaluate our personnel needs. We needed to identify which Cellport employees we would need to retain in order to satisfy the Ford purchase orders, to be able to continue to design new mobile phone adaptors for the Ford program and to find a buyer for all other purchase commitments from the automotive industry. Ralph developed a list of people he thought would make an adequate skeleton crew; it numbered less than 20.

I asked Ralph to explain his logic. His approach, essentially, was to stop pursuing new design projects for other Ford programs and to cease design work for Nissan, which we had begun the previous year, and for BMW's Mini Cooper, which had recently contracted with us to design a product that would launch in 2003 [1].

"We do not need a large staff because all the physical products are built under contract, and we just need to manage the logistics of final delivery," Ralph said.

At the end of the very long and melancholy morning, I told Ralph that I would discuss his recommendations with the Board that evening, I would call him to inform him of our Board's directives. Confident the Board would approve our recommendations, I told Ralph that I would want to meet with him and Mike Lewellen at my home Monday morning to review the final list of retained employees and to organize and schedule the day's events, which would include a very large meeting of our staff at which we would announce the layoff of most of our personnel.

Andy and I spent the balance of Sunday preparing for the evening Board meeting. Despite the unpleasantness of the tasks, there was one thing that made the process bearable and even possible: We understood our options like the backs of our hands and we were unified in our understanding of Cellport's priorities. Because the Board meeting would be such a critical one, we decided to invite our outside counsel to participate; we wanted to make sure that we received as much objective advice as possible and that we were considering all aspects of Colorado employment law that pertained to our situation. By now it was clear that we would be laying off over 70 people on Monday.

That evening, during the Board call, I summarized the events that led to the aborted Omron funding and articulated our priorities for moving the business forward. The top item on our list, I told them, was to fulfill our obligations to Ford's dealer program to get value out of the millions of dollars in inventory. The Board and I also discussed who would call Ford's purchasing department on Monday. Andy, we decided, would inform Ford of Cellport's cutbacks, assure them that our primary focus from now on was to retain enough staff to serve the dealer-install program and that we would eventually sell off our automotive purchase orders from Nissan and BMW's Mini Cooper. We also told the Board that we needed to discuss the most appropriate way to handle such a sizable layoff, both legally and ethically. To the credit of Cellport's Board members, everyone participated with sincere respect and care for our employees, customers and legal responsibilities. The discussion had a business-like and somber tone. Cellport had just become another company to fall victim to the Internet-telecom bubble implosion that had been ravaging the country for nearly two years.

There was another layer of implications as well, and that was the impact of our new circumstances on some of our most important partnerships. In Japan, Omron stopped its support of a design group it had formed to develop designs for the Cellport Global Partners program. We ended up shutting down our Cellport-Japan office and discontinuing the work Hiro had been doing for us. In Germany,

Alf Naber's company, ALAC, which was building a business as our first CGP licensee, suffered a temporary setback. It ended up forming a joint venture with Peiker to develop hands-free designs. One of the most frustrating partnership outcomes involved a fellow U.S. company, Cisco. Many of our staff had worked tirelessly to develop MobileWeb product designs for this very demanding partner and we would lose not only these employees but the Cisco projects as well.

On Monday, April 15, at 7:00 a.m., Ralph and Mike met me at my home to discuss in detail the Cellport Board's decisions. After our meeting, Mike and Ralph headed off to Cellport, while Andy and I called the Ford purchasing department. The most interesting aspect of that call, we noted, was that Ford's staffers listened unemotionally. They made very few comments, other than to say, "Keep us abreast of your progress."

We both thought the reaction was strangely muted. Andy theorized that because Ford itself had recently laid off thousands of employees, a Cellport layoff of 70-plus people was "mice nuts" to them. My belief was that Ford knew its delays had caused the financial crisis at Cellport and that its executives were afraid we would sue them for contractual negligence. Either way, we could not afford to burn a bridge with Ford, for the carmaker was our primary ace in the hole. Our bet was simple: We would start shipping the 20,000 units to Ford dealers. The strategy would give us more than enough cash and time to divest Cellport of a wonderful piece of business to an appropriate tier-one supplier. Andy said the divestiture was so important that he would start working on a solicitation document that evening.

I now had to face a business situation that was personal in every respect: laying off nearly three-fourths of the employees at a company that I had spent 11 years building.

My first priority was to give my assistant a list of about 20 people whom I wanted to meet in the main conference room at 11:00 a.m. I asked her to notify each person individually and to make sure they understood this was a must-attend meeting. These people would be the "keepers." They were top engineers and program logistics specialists whose roles were critical to either the Ford program or the divestiture of the automotive business. My meeting with this nervous group of individuals would be a necessary warm-up for a much more difficult meeting, scheduled for 3:00 p.m. that afternoon, for those who would be laid off. For lack of a better term, we referred to this group as the "non-keepers."

During the morning meeting, I gave the select audience a briefing of the failed funding effort in Japan and our new Board-approved mission to focus on the Ford program. I did my best to answer dozens of questions from a very grave but supportive group of Cellporters. One of the best questions came from a woman who asked, "If our friends from Omron essentially have no confidence in Ford, why are we betting that Ford will be good corporate citizens?"

This was indeed an excellent question. I did my best to explain that Ford would either take the products or pay for the 20,000 units that it contracted us to build. "OK, Pat, I will follow your lead," she replied, "but personally, I think Ford is a slimy organization that has been dishonest with us for months and will continue to be so."

Admittedly, I could not debate her point. All we could do was push to sell off the inventory or enforce the contract we had with Ford.

When I got back to my office after the meeting, I was surprised to find a voicemail from a writer at *The Denver Post* who wanted to interview me. The newspaper had been told that Cellport was going out of business. I realized that we had failed to preempt negative media coverage. I called Andy and our marketing director, Lori Pidick, to draft and issue a press release that afternoon. This was an obvious issue that we missed. How many other snafus had we made that would haunt us?

At 3:00 p.m., all of Cellport's employees gathered in a large room on the first floor for a company-wide meeting. While I was walking down the stairwell to this meeting, I dwelled on the number of individuals and families I was about to negatively affect with the layoff news. This would be the saddest meeting I had ever addressed or even attended in my life. There were some 80 people in the room and another 10 attending via conference call to learn of their fates. It was enormously difficult to address such a somber group and to see the concern and even fear expressed by the faces of those in the room. And, of course, I was acutely aware that my leadership failures caused this.

I spoke from a script of bullet points that covered the previous week's events in Tokyo, our weekend strategy decisions, and our Board discussions. I told everyone that to save the company, we had to radically reduce our expenses and focus solely on meeting the Ford program commitments. I was looking at a roomful of teary eyes. I told them all that unless they had met with me during the morning meeting, that today would be their last day at Cellport and that we were preparing their final paychecks. It was obvious that most of them had expected the worst. Even though Cellport's collapse took place late in the Internet-telecom bubble crash, this was the new reality: These 70-plus individuals were now unemployed technology workers from yet another company that had hit the rocks. I offered to stay as late as needed to address all of their questions.

Some of the most interesting and diverse perspectives on Cellport's circumstances and strategy came up during this question-and-answer session. "Why doesn't Cellport sue Motorola and Ford for their abuse of our company?" one employee asked. This was a tough question to answer. I replied that our objective was to win funding and sales willingly, not via the courts, however I acknowledged that at some point we might need to resort to litigation.

I had mentioned earlier in my remarks that Andy, Ralph, Mike and I, as well as a handful of others, had agreed to work for deferred salaries, and this prompted another question: What did we know about the future that we weren't communicating? This, too, was a tough question to answer. I explained simply that we were either incurable optimists or we were not smart enough to know when to quit.

Eventually there were only a few dozen or so people left in the room and no one had any additional questions. I shook each one's hand, thanked them for their efforts and wished them the best of luck.

I returned to my office and looked out the window, watching, in a sad and numb trance, as dozens and dozens of people left Cellport for the last time, carrying boxes that contained their personal items. At one point, Lori Pidick interrupted me with some startling news. She said that an angry salesperson had been talking to the press and key customers all afternoon, telling them that Cellport was shutting its doors. He had also called our key retail customers, such as Best Buy and Circuit City, advising each of these accounts to return their merchandise for credit before Cellport declared bankruptcy.

We needed to jump into damage-control mode immediately. For the next several hours, Lori helped arrange interviews with journalists from as many media outlets as possible so that we could correct the misinformation that was circulating and set the record straight about our true intentions. It was an unfortunate negative experience with the media. Throughout our history, Cellport had been viewed in the media as a high-tech darling. Now, with this public relations stumble, we were about to be roasted despite Lori's fabulous efforts to try to undo the damage. The next day, Cellport made headlines in all the business sections of the major Colorado papers and in our industry trade publications as well. The stories all conveyed a grim view of Cellport.

Late that evening we conducted another conference call with our Board to report on the events of the day and to discuss our next priorities. All of a sudden, our business seemed much less complex. We had just two primary issues to focus on in the near term: delivering product to Ford and putting together a comprehensive document to help divest Cellport of its business to tier-one automotive companies.

During the next week, Andy worked 12-plus hours a day drafting a document to solicit buyers of our automotive business. He also had to spend time that week dealing with Ford, which continually introduced a variety of new excuses to delay the launch of the dealer program. We finally decided it was time to "take the gloves off." We told Ford to give us an unequivocal launch date or Cellport would sue for payment. This was the last thing anyone in Ford's purchasing department wanted to hear. In addition to the general insecurity they felt from working amid the continuous waves of layoffs at Ford, they knew that prompting a lawsuit against their company would do nothing to enhance the security of their jobs.

In an attempt to calm Andy, who could no longer mask his agitation when dealing with the Ford team, the purchasing managers made a commitment to launch the dealer program in mid-May. They also gave us a list of companies they would like us to sell the entire automotive book of business to, including the Ford purchase agreements. The names on the list represented a "who's who" in the U.S. tier-one automotive electronics systems supply business: Delphi, Donnelly Corporation, Motorola and Visteon. While Andy was finalizing the solicitation book, I scheduled meetings with all the companies except Visteon. As hard as I tried to get a meeting with Visteon — a former division of Ford that had been spun out of the company a couple years earlier and that was still a leading vendor to Ford — I could not get this company to meet with me [2]. Nevertheless, I was able to set up a late April meeting with Motorola and meetings with Delphi, Donnelly, and another prospective buyer that we contacted separately, called Gentex Corporation, for the first week of May.

**

Motorola was the ideal company to approach first because it knew our business well, and when Ralph and I visited its offices near Chicago in late April, its telematics team already had a copy of our recently completed divestiture documents. The meeting also represented the first occasion I had to see any Motorola people since the company's Ventures unit thwarted our mezzanine financing round in late 2001.

The meeting was clearly uncomfortable for them and it was strange for me. My old friends obviously felt guilty about their company's contributions to Cellport's troubles. They were highly empathetic toward me. Near the end of the meeting, Ray Sokola entered the room. Normally chipper and friendly, Ray was as pale as a ghost — he looked at me with funereal eyes. I could see that he felt terrible about my situation, yet he was speechless. He stared at the floor while I finished answering questions from Helena Stelnicki and Mike Kraus.

After the meeting ended, Ray pulled me aside. He said he was truly sorry for the events at Cellport and, despite Motorola's reluctance to do business with Ford, he said he would talk to Marios Zenios to see if there was anything the Motorola telematics unit could do to help our cause. I bit my cheek to hold back tears, kept my chin up and told Ray that somehow, Cellport would find a buyer for its automotive business; if we were unable to achieve that, I said, we would certainly have no trouble finding a buyer for our patent portfolio. Ralph and I then left Motorola's offices to catch our plane back to Denver.

That evening, as I drove from the Denver airport to Boulder, my girl-friend, Susan, called to ask about my day at Motorola. I summarized the day's conversations for her. Even though Ray wanted to help Cell-port, I told her, I was certain that Motorola was not overly interested in our Ford business. Susan could tell I was not handling this well and she asked me what was wrong. I told her I was just a little dehydrated.

"From what? Did you have a glass of wine on the plane?"

"No," I said. "But ever since I landed and got in my car, I've been thinking about Ray's sheet-white face, empathetically looking at a nearly dead Pat Kennedy. I realized just what desperate shape Cell-port is in, and I have not been able to stop crying! The abuses that these big and heartless companies have dealt us have finally gotten to me. I am exhausted and need a new life."

**

In the first week of May, Andy, Ralph and I started a three-day road trip to present the Cellport automotive business to prospective buyers. We began outside Chicago's O'Hare airport, drove over to western Michigan and then down into central Indiana for meetings with the senior management teams at Delphi, Donnelly, and Gentex. The trip became as much a bonding and strategy session for the three of us as it was a sales mission to three tier-one automotive suppliers. Our first meeting was with Gentex, a highly regarded and profitable maker of high-tech mirror systems that also happened to dabble in the telemat-ics market. This was a perfect first meeting for our three-man sales team. The Gentex executives were polite and asked good questions, but in reality, they had little interest in our product portfolio and orders. This was not a surprise to me, but the experience we gained by meeting with them was good preparation for our subsequent appointments.

Our next meeting was with Donnelly [3], which, in contrast to Gentex, was highly interested in Cellport's automotive business. We had a most productive meeting with its executives who, at the close of the meeting, assigned their vice president of technologies to evaluate the opportunity and conduct due diligence with both Cellport and Ford. As excited as Donnelly was, I was becoming skeptical of Ford's true intentions, partially because market intelligence was coming my way and partially because I had a gut feeling that our partnership with Ford was going to completely unravel. Nevertheless, a well-regarded supplier like Donnelly would be a terrific addition to our family of licensees. We appreciated their interest and were encouraged by it.

The last appointment took us five hours south to Kokomo, Indiana, to meet with Delphi, the automotive parts supplier that had been spun-off from General Motors. Delphi had previously supplied OnStar equipment to GM before losing that line of business to Ray Sokola's Motorola.

Delphi was a most interesting wildcard; its executives talked a good telematics story at all of the important industry conferences but in reality, it had little business in this market. Taking over Cellport's automotive business would have served two of Delphi's publicly stated directions perfectly: First, the company had established an interest in offering a hands-free cellular phone technology, and the Cellport business would give them our market-leading second-generation Universal Hands-Free product. Second, Delphi was on a mission to diversify its customer base, because more than 75 percent of its business came from GM. What company would be a better customer than Ford for broadening Delphi's market?

The meeting at Delphi was friendly but the company's executives did not insert much energy into the conversation. Ralph and Andy thought they sensed a real interest, but it was obvious to me that these guys had plans for telematics that focused on something other than picking up Cellport's contracts [4]. One thing I do like about the U.S. auto market is that there are not a lot of poker players; in these types of meetings you tend to learn quickly what is hot and what is not.

**

As we drove back to Chicago to catch our flights home I received two most interesting calls, one from Ford's purchasing department requesting a meeting to discuss the sales visits we were conducting and the other from Joe Lewo, a Detroit-based entrepreneur who had invested in several prominent telematics ventures in the U.S.

The calls from Ford and Joe Lewo gave me a meaningful excuse to plan a trip for the next week to Detroit. I needed to feed my insatiable appetite for market intelligence. One thing I learned early in Cellport's history is that each incremental bit of market intelligence you obtain during the business development and negotiation process increases the prospect of creating deal heat, and that is exactly what Cellport needed: white-hot deal heat. Coincidentally, after I arrived home in Boulder that evening, I received a call from Mike Dooley, a tenured business development specialist at Motorola. Dooley said Marios and Ray had directed him to get a simple and important deal done with Cellport in short order. "OK," I said, "we have tried this twice now. Why would this opportunity be any different?"

Dooley was a very street-savvy guy who answered without flinching: "Because I am a tenured and full-time Motorola deal guy and what I set out to get done, I usually get done."

Dooley, a polite alpha male, jumped right to the reason for the deal. "Motorola does not want to see Cellport's patents hitting the auction block, so they have assigned me to negotiate a multi-million dollar prepaid license that will give you stability and that will give Motorola rights to use the balance of your patent portfolio, beyond the MobileWeb license we already have," he said. "Plus, if you can sell the Ford business to another company, all the more power to you, but," he added, "my focus will be solely on a license for Motorola and a seven-digit prepay for you."

Dooley said that to avoid the snafus that undermined the previous two negotiations between our companies, he wanted me to deal only with him and to keep everyone else out of the discussions, even Ray and Marios.

"My objective is put this deal together by the end of May," he said. "Does that work for you?"

"It works for Cellport as long as the prepay is sizable enough and the license structure is fair," I said.

"That is my job, Pat. Now, can I ask you to meet with me in Chicago next week?"

"As a matter of fact, I plan to be in Detroit on Tuesday and Wednesday of next week, so I can stop by Chicago on Monday," I said.

Finally, I sensed that we were starting to catch some breaks that would lead to deals. Furthermore, Andy later reported that after he returned home he had received emails from several European companies that wanted to consider purchasing our automotive business and wanted copies of our solicitation documents.

The next week I traveled to Chicago and met with Mike Dooley and Mike Kraus at Motorola to hear what they had in mind. On the surface, the deal they were suggesting was a fascinating one for Cellport financially, but it would force us to radically change our licensing model. When you are on your deathbed awaiting the recitation of your last rights, however, it is absolutely amazing how your perspective changes.

I listened receptively to their proposal. Motorola wanted a license to our five Universal Hands-Free system patents, but unlike our Cellport Global Partners who had licensed the Cellport-designed platform and patents that we had established as a way to create a de-facto global standard, Motorola wanted the liberty to provide a customized platform "if, hypothetically speaking" any of its customers so demanded. We had a poker game going on — I knew they had something up their sleeves and were covering their bets. And I knew, as soon as Motorola made this proposition, that it would change Cellport's dream of trying to create a uniform and global approach for hands-free products.

But here was Motorola now willing to pay us $5 million in prepaid royalties. I figured that they must have a contract collaboration in Europe with one of the companies that had IdeaJacked our patented designs and that they were trying to avoid a patent-crossing battle with Cellport or, worse, with the buyer of our patents. But which IdeaJacker was it? And which carmaker had they contracted with to supply a hands-free solution? Both Mikes were both smart and tough. There was no way I would get any of this information from them.

We spent the entire afternoon reviewing their licensing term sheet and haggling over the terms and conditions. They cleverly wanted the $5 million prepay applied to both the MobileWeb patents that Motorola licensed the year before — which were originally not licensed under a prepay arrangement and had not yet started shipping to a known customer — as well as our Universal Hands-Free patent portfolio that they now needed to license. As our meeting wrapped up, we discussed our schedules and the milestones we would need to accomplish to consummate the deal by the end of May. From a strategic negotiations perspective, I knew that the more intelligence I had and the more concerns I could cause them to have, the more favorable the deal would ultimately be for Cellport. I told both Mikes that we would need to do much work via email because I would be in Detroit for the next two days and then I would be in Europe most of the next week. Mike Kraus knew I was active in Europe and slyly asked if I was going on vacation. "No, it's all business, unfortunately," I said. "I will be meeting with a lot of Europeans that have suddenly developed a keen interest in Cellport. Imagine that, Mike!"

They looked at each other and asked me to check my email daily. We scheduled another face-to-face meeting for the third week of May, one week before we were scheduled to close the license contract.

I smiled as I drove off toward Chicago's O'Hare airport. I called my travel agent and told her to book me a Sunday flight to Frankfurt and a return flight on Friday of that week. Even though I did not have a single meeting scheduled in Europe, it was imperative that Motorola's executives believe I had appointments with Europeans who might want to preempt them by buying Cellport and, potentially, denying Motorola access to the critical, core patents that Cellport owned.

**

My first meeting in Detroit was with Joe Lewo. Joe had dodged the holocaust camps in Europe as a young boy and was a true grit, street-savvy Canadian entrepreneur. He amassed a fortune early in his career by selling U.S. car parts to Fidel Castro's regime in the 1960s and 1970s while U.S. companies were prohibited from doing business in Cuba.

By 2002, Joe Lewo had ownership interests in many more automotive markets, including Ford's Wingcast program. Lewo had a substantial facility in Detroit that developed specially modified vehicles for auto-makers; Ford was its largest client.

My meeting with Joe was as intense and cinematic as a high-drama movie. He multitasked continually as we talked and constantly shared deep insights that he had developed into all things automotive in Detroit. Joe informed me that Ford's purchasing crew was actually very pro-Cellport and fundamentally honest, except that they were frightened by layoff politics and intimidated by the pro-Wingcast engineers in Ford's Research and Vehicle Technology program who viewed the Cellport solution as Wingcast's nemesis. Because we had only two hours to cover a day's worth of discussion topics, I asked Joe if he would be available for dinner that evening. He said, "Yes, as long as you don't mind eating with my beautiful young wife and kids at our favorite Italian restaurant." Joe said he and his family would pick me up at 6:00 p.m. at my hotel.

That afternoon, I met with Ford's purchasing manager and the department's attorney. The meeting was interesting but not nearly as exciting as my morning with Joe Lewo. The meeting was completely cordial, but the Ford representatives seemed fairly nervous and they acted even a bit guilty at times. I pushed them for information on the status of the dealer program launch. They said that once they got their results back from the hands-free system testing program that they had begun earlier in the spring, they would make their final decision. They expected to have that decision around the middle of May. I asked for a copy of the test specifications or even a copy of the testing methodology. They acknowledged that these documents weren't available, but they did let me know that the Cellport product-testing effort was being aided by our "good" friends at Research and Vehicle Technology. When I heard that, I knew the program was doomed.

As the afternoon progressed, the Ford purchasing executives asked me a lot of questions about Donnelly's interest in picking up our automotive business and the likelihood that this would occur. I guarded my answers but did tell them that Cellport would do everything it could to transition the business successfully to where it belonged in the first place: with a tier-one automotive supplier. When queried about Cellport's future, I responded that we were exploring numerous options that ranged from a large license transaction with Motorola to the sale of the entire business to an interested European buyer. I asked them if the outcome mattered to them. They said they clearly preferred that we form a licensing deal with Motorola and that Cellport continue to exist as a telematics technology development lab and open licensing entity.

Joe Lewo had the Ford guys down in spades: They were slow-rolling us. Their primary concern was to not make a mistake or worse, get sued, especially in the context of the company's massive layoffs and Bill Ford's back-to-basics campaign. During our meeting, I suggested that Ford could easily distribute the 20,000 units via sales to its fleet customers and thereby avoid a sloppy dismount with Cellport. They smiled and thanked me for the idea.

Dinner with Joe Lewo and his family that evening was a major event for me. I was able to use the occasion to pick up additional market intelligence from Joe and to plant some important messages with him that I believed could find their way back to Motorola.

During dinner, I learned that Joe had been trying to hire Ray Sokola for years and that he had developed a close personal relationship with him. Later during our dinner, Joe asked me what Cellport's options were in light of the setback at Ford. I told him we were working on an attractive offer from Motorola and that the next week I would be in Europe talking to Nokia and several other companies that had each expressed interest in a transaction with us.

While it was critical that I keep my word to Motorola's Mike Dooley and not talk to Ray or Marios about our negotiations until our pre-paid royalty deal was finished, I was not restricted from talking to Joe about it and using Joe to conduct some important messenger work for me. My bet was that within 12 hours, Joe would call Ray to tell him that Nokia might buy the destitute Cellport's patent portfolio and that Ray and Marios, fearing that Motorola's rival, Nokia, might pick up patent rights that were fundamental to the future of telematics, would leverage their competitive fears to close our transaction quickly.

An additional insight Joe shared with me was that in the late 1990s, Ford's executives were concerned that GM's OnStar program might leave Ford at a competitive disadvantage in the telematics market, so it relied on Joe to help create and initially fund Wingcast for the Ford management team. However, after the Wingcast business launched, Ford took control of the program and turned it into a goliath research and development project that by now, after just four short years, was burning through $10 million per quarter and had now cost more than $140 million even though it never delivered a single product to the market. Joe said Wingcast's excessive wastefulness was a prime example of why Bill Ford chanted his "back-to-basics" mantra so often. The entire organization had become both risk-averse and highly political, which affected the launch of the Cellport program.

Coincidentally, as we left the restaurant, Joe received a call from Harel Kodesh, the president of Wingcast. Harel told Joe that that Wingcast's fate was on the agenda of the next meeting of Ford's Board of Directors. Harel feared that like most other new technology initiatives at Ford, Wingcast would likely be shut down. After the call Joe looked at me and said, "You can imagine how Harel feels. This is a dangerous time to do business with Ford."

**

When I arrived in Frankfurt the next week to conduct the various meetings I had hastily organized, I contemplated the impact that this trip would have on Cellport — it would be either a brilliant strategic move or a major waste of time and money. My first meeting was with the "Joe Lewo" of Germany, a man by the name of Hugo Scheiner. Hugo was a self-made, high-energy entrepreneur who was trying to vector into the telematics business after having recently sold his own company that developed navigation software. Beginning my itinerary with a meeting with Hugo proved to be a very worthwhile approach. In fact, I was shocked by the amount and nature of the local market insights he gave me. What I learned from Hugo was that several of the IdeaJackers who had copied Cellport's first-generation Universal Hands-Free system had happily copied our second-generation system as well, and that they were receiving orders from German vehicle producers in volumes that were increasing dramatically by the day.

I pushed Hugo for some insight as to which company awarded Motorola a contract for a Universal Hands-Free product solution. He had only heard a rumor of an award to Motorola; it was from either Mercedes-Benz or Opel, but he was not certain of the award amount or the company involved.

The first company I visited was Wolfgang Cullmann's firm, and true to the information I had obtained from Hugo, Wolfgang's design team had indeed IdeaJacked Cellport's second-generation design that I had shown him and Thomas Schlegel during their visit to Boulder less than two years earlier. I confronted Wolfgang about the knock-off, but he danced around my questions. He told me that the Cullmann product had a different connector than the one we had designed. The world moves on, he told me, and he needed to update his design or become an obsolete vendor in this market. Honoring my personal philosophy that one should burn bridges only as a last resort, I warned

Wolfgang that unless we settled on a patent license, things could get ugly between us.

Wolfgang smiled. "Pat, I warned you about doing business with American carmakers," he said. "If you are still in business in six months, we should talk then."

I felt such convoluted emotions when I drove away from the Cullmann offices. On one hand, I was proud that our design efforts had, once again, paved the way for such great innovations, even though they were flatteringly IdeaJacked. On the other hand, I was furious that Cullmann was expanding its operations to satisfy a growing volume of orders from Audi and Volkswagen while I had just laid off the bulk of Cellport's employees, whose families were now struggling to get by. It was horribly unfair.

My next meeting in Germany was with the recently appointed head of Nokia's telematics business unit, Razvan Olosu. In the middle 1990s, Nokia had eclipsed Motorola as the world's leading supplier of mobile phones, yet the Finnish company was not pleased that in turn, by 2002, Motorola had obtained numerous large telematics contracts, leaving Nokia in the dust in this new and potentially very lucrative market. Razvan's job was to turn Nokia's telematics business around to eclipse Motorola once again, and he wanted to understand how Cellport's patents and technology could help his company do that. Being charmed by this shrewd wireless industry warlord was a flattering experience and an eye-opening one. As our meeting progressed, I began to realize the depth of Motorola's justified fear of Nokia. If Nokia did own Cellport's patent portfolio and inventive prowess, it would soon wage patent wars against its competitors and I would be in the middle of a legal and market battle that would affect the industry worldwide. Razvan wanted me to sign a two-year employment contract and be available for patent litigation disputes for the life of the patents. I felt like I would become the singular person who owned a nuclear-trigger technology that could influence the outcome of a battle between two bomb-building and market-crazed organizations.

But I also knew that any transaction with Nokia would take months to consummate, and, in my heart, I also understood that the sale of Cellport's pioneering telematics patents to Nokia — rather than promoting the safety features and potential new applications our technology could provide — could have a regressive effect on the market we had been trying to build for so many years.

At dinner that evening, I asked Razvan how Nokia would share Cellport's core technologies with others. His answer was simple: "We would use Cellport's patents to dominate the market for the benefit of Nokia's shareholders, of which you would be one," he said. His frankness convinced me that it was critical for Cellport to remain independent so that it could promote open licensing of its patents, and that Motorola had a legitimate fear of being cut out of the telematics market if it failed to secure a license for our five patents that covered the Universal Hands-Free design. Motorola and I were in the same boat. We had to have a deal if either of us was to continue to prosper. The worldwide telematics market was then worth nearly $1 billion in annual revenues and on a growth track to easily surpass $5 billion in the next 10 years [5].

**

I was exhausted after this enlightening but scary trip, and as I drove home to Boulder from the Denver International Airport, my teenaged son, Matt, called me. Matt told me, in a trembling voice, about a very bad experience he had at school that day. His language arts teacher had asked each of the students in class to select a section of newspaper out of a large pile of newspapers on her desk, and to then pick a news article that interested them and write about it. She wanted each student to discuss the meaning of the news article they had selected and to explain what it meant to them personally. Unfortunately, Matt had grabbed the business section of *The Boulder Daily Camera*, dated April 16, 2002. The headline told of the massive Cellport layoff the previous day. The challenge of writing about the huge body blow his father's company had taken, and how the company was now threatened for its very existence, upset Matt greatly. He asked me if it was true that Cellport was most likely doomed and wondered what our family would do without a business and money. I asked him what he thought would happen.

"Dad, I'm afraid that we'll lose everything. How will we eat?" he asked.

His words were genuine and spoken from the heart of a 15-year-old. While his pleas crushed me emotionally, I instinctively, as a father, recognized this moment as one of those seminal times when a parent has an opportunity to offer guidance in a way that might perhaps help shape their child's perspectives and ability to deal with the challenges they will inevitably face throughout life. I said, "Matt, there is no doubt these are difficult times. But in life you will find out that not all things are easy or fair. For sure, you will have a friend who will try to steal your girlfriend and maybe someone will try taking your business or job. Maybe they will IdeaJack your great ideas, just like I experienced for the second time in Europe this week. Should I give up? If I give up working toward my goals, our future will be full of sadness rather than confidence and opportunities. If you work hard and fight hard to survive, most times you will eventually find a way to succeed. This is your father's battle on the front lines. Stay strong with me, and I will do my best for our family, investors and all the employees we still have at the company."

**

When I got home that evening, I read an email string between Andy and Ford's purchasing department that indicated the carmaker would send us a letter canceling the entire order of 20,000 units and spare parts that we had already built and stocked, ready to deliver, in a warehouse in Colorado Springs. Strangely, I found that I was relieved that the nightmarish saga had come to an end. Even though the conclusion of the Ford relationship was substantially disadvantageous to us, it would expedite the urgency of the Motorola prepay license. Motorola knew that Cellport would never file for bankruptcy. From Motorola's perspective, the prospect was now more real than ever before that Cellport would unload the company in fire-sale transaction with Motorola's nemesis, Nokia.

With all the players in my world moving like pieces across a board of Chinese checkers, I realized just how critically important it was for Cellport's patents to remain independent as we closed our deal with Motorola. I needed to consummate the agreement while the deal heat was to my advantage. And indeed, Motorola was agitating to finalize the agreements. During my trip to Europe the previous week, Motorola had insisted on two conference calls to hasten the process of drafting and reviewing the contract, and it had scheduled a final face-to-face meeting with the Mikes — Dooley and Kraus — and me for the last week of May to conclude our contract negotiations.

At this late May meeting, the three of us shook hands on what we considered a win-win license contract, and now, finally, I was allowed to visit with my old friend Ray. Over coffee, I thanked Ray for his help at such a critical time in Cellport's history and for taking the high road by licensing our two patent portfolios. With typical modesty, Ray downplayed his role and gave credit to Motorola's senior leadership team.

"Yes, I understand all the great support you had from your associates for this financial transaction. But as a fellow inventor, it is your respect for Cellport's inventive contributions that ethically anchored our long-term partnership," I said to him.

On Friday, May 31, I sat in the office of our outside counsel, looking at Boulder's spectacular Flatiron peaks, listening to the Cellport and Motorola attorneys, in a conference call, refine a few minute contract details for a Universal Hands-Free license that was free of platform design restrictions. At about 3:00 p.m., I heard the attorneys agree that the document was ready for signatures. After two failed attempts to forge a partnership with Motorola, we were finally about to consummate a deal closing. Ray would sign a financial prepay of $5 million and take out additional patent licenses with Cellport, a company that had eagerly taught him about the art-of-the-possible in telematics architectures. Five minutes later, I watched the fax machine print out a 22-page, $5 million prepay license contract with Ray's signature on the fourth from last page. It was a wonderful visual sensation. After a quick review by our attorney to ensure that the Motorola-faxed document matched his record as the final copy, I counter-signed the contract and faxed it back to Motorola. Fifteen minutes later I got a call from Ray. With him on the call were Mike Kraus, Marios and Helena all wishing me well. I conveyed my heartfelt thanks to each of them and they all laughed. Helena said they were sorry it took so long, but in the end, she and her colleagues at Motorola wanted to be fair. We all chuckled and I wished them all a wonderful weekend and a final thanks.

This deal-closing ceremony with Motorola was much like the New Year's Eve contract-signing drama I had conducted with FLV several years earlier. The peaceful euphoria that comes over me after successfully consummating these types of large financing deals also gives me a sustained adrenaline rush. That evening, I went for a long bike ride, smiling to myself the whole time, before meeting up with some close friends for a relaxed and celebratory sushi dinner at a favorite local restaurant.

On Monday, June 3, as I drove to the office I called our accounting manager with instructions to issue sizable bonus checks for all the employees who had stayed with us for the preceding six weeks when Cellport desperately fought, against the odds, for its survival. During the drive I received another call from Joe Lewo. Anxious to hear what Joe heard about our deal with Motorola, I took his call. "Pat, I heard that Friday was a super day for you. Congratulations," he said. "By the way, Ford's back-to-basics program struck again today."

I asked, "What do you mean?"

"Early this morning, Ford fired all of its Wingcast employees and had private security guards supervise them as they exited their building. Plus, it secured all their PCs and shut down their communications networks," Joe said.

After all of our years of work with Ford and nearly $140 million dollars wasted in Wingcast, Ford was now an even more basic car company.

13 | Modifying Our Game Plan

1991
1992
1993
1994
1995
1996
1997
1998
1999
2000
2001
2002
2003
2004
2005
2006
2007
2008
2009

Even with the good fortune Motorola brought us, we were still devastated by Bill Ford's back-to-basics mandate. I felt betrayed — especially after the distasteful experience of having to lay off most of our personnel. And now at Cellport, we had to make many financial decisions that would have long-term effects on the company's future and we had to make these strategic decisions in a matter of weeks. Wolfgang Cullmann was correct, Detroit-based vehicle producers were notoriously bad partners.

Andy and I divided up the most critical responsibilities, and his task became known in the company as "the cleanup." His jobs were to get us out of debt, deal with creditors, find prospective buyers for our automotive business, and try to negotiate a settlement with Ford. Andy's work was truly the most difficult in the company at the time, and the task of approaching our creditors was extremely unpleasant.

Many of our creditors found it difficult to accept the Ford cancellation story; they were understandably angry with Cellport and tried to take it out on Andy. Fortunately for us, Cellport's collapse came late in the Internet-bust period, and most of our creditors by then had seen many of their failed Internet-telecom customers simply close shop and abandon their debts. Thus, when our creditors realized that

Cellport had a real human being — Andy Quartner — to negotiate with, most considered any type of payment to be a positive outcome. Many were willing to settle for reduced payments, though some of these companies were skeptical that we could make good on any type of payments and wanted their money "yesterday." Some of our creditors threatened to sue us, and several did [1].

My first priority was to find ways to bring money in the door so that we could turn the company around and resume developing another innovative technology platform and to further expand our patent portfolio. This strategy ultimately resulted in our "Mobile Multimedia Connectivity" patent portfolio. Unlike earlier times when the world was awash with investment capital for cutting-edge technology opportunities and one could raise money with little more than a compelling strategy and good fund-raising skills, funding for technology companies in 2002 was nearly impossible to come by. I could identify only two approaches that seemed worthwhile for generating revenues in the near term: selling off the over $6 million in cancelled inventory we built up for Ford and securing additional patent licensees from the growing number of companies that had copied our product designs and their underlying core Cellport patents.

Much to our relief, as the summer progressed, Ford found a new need for Cellport's assistance. Hewlett-Packard (HP), Ford's large fleet customer that purchased tens of thousands of Cellport Universal Hands-Free units from Ford in years prior to the failed dealer program, insisted that Ford install the Cellport Universal Hands-Free system in all of HP's new company cars. Ford needed to buy at least 5,000 units: the very same Cellport units that just four months earlier supposedly failed Ford's obscure (if they existed at all) test specifications.

Corporate fleets such as HP's were the best prospects to buy the 20,000 units we had built, so I assigned Ralph Poplawsky to a new role as head of our sales initiatives. To sell off this inventory over the course of one or two years, we would need to invest more than $1 million to develop and build phone adaptors for a representative handful of new mobile handsets entering the market. The need to build a half dozen or more phone adaptors in order to sell off 20,000 units to fleet customers was an exercise in diseconomies at its finest. That $1 million would have been inconsequential if Cellport had additional supply contracts in place or if it was benefiting from the hundreds of thousands of units that European IdeaJackers were selling to automotive producers on the continent.

We had other costs associated with selling to fleet customers as well, and these expenses came from the need to rebuild a marketing, sales and customer service infrastructure. As I added up the expenses we would incur trying to sell 20,000 units to fleets, it was obvious we would barely break even over a two-year period. But recovering our investment in these products was not our only objective: Andy continually reminded me that as painfully slow as the process to sell these units might prove to be, it would eventually enable us to pay off our creditors, both the friendly and unfriendly alike. As a matter of good business practice and out of basic self-respect, financial integrity was something we all wanted to preserve.

We were thrilled to receive two bits of good news in early 2002: the U.S. Patent and Trademark Office awarded us two patents, one for the Dual-Processor Multi-Bus and the other for the Adaptor Latching System, which we had architected in 1998 and developed in 1999. The timing of these patent awards was ideal for our critical licensing initiatives because it further established our leadership with core telematics patents and it would help bring in additional revenue to pay off the Ford-related inventory debts. These two new patents strengthened our portfolio of hands-free technologies and would make it more difficult for reluctant companies to deny our design leadership and the resulting patents.

By now in 2002, I had come to know the leaders of Cullmann, Dabendorf and several other European companies that had IdeaJacked Cellport's telematics technologies. I observed these individuals to be neither overtly unethical nor unlikable but, rather, tough entrepreneurs who had a different perspective on invention ownership and Cellport's role in the telematics industry [2]. In view of our critical need to generate revenues from these companies, and to set the historical invention record straight, I decided to create a definitive communications tool that would substantiate our record of invention and product development and that would take any doubts about our claims off the table once and for all. This communications tool was a horizontal scroll that was 10-feet long by 8.5 inches high that I developed to plot, in graphic fashion according to a timeline, the invention and business milestones in Cellport's history. I called the document a "histograph." It delineated, in chronological fashion, each step in the development of the Cellport business, whether that step was an invention, patent filing, patent award, investment, licensing agreement, product order or shipment or other significant business event. I later added photographs of all of our Universal Hands-Free and MobileWeb products, aligning each of these images with the year of the particular product's release.

I knew this would be a powerful communications tool. I knew that none of the European IdeaJackers, for example, was in the Universal Hands-Free business in 1995 when our original design first shipped and, more importantly, that none had accomplished the Dual Processor Multi-Bus and Adaptor Latching System used in our second-generation design until at least 18 months after they saw our early prototypes in 2000. The histograph laid out the proof of all of our accomplishments in cumulative order, for all to see. I showed the histograph to various friends at Cellport, Motorola and Omron for their critiques, refined the document based on their feedback and produced several copies to take along on a trip to Europe, where I would begin my campaign to convert our IdeaJackers into bona fide licensees. I scheduled the trip for September.

**

That summer, fortuitously, I received calls from two of my favorite out-of-the-box thinkers, Chuck Spaur and Dr. Axel Fuchs.

Chuck told me that after his two-year sabbatical, he was anxious to get back to working on "tough stuff, Cellport-style," as he described it. With his experimental airplane now finished, Chuck was now hoping to work on new challenges in the telematics business. He returned to Cellport as our chief architect with a focused objective to advance our new Mobile Multimedia Connectivity (MMC) research, research we had begun at Cellport in hopes of finding more flexible ways to interface phones with growing capabilities — such as playing music, video and enabling personal computing applications — to vehicle and other platforms.

Axel, I was pleased to hear, was also interested in contributing to Cellport. I first met Axel in 1996 when he worked at the Daimler-Benz Research and Technology Center in Palo Alto (the same organization that had IdeaJacked our MobileWeb Internet car technology in 1997) and we had enjoyed a good relationship. Axel, it turned out, was too much of a maverick for the ivory tower Daimler-Benz research organization. In 1998 he had joined Motorola's telematics unit as a senior project manager of advanced designs, but he had just left the company to escape Chicago's harsh winters and to move back to California with his family. Axel gained substantial and valuable empirical design experience during his four-year tenure at Motorola. Plus, he had recently finished writing a book, under contract for the Society of Automotive Engineers, on the global telematics market. He had not only sophisticated and current design experience but he understood the big-picture issues as well. Axel was looking for project consulting work; his talents and interests fit perfectly with my ambition to pursue a new inventive breakthrough to advance our "third-generation" design platform, which I was now calling "MMC," short for Mobile Multimedia Connectivity.

Cellport desperately needed an invention coup on the order of its recently accomplished license with Motorola, and the prospect of putting together an invention dream team with a clean sheet of paper and money in the bank made me more excited about the business than I'd felt since the late 1990s. To round out this all-star invention team, I asked Michael Braitberg to come out of semi-retirement to help us assess early market needs and to help fuel our art-of-the-possible strategy sessions.

During our initial strategy session we reviewed our historical telematics invention advancements and how they mapped to current market successes. Then, for the tough part, I asked everyone to deliver a presentation offering their views on a future with mobile phones as the hubs of our communication and entertainment world connected more dynamically with vehicle systems. I also asked them to describe the envisioned technical and business challenges that would have to be solved in order to design a next-generation architecture capable of delivering this vastly superior connectivity system. Everyone would deliver their presentations on the same day. We would use our findings from this session, if indeed we were able to come to any conclusions, to create a framework for our future research.

To kick-off this session, I asked Axel to give us his best shot. He predicted that Cellport's MobileWeb technology would become a market reality within a few years in the United States, Europe and Japan, but he also said that it would take much more work to create applications that would be compelling to consumers and that would address concerns the automotive industry had about maintaining the security of their in-vehicle communication networks.

Chuck, now back at work after his two-year sabbatical, came to the session with an unusual but very valuable perspective: a fresh set of eyes combined with a seven-year background contributing to Cellport's historical and cutting-edge work in this field. Chuck's presentation fit well with Axel's. He predicted that security would become a more complex issue in mobile devices and telematics in general than it had already become for consumers and businesses that use the Internet. Therefore, he asserted that a new security architecture would be needed if the industry had any expectation of encouraging adoption of telematics products and services at levels that would satisfy the automotive companies' revenue ambitions.

Michael's perspective was different but again seemed complementary. He believed that next-generation telematics systems would need to give the automotive producers a reason — above and beyond driver safety — to continue to invest in telematics, so he called for developing the capability to offer more creative and enhanced applications as well as the means to use the technology to generate revenues for car makers. Adding e-commerce, or digital-wallet capabilities to telematics systems, was one illustration of the kinds of revenue-generating applications he was looking for. The digital wallet, for example, could be used to pay road tolls, fuel costs or a whole host of other applications that could provide conveniences to consumers and revenues to automakers, vendors and system operators.

I was encouraged by the presentations because our network experts agreed that security in mobile devices and telematics was fundamentally important and that it would require a very unique solution, which would justify our focused research. Michael's vision of popular revenue-generating applications was complementary and would require improved security as well.

My presentation was, perhaps, too influenced by my work of the preceding few years to architect and commercialize the Universal Hands-Free solution. I predicted that within a few years — if it had not occurred already — the most powerful computers found in an automobile would be the computers built into the driver's or passengers' mobile phones, and that these powerful new devices would create terrific new opportunities for mobile-influenced telematics applications. I proposed that a next-generation telematics system would need a more sophisticated approach for creating a universal interface between the increasingly powerful — but still disparate — mobile handset designs and the rudimentary computing devices and various proprietary networks used in automobiles.

At the conclusion of this day-long session we were completely convinced that there was plenty of very promising work to do. We agreed to meet each week for a day or two to continue our discussions and made it our goal to refine our ideas in a way that would direct us to an architectural solution that could solve many of the challenges we had discussed that day.

**

By the late summer of 2002, Ralph's fleet sales efforts had borne fruit. He had sold the 5,000 Universal Hands-Free units that Ford needed for the Hewlett-Packard commercial fleet order. It was a diplomatic face-saving solution for all parties involved. Plus, with our new third-generation telematics research team off to a terrific start, I was now ready to attack my other revenue-generating objective: getting the Europeans to recognize and license Cellport's technology. I hoped the histograph would prove to be a convincing communications tool, but to increase my chances of delivering a slam dunk performance in Europe, and to shore up my very limited German language skills, I asked Axel Fuchs to join me on this trip. Not only was I looking to persuade our IdeaJackers Cullmann and Dabendorf to license the Universal Hands-Free technology patents they were already using, but I also wanted to meet a new participant, Peiker, which had won the Mercedes-Benz business with Motorola. I also wanted to visit several of the leading German automotive producers to learn what I could about challenges they had in the telematics business and their visions for its future.

Taking Axel to Europe proved to be a spot-on decision. He shared with me many fabulous perspectives on German society I had been unable to derive on my own — the sort of perspectives that are of practical importance in business and everyday interactions with Germans. In particular, he explained to me that Germans accept very little on face value and thus they are inclined to view new concepts cautiously. This is one of the reasons German people are so detail-oriented and have a propensity for precision, he said. In fact, he added, Germans are trained to develop those skills; they are challenged both at school and at home to carefully explain or prove any position they might take on an issue to prove a point.

"This is why your histograph will prove to be effective, for they want you to work seriously to convince them that they crossed Cellport's patents," Axel told me.

This was certainly a most valuable cultural understanding for me to have. Axel's teaching in this regard was similar to the various perspectives about Japanese society that Hiro shared with me as we began establishing our numerous relationships in Japan.

During a week-long trek across Germany, Axel and I met with Audi, BMW and Daimler-Benz. We gained significant understanding of their telematics ambitions as well as their business challenges and learned that they considered security issues to be an emerging concern. Our findings gave us solid encouragement that the industry needed more innovative connectivity and security solutions, which was now the focus of our third-generation MMC research work (see p327 for a diagram of the MMC Portfolio.)

The meetings with Cullmann and Dabendorf were also enlightening. Every one of them told us that when they learned of the Ford cancellation of its Cellport contract, they had assumed that Cellport would fold and that they would not have to worry about our patents. Wolfgang Cullmann told me securing Motorola as a licensee spoke loudly in Europe. During the meetings with each of these companies, I spent several hours going over the histograph in thorough detail, and although I knew they wanted to scream "Enough already!" during my presentation, I did not let any of them off easily. I proceeded carefully with my presentation until I was finished and certain that I had conveyed the unassailable strength of our patent portfolio and inventive history to them.

Both these companies copied one or both generations of our Universal Hands-Free system designs and the moments when these companies reviewed the histograph revealing their blatant intellectual property theft were certainly cinematic.

During these various meetings we learned that Audi, Daimler-Benz and Land Rover all planned to bring, to the U.S., automobiles equipped with European-supplied Universal Hands-Free systems. I knew that these companies would demand that their suppliers license Cellport's patents rather than risk lawsuits or potential import restriction rulings from the U.S. International Trade Commission. It seemed quite likely, now, that we would be able to consummate licenses with over a half-dozen IdeaJackers within a few years.

One cinematic moment occurred at Cullmann, when the forceful and effervescent Wolfgang Cullmann started, in his discussion with me, to dwell on differences in connectors between the Cullmann and Cellport products, among other details he claimed differentiated our approaches. I looked him in the eye and said, "Wolfgang, I am anxious to hear you explain, to an American jury and with your German accent, your 'accidental' history of knocking me off not once, but twice."

Wolfgang was not at all taken aback. His blue eyes twinkled and he said, "Pat, I told you if you lived I would license your technology. You will find me completely tough, but I am also a man of my word."

With that, I shook Wolfgang's hand and said, "Great. Cellport's research abilities will march on. I look forward to consummating a license with you."

Wolfgang laughed and "Ya ya, Pat, you'll see that I am a man of my word. Let's work together."

"Wolfgang, you have my word for our close cooperation in the future," I assured my new licensing partner.

Back in Boulder, I was pleased to report to our team that the trip to Europe had some noticeable impacts. Our gesture of reaching out to these companies convinced each one of them that not only had Cellport survived the Ford contract cancellation, but that it had every intention of assuming its deserved leadership role as a pioneer and ongoing innovator in the market. Further, I told them, the presentation of the histograph proved to be very effective and underscored our intention to enforce our patents across two generations of design. And our timing couldn't have been better, I said, explaining the new and credible information we received about the European car makers' plans to bring their systems to the U.S.

What was concerning me, by now, was the level of operational support we needed to sustain to sell off the Ford inventory; the process was much more expensive then we originally forecasted and the sales cycle for fleet vehicles was much longer than we initially expected, which adversely affected the pace of our sales and, by extension, our financial recovery.

Further, our plan to sell the automotive business was proving to be a challenge. Since our encouraging initial meeting with our prospective buyer, Donnelly, in May, we found that the vice president of technologies — who was charged with conducting the due diligence on the purchase of Cellport's automotive orders and tooling — had become distracted from the process. Donnelly was now itself being acquired by Magna International. And since Ford had cancelled our purchase orders, there was little for Donnelly to buy from Cellport anyway.

With Donnelly's interest in buying our automotive business essentially dead, I decided to introduce the prospect of selling our automotive business and platform design to Cullmann, Dabendorf and Peiker, because each had ambitions to follow their automotive car customers into the U.S. market. Although each of these companies articulated interest and went through the motions of studying our financials and supplier lists that they requested, the reality was they had no intention of perpetuating Cellport's vision of a single design platform. It seemed that so many wanted to bury the Cellport universal interface vision and live as suppliers of fragmented design silos tied to different German auto makers.

Throughout the fall of 2002, our third-generation telematics design team worked diligently to develop what we were now calling the Secure Telematics Framework patent, the first of many MMC patents. Our intention was to have this architectural breakthrough ready for a patent filing that December. We made steady progress that fall, and, as I expected, Chuck became the leader of the team. But in a private conversation with me he voiced concerns that we were working outside our area of expertise. As Chuck described the problem, our invention team had developed some great ideas for new applications that consumers would value and that would provide additional profits for vehicle producers, but he was unsure that we were addressing the security aspects as innovatively as was needed. It was a very valid concern; while everyone on the design team had expertise in mobile phone and vehicle telematics designs, no one had a strong background in the arcane and complex world of security. The originality of our architecture, and its marketability to the industry, demanded that we consider state-of-the-art security technologies in our research and design work to anticipate future advancements in that field.

As luck would have it, I was in the Detroit airport the very next week, waiting to catch a flight to Denver, when I ran into Ken Klingenstein, the University of Colorado professor who had helped us develop the Link Select patent back in 1997. Ken was on his way to Denver with his son, Nate. This father and son, a two-man team of traveling scientists, had traveled to Michigan to attend a meeting for a technology committee that was developing security solutions for Internet2 — a consortium of government, academic, and industry researchers that were working to develop revolutionary network technologies. When I heard Ken mention the word security in relation to their Internet2 contributions, I realized this could be a fortuitous encounter.

Ken and Nate gave me a fascinating briefing on their work toward the next-generation Internet and afterward I took an opportunity to tell them about Cellport's Secure Telematics Framework research and our growing interest in, and need for, a more sophisticated security approach. Nate quickly asked, "Are you considering the federated security model?"

"I do not believe so," I replied, "But frankly, Chuck is concerned that we need to do more work on the security front. Given your interest in next-generation designs as well as security, would you be interested in helping us advance our Mobile Multimedia Connectivity research?" I asked.

Ken responded that he was really overbooked but suggested that he could attend an initial meeting at Cellport. "Thereafter, if you like our insights on security innovations, Nate should be able to afford more time to help advance your project research," he added.

The federated security model, I later realized, would have strategic importance to many mobile and telematics applications. At the time, the federated model was new to the networking world. Its premise is that it will make it possible for service providers and businesses that partner with each other to pool security services for end-users. It is also intended to make it easier for customers to make electronic payments for Web-based services delivered through multiple providers or businesses and via a variety of networks and devices — as would occur when an end-user uses his or her automobile as a digital wallet to pay road tolls and to purchase both fuel at gas stations and fast-food at drive-up windows — because it would enable the vendor, the end-user's bank, and other businesses involved to manage the billing and other accounting processes behind the scenes without creating a hassle for or violating the privacy of the customer.

As busy as the Klingensteins were, it took a month before we could hold that initial meeting, but the wait was well worth it, for both Ken and Nate added substantial and valuable perspective that underscored the need to make the security component of our Secure Telematics Framework much more dynamic and agile to the future. And indeed, adding the federated security model to our architecture and patent application gave our architecture the thoroughness and caliber of vision-ary considerations that we felt were needed if we intended to main-tain Cellport's track record of core pioneering invention research.

The technology also fulfilled one of our strategic objectives with the MMC innovation platform: to provide a greater economic motivation for automotive manufacturers to adopt our MMC work and promote its use. The digital wallet capabilities enabled by the Secure Telemat-ics Framework would give car manufacturers — which already have very profitable credit operations for customers — an ongoing source of customer revenue long after a vehicle is sold and paid for by the customer (see p327 for a diagram of the MMC Portfolio).

Although the final Secure Telematics Framework patent filing was delayed until the spring of 2003, everyone was pleased with our advancements. Suddenly, our patent portfolio included a full-featured universal interface between in-car and mobile cellular phones; the MobileWeb family of patents made it possible to connect automobiles to the Internet, and now the Secure Telematics Framework would add e-commerce and other revolutionary capabilities to automobiles (see Fig. 9).

**

In early 2003, as I had predicted months earlier, Funkwerk Dabendorf of the old East Germany approached us to secure a patent license for our Universal Hands-Free patent portfolio. After a fairly efficient exchange of documents between Andy and Dabendorf's lawyers, we added our first new licensee since we signed Motorola nearly eight months earlier. The Dabendorf license, which came with a significant initial prepayment of royalties, was a financial shot in the arm that we desperately needed. We had been using much of our cash from the Motorola license to pay off what seemed to be a mile-long list of creditors from the cancelled Ford program. By this time, no one could question our will to survive, but the burden of cleaning up the financial ramifications from the Ford deal was dampening our spirits.

In fact, our anger with Ford was growing with time and not dissipating as I had expected it would. Andy proposed that by now — nine months after the cancellation of the Ford program — Ford had had enough time to find an acceptable solution for a settlement, and that the only way to recover our losses was to sue them. In general, litigation is a pursuit I would prefer to avoid, but as Andy suggested, it appeared to be the only means available for us to recover our inventory investment and our many millions in engineering expenses that we had put into the cancelled program. After a lengthy discussion, and with the support of our Board, in May 2003 we filed a lawsuit against Ford. Our purchase contract with Ford stipulated that any litigation potentially arising from the contract would have to be conducted in Michigan and under the rules of binding arbitration. This was a big roll of the dice for tiny Cellport. Not only were we suing a nearly bankrupt Fortune 500 company on its home turf, but the arbitration trial would take place in the bankrupt city of Detroit. As ones who had worked hard to settle our debts honestly and with clear consciences, we became emotionally and intellectually convinced that we were wronged by Ford, that Ford had concocted a reason for cancelling the project, and that justice would prevail regardless of any hometown bias we would encounter in Michigan.

We were also quite aware that filing a lawsuit against a car manufacturer would surely harm Cellport's prospects of ever supplying telematics equipment to that company again. Litigation would have other indirect consequences on our business as well. We would have to license our pioneering technologies more aggressively to generate revenues needed to pay for the Ford litigation and for our research to develop new cutting-edge technologies that would sustain us in the years to come.

I could not help feeling a bit of déjà vu; we were morphing back to the research-intensive days when we founded the company and named it Cellport Labs. I considered the evolutionary change in our business to be a healthy thing and did not concern myself about it too much, for I knew that Cellport was without peer in the core wireless connectivity business community thanks to the technologies we invented and promulgated.

A major aspect of Axel Fuchs' consulting work on the Secure Telematics Framework project was that we gave him full access to some of our most detailed technology development documents. To help orient Axel with Cellport's long list of mobile and telematics connectivity technologies, Mike Lewellen dusted off the communications software language document we had developed to implement our Dual-Processor Multi-Bus invention, and he gave it to Axel to study. With a highly creative nature, more than a decade of experience working at the large institutions of Daimler-Benz Research and Technology Center and in the Motorola telematics unit and, now, experience working in Cellport's art-of-the-possible inventive environment, Axel was primed to come up with a big breakthrough for our group.

After studying this intensely detailed document and reflecting anew on the third-generation MMC objectives list, Axel came up with a big idea. He brought it up at our next third-generation technology design team meeting by asking a great question: "What if we extended the Dual-Processor Multi-Bus communications capabilities so it would become fully bi-directional and network-like in its agility?"
The Dual-Processor Multi-Bus, which had played such an important role in our second-generation Universal Hands-Free system, made it possible — via use of microprocessors, a common software language and middleware — to transmit data from the Internet or remote sites to a vehicle's electronics system via a mobile phone. But its commu-

nications with a vehicle's network were primarily one-directional and used mainly for voice recognition dialing and other functions commonly found in mobile phones circa 1999.

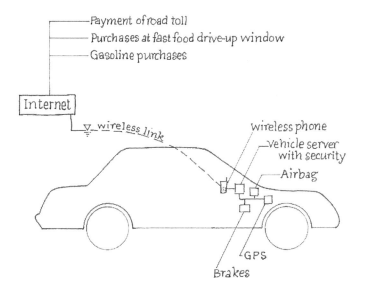

Figure 9: Secure Telematics Framework

The Secure Telematics Framework invention established a new server-based architecture for Internet-connected automobiles that provided the security features needed to add "digital wallet," or e-commerce capabilities, to Internet-connected cars. Security techniques make it easier for customers to make Web-based payments from an Internet-connected car and to control how their private information and financial data are used.

Axel's idea matched with Cellport's hypothesis that as mobile handsets' applications become even more powerful, they could share their capabilities with the vehicle network, a breakthrough that would create a huge new market for MMC telematics applications. Axel concurred with me in my strong belief that mobile phones had much more powerful computer processors and application environments than any computing resources native to an automobile. This trend would enable mainstream mobile phone consumers to use their handsets not only for voice and data communications but also to play digital music and, by the end of the decade, to receive and play mobile videos on their phones. And indeed, these features are widely available in the mobile phone market today. What Axel was asking then, in 2003, was this: Is there a way to better share the mobile phone's capabilities with an automobile?

The development to create an agile bi-directional protocol across the completely different operating systems and network links that automobiles and mobile phones use was indeed a clever concept, but accomplishing it would require a far more sophisticated technology solution than Cellport's previous inventions of adaptors and gateways between networks. But as Michael frequently reminded us, the tougher the problem, the greater the chances we'd come up with a groundbreaking — versus incremental — invention.

The timing of Axel's "what-if" question was ideal, for our work related to the Secure Telematics Framework was nearly finished; we were in the final stages of reviewing drafts of the patent application. A fresh challenge was just what the third-generation MMC design team needed.

As time went by, I felt increasing pressure to grow the number of licensees to generate more funds for the company. Ralph managed by May 2003 to sell nearly another 5,000 Universal Hands-Free units to Agilent Technologies, the former Hewlett-Packard test equipment division, which wanted the products for its upcoming 2004 fleet vehicles, but the margins were narrow going on negative because Agilent's purchasing team knew that our inventory was getting staler by the day. Our email dialogue with Wolfgang Cullmann on a draft license agreement was progressing, but ever so slowly. I decided to make another trip to Europe for some face time with Wolfgang to advance the license drafting work. I asked Andy to join me, believing that he might be able to help expedite the process.

The trip to Europe was a major eye-opener for Andy. We visited Cullmann, stopped by Nokia's telematics headquarters in Düsseldorf, Germany, and spent time with Hugo Scheiner, who gave us a helpful update on the European telematics market that so loved Cellport's multiple design innovations. Andy began to see just how fast the Universal Hands-Free business was growing in the safety-conscious European market and he started to share my optimistic excitement about it. We learned that sales of the Universal Hands-Free system in Europe were forecast to reach 250,000 units by the end of 2003, and sales for 2004 were expected to increase by more than 40 percent.

Cullmann had a new and very large manufacturing facility that we were able to tour, and there Andy saw firsthand just how extensively Cullmann profited from its contracts with partner-oriented vehicle producers Audi, Skoda Auto and Volkswagen. Cullmann's healthy business operations showed just how much potential our Ford contract could have had if Ford had been a comparable partner.

Our negotiations with Wolfgang and his patent lawyer went well. While they were not ready to sign an agreement, not even after a full-day meeting, I became tremendously more confident in Wolfgang's promise to me that he would take a license. I felt especially good about this after he shook my hand and said that we were very close to consummating a license with a sizable prepayment. Then, in an attempt to strengthen the bond we were developing, Wolfgang pulled me aside. He said, "Now that you have me convinced, I will introduce you to Harman/Becker, for they are supplying the replacement to our docking station electronics in the 2004 Audis. They too should respect your historic invention and patent work."

Our next meeting was with Nokia. Prior to attending the meeting, Hugo warned us that the animosity that Nokia had publicly displayed against Qualcomm's wireless patents would soon take aim at Cellport, that is, if we did not show the mighty Nokia submissive respect. And that did prove to be the case. Our meeting with Nokia, which took place at their ultra-modern facility in Düsseldorf, was right out of the theater of the absurd.

The meeting started off with a sustained greeting session that could have taken place in Japan. But as Nokia's executives said they were honored to host our visit, they said they looked forward to a close partnership "between two great telematics powerhouses." Their use of that characterization of our companies to set the negotiating table made me lose my appetite for the tasty cookies that they offered us. Nokia had, in fact, invested tens of millions of dollars in the pursuit of telematics projects, and they had designed embedded telematics solutions for BMW and Mercedes-Benz, but their products in the European markets had serious drawbacks — such as the lack of carrier roaming agreements — and thus it could not build a sustainable volume market pan-Europe. The Ray and Marios team at Motorola had actually out-foxed Nokia when they shifted Motorola's European strategy toward Cellport's Universal Hands-Free architecture for portables, because the strategy left Nokia to chase embedded solutions that became complete nonstarters due to their lack of roaming agreements throughout Europe. I found it audacious for Nokia to put itself in the same league as Cellport's $40-plus million in investments and its development of the market's two leading technology portfolios full of core patents.

As the meeting progressed, the Nokia executives asked us to prove how our patents could possibly apply to their planned projects, yet they would not reveal many details of these projects to us. Andy started to lose his temper. He yelled at the Nokia executives for flattering Cellport's work and then, in the next breath, directly insulting us. Andy is a super straight negotiator, and, unfortunately, his mood began to deteriorate. As the meeting went on, his attitude went from bad to ugly. I had never seen Andy more pissed off.

If the daylong meeting, such as it was, produced any outcome at all from Cellport's perspective, it was progress in the wrong direction. At dinner that evening, as Andy and I discussed what we considered to be a charade of a meeting, I realized that Nokia had possibly gained two important benefits from it. For one, Nokia executives could now tell their European customers that they were in licensing discussions with Cellport, which would buy them time to provide products for a number of years before actually needing to close a final license agreement with us. In addition, we had shared with them our perspectives on what we believed were our patents' strengths; thus they now had a more detailed understanding of our technologies and market advantages than they might otherwise have had as a non-licensee.

While dealing with patent adversaries is part of the technology pioneering business, this negative outcome was not a great ending to an otherwise very productive trip. Now I better understood why Motorola was afraid that Cellport would sell its patent portfolio to Nokia. I was convinced that if Nokia owned Cellport's patent portfolio of core innovations, it would use the monopoly power of our pioneering telematics patents to shut down competition, not to keep the market open. In contrast, both Motorola and Ford, in our dealings with them, said they desired the open licensing model we employed and encouraged us to maintain it.

After suffering through the overtly prejudicial and oppressive meeting with Nokia, I found that I was completely fired-up to out-invent the powerful company. During the flight home to the states, I drafted an email to Chuck Spaur. I instructed him to "put the pedal to the metal" in pursuit of Axel's challenge for a new paradigm that addressed a bi-directional protocol with link and operating platform agility. Much to my delight, on my first day back at the office, Chuck reported that he had been feverishly working on Axel's challenge and that he had a major breakthrough to announce to everyone at our next meeting. I was thrilled to hear this; we needed to keep pushing the art-of-the-possible to maintain our architectural leadership in the pioneering telematics invention business, for it had become clear that we had little prospect of surviving in the product business. And Andy and Mike Lewellen were now gearing up for an ugly legal fight with Ford, which would drain a lot of money and precious human energy out of Cellport. I knew that Chuck's proposal would give us all a big emotional lift for the future.

**

At the next third-generation telematics team meeting, Chuck laid his bombshell of an idea on us. For the past few months he had been working with one of our brightest software engineers, Jay Plucienkowski, to develop a connectivity design that would revolutionize not only telematics but other technology markets as well. Chuck and Jay proposed an architecture that we would call CP-Connect. The essence of their brilliant idea was to allow applications that worked on any mobile phone, such as a navigation map or a music playlist, to also work remotely from the phone to any vehicle display and audio systems.

Imagine, for example, that a customer used a message in Sean Connery's voice for a mobile phone ring tone. CP-Connect could apply that voice to a car application, such as a door-is-ajar warning. With CP-Connect, instead of hearing the annoying ding-ding-ding to warn that a door is open, a consumer could hear Sean Connery, in his gentlemanly brogue, saying "Please close the door, my dear sir."

Similarly, the information resident in an automobile could be shared with the mobile phone; high-accuracy GPS data, for example, could be used in conjunction with a mobile phone's navigation program.

It was hard for me to believe that this was not possible before, but both Axel and Michael convinced me that Chuck's CP-Connect design established between systems communications that were previously not possible due to differences in either the operating systems or communications links. While I thought the new CP-Connect architecture brilliant and beneficial to society, the detailed mechanisms that made it work were still technically over my head. Nevertheless, as I watched our gifted engineering team dance around the conference room in youthful excitement, I was comforted by their exuberance. Confident that licensing revenue from Cullmann was right around the corner, I instructed Chuck and Jay to work diligently to design a CP-Connect prototype that we could use to experiment with the design and to work with Michael to turn this latest epiphany into a patent application with Dave Zinger (see Fig. 10). Separately, I asked Axel to develop scenarios that would explain how CP-Connect applications could be used in consumer and other markets. We could use these scenarios for our own edification in getting to know this new technology as well for our eventual need to launch this radically clever connectivity and application-enhancement solution in the market. Of course, like any new paradigm-changing technology, CP-Connect would take several years to launch. And because vehicle telematics would be its primary market, it would not be unusual for the adoption period to take longer than five years.

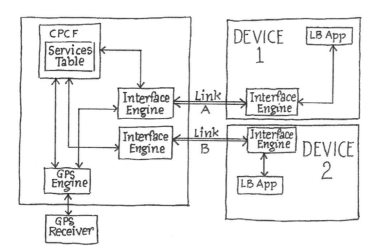

Figure 10: CP-Connect

This adaptation of a drawing from the CP-Connect patent application illustrates how this architecture invention would allow a mobile phone to share its powerful data and computing features with electronic devices in an automobile, despite the different operating systems and network links used by the phone and automotive technologies. For example, a consumer could program their phone's ring tone to play in lieu of conventional car-door alerts, or import the car's GPS data to the phone for use in hand-held navigation software.

By late spring 2003, it had been a year since the Ford contract cancellation and the massive layoffs at Cellport and we had been battling for the company's survival the entire time. We all still had much work to do to recover the millions we invested on the Ford nightmare, to help reestablish Cellport's balance sheet and to accelerate the progress our invention team was making. Nevertheless, this time was full of promising licensing opportunities. I was now convinced that both our Universal Hands-Free and MobileWeb patent portfolios would be used in millions of telematics solutions annually within the next three to five years. Cullmann's attorney and Andy were refining the last issues remaining in their licensing negotiations and our companies were nearly ready for a contract signing. I was now advancing licensing discussions with Harman/Becker Automotive Systems.

With our circumstances now looking more promising, I felt it was time for a big shot of family enjoyment. I decided to take my sons to the living museum of Europe that summer. Of course, a side benefit of announcing a trip to Europe with my family was that I could use the trip to help accelerate closing the Cullmann license. Wolfgang Cullmann was very family-oriented, and over numerous dinners and drinks that we had shared in the past few years, we talked extensively about our families. I knew he would want to meet my sons, and that the meeting would be much more meaningful if he were a new Cellport licensee rather than an IdeaJacker, which was his current status. Sure enough, just a few days after I sent him an email telling him about the three-week tour of England, France, Switzerland, Austria and Germany that I had planned with my sons, I received word that the Cullmann license was ready to sign and fund.

That summer, both boys loved the many sights, museums, back-road adventures and numerous dinners we enjoyed with our many European friends and their families. My youngest son, Brian, was most fond of our experiences in Austria and Germany. He loved, and still talks about, the large Kaltenberger Renaissance Festival that was a surrealistic display of European life 500 years ago. When the German Prince Von Luitpold, who sponsored the festival, spoke to the audience before the start of the jousting events in the grand arena, Brian asked me what the "Von" stood for in the Prince's last name. I explained that it most likely meant that he was from royal blood lines.

"So does that mean if the German ancestors from Grandma's side were Von Geiger instead of just plan old Geiger, we would be from royal blood?" he asked.
"Well, yes, I guess so," I replied.

"Dad, from here on out, we'll be known as Von Geiger-Kennedy, how does that sound?"

Leave it to an exuberant teenager to re-brand a family.

As our magical trip across Europe wound down to its end, the boys' last experience in Germany reinforced another perspective I had shared with them about the cultural differences between our two countries. We flew out of Munich, which is easily one of the world's most beautiful airports and my favorite. When we reached the boarding gate, I asked the United Airlines agent if we could place our names on the upgrade list for business class seats. The agent responded and said, "Mr. Kennedy, given your frequent flyer status, I can accommodate you immediately, but as for your sons, it looks doubtful."

This was of course disappointing and Brian, who was the youngest, looked dejected. I couldn't help but take this opportunity to share another important cultural perspective. I told him, "Brian, as my good friend Axel Fuchs taught me, German people do not like to overpromise and would rather give you bad news or a challenge upfront than disappoint you or oversell something to you. Let's just sit here and see who shows up for this flight. Who knows, we may get lucky."

Within 20 minutes, the boys had given up all hope for an upgrade. But as we were preparing to board the plane, Herr "Gate Agent" called their names. Responding as if they had just received Christmas presents, the boys briskly walked over to the agent and exchanged their coach tickets for business class seats. The agent informed the boys that this was their lucky day and to travel well.

As we all walked away from the agent, Brian looked at me. "I could get used to this German approach," he said. "It is very different than Americans, who can overpromise and then, at times, disappoint you."

14 | Cellport vs. Ford Motor Company

1991
1992
1993
1994
1995
1996
1997
1998
1999
2000
2001
2002
2003
2004
2005
2006
2007
2008
2009

As the vividly pleasant memories of our European summer vacation began to fade, the market intelligence I picked up during my several recent trips to Europe took on greater clarity. All of the European luxury car producers that offered full-featured Universal Hands-Free solutions reported sales growth figures that exceeded everyone's expectations.

Yet Cellport, the very company that pioneered two generations of the Universal Hands-Free design, was still trying to climb out from under the millions of dollars in inventory and expenses resulting from the Ford project cancellation. The irony was bittersweet.

I could explain the discrepancies between European and U.S. market conditions by the vast differences in the types of relationships that European and American vehicle producers have with their vendors. The dynamics gave European vendors all of the market's opportunities, however, and unfortunately, Cellport was on the wrong side of the ocean to reap the benefits. Indeed, Wolfgang's advice back in 2000 was more insightful than I gave him credit for during my myopic promotion of the Cellport CGP program. On the other hand, we had been able to raise more than $40 million between 1995 and 2001 to develop our cutting-edge telematics architectures because we enjoyed two benefits here in the U.S. that our European counterparts didn't have: a funding environment that was responsive to risk-takers and a less-restrictive patent system that encouraged and rewarded the entrepreneurial ambitions of both individuals and companies. As innovative entrepreneurs, we had our roots in the right place.

Finally, by late 2003, after years of negative earnings and cash flow, Cellport's two patent portfolios, the Universal Hands-Free system and our MobileWeb vehicle networking technologies, began to generate predictable and growing revenues. I had very real reasons to be enthusiastic about further developing our patent licensing business: It had high margins. And I had renewed enthusiasm to work with our design team to pursue more third-generation telematics innovations. I believed that our licensing agreements could deliver steadily increasing cash flows that could fund a small but potent art-of-the-possible research team. We would need a staff of six, at minimum, to a dozen people over the next few years. With Cellport's business charter again targeted at architectural research and licensing, we were now more a lab than ever!

Unfortunately, however, as positive as our revenue growth from licensing was, a large portion of those royalty revenues was being used to settle outstanding debts from the cancelled Ford program. To finish cleaning up these debts and to properly launch and market CP-Connect, we would need to invest millions of dollars in marketing initiatives. The most likely near-term source of this funding would be the contract violation award we expected to receive in our suit against Ford. But this payment was not likely to come our way for months.

Nor would our hardware business do us much good, we finally began to admit to ourselves. In early 2004, still desperate to pull a rabbit out of the hat and bring in some income from the Universal Hands-Free system inventory, we started to advertise our products directly to end-users via Google-sponsored links on the Internet. Selling to consumers directly actually showed promise, but this was not Ralph's calling so he left the company in late 2004 and became the chief technology officer of an equipment test company based in Denver. Ralph's departure was an eventuality that he and I had anticipated and discussed in late 2003, but even so, after his eight-year career at Cellport, I was sad to see him go. I was disheartened with the hardware business after the Ford cancellation — a wasteful disappointment — and, preferring that Cellport focus on new architectures and licensing, was not driven to manage online sales either. We ended up shutting down all sales in May of 2005 and disposing of over a million dollars in hardware inventory. It took four people three days to empty our warehouse in Boulder. We recycled what we could, but sadly filled eight 20-feet-long mega-dumpsters with the remaining Ford inventory.

The objective and studious side of me tended to view the changes at Cellport within the larger context of economic theory. One of history's brightest economists was the Austrian-educated Joseph Schumpeter. He lived from the late nineteenth to the mid-twentieth century and taught at universities in Germany and at Harvard in the U.S. One of Schumpeter's most brilliant economic theories was that the economic turbulence that churns in society as a result of innovation and the development of new ideas is healthy. He said that the process is driven by man's historical propensity to invent. At a micro-level, one of the consequences of innovation is the birthing of new businesses or services and the atrophy of obsolete or marginal ones. At the macro-level, groundbreaking inventions solve deficiencies in earlier methods or institutions and reinvigorate an economy at a more accelerated rate compared to typical economic influences. Schumpeter referred to this phenomenon as "the perennial gale of creative destruction." Schumpeter's theories articulating how this process creates a wealthier and more vibrant society were considered insightful in his time and are still considered brilliant today for helping to explain the pace of innovations and economic activity in our ever-shrinking world [1].

Schumpeter acknowledged that creative destruction can cause painful adjustments for those caught at what he called a business's "biological" level in the eye of turbulent change, but he argued that in the long run, that turbulence is what motivates a company to clean out superfluous or poorly performing businesses or services. I viewed the painful loss of Cellport's Universal Hands-Free platform business from a Schumpeter perspective: It came out of a painful period in Cellport's history caused by the perfect storm at Ford Motor Company, but these challenges brought about necessary adjustments for Cellport that could make us stronger.

**

Cellport filed a patent application for CP-Connect in the spring of 2004, our second in the MMC portfolio (see p327 for a diagram of the MMC Portfolio). Throughout the year, Chuck and Jay Plucien-kowski endeavored to develop applications based on the technology's design and they came up with a working software framework for a suite of CP-Connect demonstration applications that proved to be far more compelling than any of us had initially imagined. Loading the CP-Connect software on devices was not difficult and it worked as we theorized, but the real challenge we faced was in launching its availability and value to the various and vastly different markets it served: consumer electronics, automotive and software product companies. We needed a marketing model that would resonate with these different communities.

Fortunately, Axel Fuchs was spending the majority of his consulting time with Cellport, and with his help we were able to make CP-Connect's seamless connectivity story compelling to device makers. We picked up support for the technology from senior executives at Cullmann, Microsoft, Qualcomm, and Volkswagen's research organization in the U.S. All of these companies voiced the same question that bogged us down when we were trying to craft a market roll-out model: How does Cellport launch the fabulous new CP-Connect solution across the diverse markets that it addressed? Herding all these cats, each with their own disparate marketing agendas and product design cycles, presented an enormously complicated challenge. Plus, it was unclear how Cellport would make money on a solution whose market acceptance, we believed by now, would be viral by nature.

Hiro made several trips to Boulder to help us brainstorm this problem. After he studied CP-Connect and its capability to ignite an entirely new world of cross-device applications he, too, fell in love with it. But Hiro, unfortunately, shared our dilemma of how to profitably achieve broad adoption of it in the consumer market. For a company that was built by taking on seemingly insurmountable technical and market challenges, this new market launch and monetization challenge promised to be the most difficult of all.

Both Axel and Hiro were gifted marketers, and if anyone could come up with the secret to a successful CP-Connect cross-market launch, they would be the ones. I was convinced that the Ford arbitration hearing, which by now was scheduled for the fall of 2004, would yield us millions in compensation and I planned to use the settlement to push for at least $1 million to invest in a market launch of CP-Connect connectivity software.

CP-Connect would also, happily for us, accelerate the use of our Universal Hands-Free and MobileWeb patent portfolios, which in my mind was sufficient economic justification to budget $1 million to market the new software. But before proposing this investment to the Board, we needed to develop a strategic marketing plan that would document support for the technology from leading companies representing our key customer segments. Our goal was to bring in vendors to join with us to develop a proof-of-principle study of CP-Connect and to build prototypes that we could use to demonstrate the technology's feasibility for the consumer electronics, automotive and software developer markets that needed to buy into it.

Axel and I made several trips to Europe to promote CP-Connect and during one of these trips we briefed our licensee, Wolfgang Cullmann, on the technology. After Axel delivered his CP-Connect spiel in German, Wolfgang looked to his trusted chief engineer, Thomas Schlegel, for his opinion and got a double thumbs-up. I had learned by now that Wolfgang was a no-nonsense guy and that when presented with the facts and proof in a situation he was a man of integrity and action. He made a verbal commitment to invest engineering dollars to help launch CP-Connect with Cellport and he intended to weave the solution into his next-generation telematics product plans. With Cullmann, we had our first partner to help bring CP-Connect to market.

Unfortunately, about a month later we learned that Wolfgang was about to make some monumental changes in his personal life and business that would make this new CP-Connect partnership with Cullmann problematic. He was selling his majority ownership of his Cullmann company for estate planning purposes. For him, the sale would yield tens of millions of dollars in profits. I was nervous about it, however, because we had no way of knowing how the new majority owners might support his commitment to CP-Connect.

Fortunately, around this same period of time, we picked up support for the program from Paul Jacobs, the president of Qualcomm's wireless and Internet group. As a minority investor in Ford's $140 million Wingcast telematics program — Qualcomm had put about $25 million into that initiative — he knew the industry's challenges very well and had a keen appreciation for CP-Connect's ability to share applications across operating systems. Furthermore, CP-Connect could be conveniently deployed within a commercially popular applications environment that Qualcomm offered for mobile phones, called "BREW," to extend handset applications to vehicles and other devices.

The approach would advance Qualcomm's ambitions. But Qualcomm's BREW team was extremely leery about pursuing a telematics product line because the company had lost its investment in the field when Ford ungracefully shut the Wingcast program down in 2002.

That bitter loss still reverberated across Qualcomm. Paul Jacobs did support Chuck and Cellport by lending BREW experts to participate in software development and critical demonstration tests of CP-Connect applications operating on the BREW platform, but he was loath to invest much more of BREW's development time, services and equipment into the now profane word, "telematics," unless Cellport could bring an automotive producer to the table that would provide a real tangible business opportunity.

Microsoft was also coming into the picture. Axel and Mike Lewellen had done a terrific job of introducing CP-Connect to a few Microsoft telematics team members based in the Detroit area and before we knew it, we were getting free software and a lot of helpful support from their telematics engineers. Axel's and Mike's inroads at Microsoft complemented access that Chuck and I were making into the company; during the spring of 2004, Chuck and I had met several times with the Microsoft telematics team in Redmond, Washington about our CP-Connect breakthrough. Seemingly impressed, they asked me to deliver a presentation about the technology during a panel discussion Microsoft was sponsoring at an upcoming telematics conference in Detroit. We must have struck a nerve with Microsoft because right after the panel discussion concluded, some of their executives asked if they could assign an engineer to join me on a visit I was planning that summer to see Cullmann in Germany. Microsoft was interested enough to want to come to Germany to gauge Cullmann's interest in CP-Connect and telematics before fully committing to support our technology.

We now had Microsoft, Cullmann and Qualcomm all agreeing that CP-Connect had important value as a technology and all were committed to participating in a proof-of-principle demonstration. But a full-blown demonstration could not be conducted without the participation of an automobile manufacturer. Fortunately, Axel was persuading Bret Scott of Volkswagen (VW) of America's Electronics Research Laboratory in California to participate in a CP-Connect demonstration that would use a Cullmann-manufactured Universal Hands-Free system, Qualcomm's BREW application environment and Windows CE, the operating system that Microsoft developed to make Windows run on compact, consumer electronics devices.

VW's Bret Scott had previously worked in advanced research at GM, where he became acquainted with some of the classic telematics connectivity challenges, and where he also gained exposure to their now successful OnStar telematics products and services. To further encourage VW to join in the proof-of-principle study, Axel arranged a meeting in San Diego between Bret and Qualcomm's business development team. The meeting incited sparks of enthusiasm, Axel reported to me later. Axel had developed a variety of CP-Connect applications that he showed off at the meeting and some became clear-cut favorites, in particular the ability to download celebrity voices or songs from a mobile phone to the car to replace standard electronic alerts indicating that a seatbelt is unbuckled or that a door is ajar. He showed how Web-based maps and current traffic data could be sent wirelessly to a mobile phone and, from there, seamlessly linked to the attractive color display on the dashboard. The mobile phone navigation application could be used to replace the expensive in-car DVD mapping computers that add thousands of dollars to a car's purchase price and that need to be updated regularly at additional cost to the consumer.

By now the prospect of signing Cullmann, Microsoft, Qualcomm and VW to the proof-of-principle study and development of a prototype system looked certain. We expected that once these companies formally signed onto the project, we would be able to show the world, within six months, a killer CP-Connect demonstration that would articulate the value of sharing applications across devices for use in automobiles. These companies' participation would help our cause tremendously. We hoped to announce the collaborative demonstration partnership by late summer 2004.

Unfortunately, just as we were starting to prepare to sign the documents launching the CP-Connect project partnership, several unpleasant-looking clouds started to appear on the horizon. First, Cullmann began showing signs of instability following its sale to a new majority owner and Wolfgang's own tenure at the helm of the company he had founded became questionable. Next, Andy reported that the arbitrator initially appointed to conduct the hearing against Ford in the coming fall had resigned from the case. This disappointing development meant not only additional legal expenses but further delay before we would be able to get our much-needed compensation from Ford for having cancelled the dealer program in 2002. We would have to delay the launch and marketing of CP-Connect until mid-2005, at least nine months away.

An even more ominous cloud emerged from what can only be termed a classic case of unintended consequences. In January 2004, Cellport had sued THBury of Germany for selling a Universal Hands-Free solution without a technology patent license from Cellport [2]. THBury was chosen to be the supplier of Volkswagen's new Universal Hands-Free systems; Volkswagen's senior management became angry over news of Cellport's legal action against a fellow German company and its own vendor of Universal Hands-Free technologies. In rapid order, Volkswagen's research arm in California terminated its relationship with Cellport and withdrew its promised funding for the project. Not only was Volkswagen's withdrawal from the project frustrating for us, but it had catastrophic fallout. Without an automaker participating in our CP-Connect project, Microsoft and Qualcomm both dropped out of our proof-of-principle projects. We now had cash flow problems related not only to legal expenses from the Ford suit but to the THBury situation as well. We were very stressed for cash.

At Cellport we needed to reduce expenses and Axel was one of several unfortunate personnel losses. Losing Axel cost our CP-Connect marketing effort tremendously. I was not worried about our prospects for marketing CP-Connect in the long-term, because by this time we were making solid progress developing licensing partnerships for — or earning royalties from — our Universal Hands-Free patents with Motorola, Harman/Becker, Cullmann, Peiker and others and our profitability prospects, at least in the mid-term, looked good. Unfortunately, we were in an awful condition to support the short-term promotional needs for moving CP-Connect forward. Worse yet, our partners sensed our slippage.

**

By the fall of 2004, Mike Lewellen and Andy were spending almost all of their time preparing for the Ford arbitration, which was now rescheduled for April 2005. Our case was simple: In the spring of 2002, Ford had cancelled a confirmed purchase order to Cellport to build and deliver 20,000 units to Ford. We wanted Ford to pay us millions of dollars for our inventory investments as well as for engineering costs that Cellport incurred on behalf of the Ford program. Ford's counterargument was that, according to a clause in the "global terms and conditions" section of its contract with Cellport, once we "offered" our "means of production" to companies such as Delphi, Donnelly, Gentex, and Motorola, Ford was permitted to cancel any outstanding purchase orders. Their stance was that because we had been trying to sell our automotive design business and contracts along with our contract manufacturing the resources that produced the Ford product, they were permitted to cancel any outstanding purchase orders. We successfully secured testimonials from Ford's own executives in which they stated that they helped us draft a list of acceptable buyers for our automotive business and encouraged us to sell the business. As one would expect, however, Ford had a resource-rich, top-tier Detroit law firm assigned to take on the weary and cash-strapped Cellport team.

Andy believed that we should try our case according to the pure letter-of-the-law established in Michigan's own Supreme Court decisions on contract interpretations, which he said read in our favor based on the court's interpretation of the meaning of the word "offer." He did not want to over-complicate the case with all the internal political reasons, within Ford, for cancelling the Cellport order. Andy's argument was that we had not made what could be legally defined as an "offer" because our solicitation documents did not name a price. Nor did we actually "own" the "means of production," according to Michigan law, because all of our manufacturing was contracted from suppliers. Andy was absolutely confident that the law was completely on our side.

As fundamental as the case was to us, the crumbling and reorganization that Ford went through between 2001 and 2003 was enormous and ensured that the Cellport litigation was only a minor sideshow for the giant company by 2004. Ford's corporate treasury had negotiated settlements for many large program or contract cancellations that came out of its back-to-basics restructuring campaign budgets, but Cellport was not one of those, even though a settlement with Cellport would have amounted to no more than a rounding error in the billions of dollars of write-downs Ford took from its restructuring program. Cellport's contract was trapped inside a specific Ford business unit that had ordered our engineering work and products and our purchase order was that group's specific problem. That business unit did not want its profit levels affected with a costly Cellport settlement, particularly at a time of harsh profit-and-loss reviews across Ford.

Andy and Mike worked hard to keep our outside legal costs down, but we knew that Ford could afford to pay millions to the Detroit

blue-blood law firm it hired to defend itself. For the first time in
Cellport's history, I was completely bunkered-down with virtually no
funds. We were unable to promote CP-Connect. Most of our time and
monies were going toward the big event in April 2005, when Cellport
would finally have its arbitration hearing date with Ford in the Motor
City. Also, for the first time in the company's history, Andy was the
commanding general of Cellport's number-one priority: recovering all
or some of the badly needed cash Ford owed us.

On a theoretical level, I recognized that the changes taking place at
Cellport did not have the clean-up effects of Schumpeter's creative
destruction theory. The changes we were going through were caused
by several independent cases of bad timing, such as the new instability at Cullmann and Volkswagen's withdrawal of support because we
sued THBury for multiple patent violations. The realization was not
reassuring.

For several months before the Ford arbitration began, Andy worked
60-plus hours a week conducting depositions of nearly a dozen Ford
staffers, preparing the accounting of the damages we incurred, developing presentation materials for our four witnesses and numerous
display boards to help tell our story of a relationship built up by Ford
and then abandoned. Smart lawyers advise against engaging in high-
stakes litigation except as a last resort because it disrupts business, is
costly and it can introduce unknown risks. And over the years I had
received plenty of warnings against entering into automotive supply contracts with Detroit companies. In retrospect, I guess it was a
combination of ego and greed that convinced me to change Cellport's
business model from that of a "lab" that conducted research and
small product development projects to that of a "systems" developer
that would deliver volumes of products to the automotive community. Nevertheless, we felt Cellport was clearly wronged and that Ford
should be told to compensate us, at the very least, for the lost cash.

In the spring of 2005, life in the litigation mode at Cellport was
depressing. To make it worse for me, CP-Connect was still stuck in
marketing limbo. One unexpected ray of sunshine from the delay
of the CP-Connect launch was that Chuck and Jay had plenty of

development time to come up with a new invention, and invent they did. Most helpfully for Cellport, their new idea was based on the CP-Connect architecture, and it was a promising one. Because of my all-consuming involvement in the Ford litigation, however, I could not afford much time to participate in the new technology development process that I loved.

**

Chuck's and Jay's latest big idea was a new technology enhancement for CP-Connect that would make it possible to seamlessly export the digital music playlist from a mobile phone's screen to the larger screen on a vehicle dashboard. The user would be able to control the phone's playlist via the controls on the steering wheel in the car. We knew we were hitting on what appeared to be a mother lode of new capabilities: the exportation of images from a phone to a car's display and the remote control of applications that were transmitted across various devices, in-car and Internet systems and platforms. Chuck and Jay sold me on this new extension of the CP-Connect technology. We would call it the Human Interface System (HIS) and in the spring of 2005, after less then five months of architectural and code development work, we would file the patent application for it (see Fig. 11).

The decision to pursue this patent application was not taken lightly at Cellport. Because the foundation of Cellport's contributions to both society and our shareholders is its invention process, and because of the investment in time and money it takes to pursue patentable projects, we take each development that the invention team makes and each patent application effort very seriously. Beginning with the first patent that Michael, Hiro and I had collaboratively developed in 1991, our policy at Cellport was to apply only for patents that we hoped would become core architectural technologies in the telematics field. Although we were dirt poor, cash-wise, we absolutely needed to consider the Human Interface System, which was an extension to the CP-Connect patent, to be a core architectural innovation opportunity.

Different companies promote patenting in different ways. Many large institutions rely on sheer quantities of patents as a way of measuring the results of their research investment and therefore these companies tend to file patents for all kinds of innovations, even small incremental steps toward a product design. Some companies become patent-filing mills in order to establish blanket ownership of inventions in hot new areas of technology. A cost of $10,000 or less per patent application may suffice for these higher volume filings.

Because of Cellport's objective of staying two to five years ahead of the telematics market in our invention methods and strategies, we have tried not to submit an overly large number of patent applications. The depth of cutting-edge technologies employed in and created by our solutions required a significant level of initial drafting and editorial input by all the inventors. Searching the prior art and working through countless drafts and reviews of a patent application would cause us to spend, at times, far more than $50,000 to prepare a core architectural patent application.

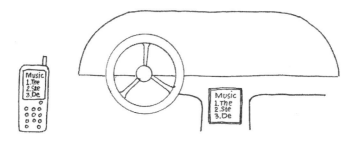

Figure 11: Human Interface System

The Human Interface System invention, an enhancement of CP-Connect, made it possible to seamlessly export images from a display of one device to the display of another and to remotely control applications transmitted in this manner via remote commands. The invention can be used, for example, to transfer the digital music play list from a mobile phone's screen to the larger screen on the dashboard, and to control the playlist via the controls on the steering wheel in the car. The music, delivered from the music player embedded in the mobile phone, plays over the automobile's sound system.

Yet ever-more confident that the case that Andy and Mike were putting together against Ford was well grounded and would produce an arbitration award for us of at between $4 and $13 million, I gave Chuck and Jay the green light to file a new patent application for the Human Interface System that they derived from our CP-Connect advancements.

**

As we finished packing our legal ammunition for Detroit, I was relieved that three challenging and torturous years would soon be behind us. The Ford arbitration hearing could not happen fast enough for me: We had lost an immeasurable amount of business opportunities as a result of Ford's contract cancellation, not to mention the business toll incurred during the litigation process, and I wanted to move on from this stage in our company's evolution.

The arbitration hearing took place in a conference hall that was about five times bigger than an average conference room. We were now face-to-face with Ford's lawyers and the arbitrator. After opening statements by Cellport and Ford on day one, Andy put me on the witness stand for six hours of testimony and cross examination by Ford's lead attorney. At the hearing, I presented what I knew to be the absolute truth in answer to questions from both Andy and then, on cross-examination, from Ford's lead attorney.

My biggest mistake, it turns out, was not taking the high road with Ford's attorney during his cross examination of me. Ford's lawyer was an older John Wayne-type of character who, during the deposition process the previous year, had mocked and harassed Andy numerous times for Andy's rusty use of certain procedural protocols while questioning Ford employees. While he presented himself as if he were riding a legal high-horse, I thought he was ignorant of technology and insensitive to small business challenges. On several occasions during the deposition breaks the previous year, I noticed that this lawyer hand-dialed his cell phone to reach his wife and daughter.

At one point I asked him why he didn't store commonly dialed numbers in the speed-dial directory. He responded that he wouldn't use the speed-dial functions because he hated technology. As soon as his wife lets him retire, he said, he was going to throw his cell phone into the Detroit River.

This comment, of course, hit me as blasphemy. As a resident of Boulder, Colorado my first thought was, "What an ecology-insensitive klutz." Plus, he clearly did not understand all the fun and efficiencies that mobile handsets have brought to our lives. I thought he was obtuse.

During cross examination, virtually any time he asked me a question about a technology or product scenario related to the case, he got completely twisted in his underwear. He convoluted just about every technical scenario he tried to use in his questioning and I lost my cool with him.

"John, if you do not understand the technology, or how the product works, how can you ask me any meaningful questions or even understand the merits of this case?" I asked him.

He made several more gaffes of technical illiteracy that compelled me to send a few more criticisms his way and he finally got angry at me for being disrespectful. Despite this, however, everyone on our team felt that we told the Cellport story effectively and well. And the arbitrator appeared to be attentive and taking good notes, although we did notice him taking a 10-minute doze after lunch.

The next day, Mike Lewellen sat at the witness table all morning and did a good job delineating the Ford product development and inventory costs. Ralph Poplawsky finished out the afternoon, describing the relationships we had with senior management at Ford, our various communications with Ford documenting the product deliveries that satisfied our contractual obligations, and orders that were still pending at the time of the contract's cancellation. We all felt good about the testimony, but we had no frame of reference to assess how the case was going; we were confident, but were we entrepreneurs reading our own mail?

The third day told us a lot. That day, the Ford business unit's purchasing leader testified. He volleyed a few easy questions from John Wayne, and then it was Andy's turn to get this fellow to admit that Cellport had been wronged. The purchasing manager was candid and several times said outright that Cellport did everything it committed to do and that we were honorable people. Nonetheless, he stuck tightly to the Ford story that the company simply exercised its cancellation rights because we "offered" our automotive business up for sale. Andy had worked to make our case simple and to follow the letter of contract law, and Ford made the case even simpler yet: Ford asserted that it had a cancellation loophole that gave them a "heads I win, tails you lose" way out of the contract. The court, we believed, would not respect a loophole.

At dinner that evening, we all felt good about our testifying and we all felt that we performed better than Ford's witnesses. That evening Andy relaxed and even smiled for the first time since we had arrived in Detroit that previous Sunday afternoon. Andy wanted a victory over Ford and its lawyers more than any of us, and now, finally, through the process of testimony, the heartlessness of the case was exposed and Ford's case was every bit as bogus as we claimed in our initial litigation filing against the company. The next day's calendar was filled primarily with testimony from two expert witnesses from accounting firms representing Ford and Cellport. Needless to say, our respective accountants agreed on very little and the differences were so extreme that I was amazed that both experts were professionals in the same rule-driven numbers world.

On the fourth day, I realized that I might have made a faux pas during my first day of testimony. Just before the hearing started that day, the arbitrator attempted to make a call on his cell phone. He made John Wayne look like Apple's CEO Steve Jobs on stage. Then, at lunch time, because everyone anticipated the hearing would conclude before 2:00 p.m. that afternoon, the arbitrator expressed interest in catching an earlier flight home than he had originally scheduled. He asked an administrator at Ford's law firm to inquire about the availability of seat space on an earlier flight. She returned promptly and told him that there were plenty of seats; all he had to do was show up at the airport early. The arbitrator's response was telling: "If they cannot fax me proof of the change, tell them to forget it. I will take the late-night flight." While it was common by now in the U.S. for airline travelers to use online reservation procedures and email to confirm flight arrangements, he insisted on having a paper contract assuring him that he could change flights.

This did not sit well with me. The arbitrator was as old as the John Wayne lawyer for Ford, and now I was convinced that he was more out of touch technically than anyone in the room. Andy said not to worry about personalities. He was growing more hopeful that the arbitrator was a letter-of-the-law man and that he would read the Michigan Supreme Court's rulings on the "offer for sale" sections of contracts clearly in Cellport's favor and not side with Ford's "caught you in a loophole" argument.

We were all emotionally exhausted after the hearing and ready to get home. Back at Cellport the next week, I worked with Chuck and Jay on the HIS patent filing, which, in our opinion, had become a very impressive core-architecture patent application. Additionally, I was trying to ascertain if Wolfgang would survive as CEO of the now-turbulent Cullmann company. Andy warned us not to expect an award notice from the arbitrator until June, so I kept busy planning the market launch of CP-Connect, which would now be possible with the expected Ford compensation payment.

But June came and went with still no ruling. July got off to a good start because we received very good reports on current sales volumes from our licensees in Europe, plus my market intelligence sources informed me that many new vehicle platforms would use our MNT patent portfolio technologies. Since Motorola was both the primary supplier for these rumored internet-connected vehicles and a Cellport licensee, Cellport was finally assured that it would reap meaningful benefits from the tens of millions of dollars we had invested to create the network-connected vehicle.

All summer, I had been losing patience over the delayed arbitration ruling, and as the month of July wound down and I realized summer was passing by, I hastily put together an August vacation on the beach with family and old college friends. On the third day of the vacation, after a wonderful day at the beach, I had a voice mail on my cellular phone from Andy. He said, "Pat, we heard today from the arbitrator, and he awarded Cellport zero. I am very sorry and probably like you right now, I am pretty disappointed."

15 | Great Karma and Reunions

1991
1992
1993
1994
1995
1996
1997
1998
1999
2000
2001
2002
2003
2004
2005
2006
2007
2008
2009

Never in my entire life had I felt such a massive body blow. I quickly laid down on the couch in a semi-fetal position, clutching a bottle of water, because my throat had suddenly tensed up so much that it felt like it would close shut on me. I told the friends I was vacationing with about the message from Andy, and because I had previously shared with them some of the history of the Ford case and my feelings about it, they understood what I was going through. These were my friends who had teasingly nicknamed me "captain of industry" during our beach-house vacation four summers earlier, when Cellport was flush with funding and customer contracts and riding high in the media. I was anything but that today. The news I had received during this intended refuge from work was stunning for all the wrong reasons. For days I kept repeating, "This ruling is so unfair. It changes everything."

Getting zero compensation from Ford was unexpectedly jarring and the next week, when I returned to work in Boulder, I quickly learned that many others at the company were in a state of shock. A few people were showing signs of outright depression. Over and above the very real need of having to deal with our emotional responses to the ruling, we would now need to create a new business model that did not include millions of dollars in cash compensation from Ford to finally pay off the last of our debts and launch the CP-Connect marketing campaign. I spent all of my time at work for the rest of the month feverishly modeling our options and in late August 2005, once again downsized Cellport's business and started to develop a new strategy with more modest and attainable goals.

I recognized quite easily that I also needed to deal with my disappointment on a personal level, and therefore I decided to use this setback as an impetus to reevaluate various aspects of my personal life as well. The process proved to be both stimulating, highly therapeutic and full of good karma. The first thing I did was give up driving to work in favor of bicycling, which took me on a forty-five minute ride each way.

It turned out that I did some of my most productive thinking in years during these two-wheeled therapy treks. I came up with some new ideas for rearranging Cellport's priorities. From now on at Cellport, we would target fewer opportunities and pursue more collaborative partnerships — and only those that would enable us to get the greatest leverage possible from our assets. I also decided to write this book, *IdeaJacked*, in part because it would produce badly needed reflection catharsis after the injustice of the kangaroo court ruling in Detroit. I also thought it was important to share Cellport's colorful story with other entrepreneurs and most critically, from a societal standpoint, I believed it would be a compelling way to draw attention to the larger issues of idea theft that have just started to ravage the world's developed economies.

One of my new ideas for Cellport was to study how to launch more of its technologies in Japan, which is home to some of the world's most advanced wireless networks and customers and which has a community of very progressive automotive gear producers that are eager to innovate. Better yet, Japan is home for a fellow Cellport founder and dear friend, Hiro. I had sensed that Hiro was ready to move on to a new challenge after three years as the general manager of a mid-sized software company in Japan and that he would likely be happy to assume the challenge of finding business opportunities for Cellport's patented wireless connectivity technologies in the sophisticated

Japanese consumer and automotive markets. In November 2005, Hiro resigned his executive post and rejoined Cellport's efforts to promote our technologies. This would be the first time, in the 14 years since we had created the company, that we would get his undivided attention.

The two of us had come full circle: We were back to doing business in Japan and the friendly partnership from which Cellport's first technology, its "Labs" business model and indeed its name, had originated in 1991. The reunion was an exciting one for both of us.

Another idea was to put more diligent effort into creating income from our patent portfolios. Toward the latter part of 2005, Cellport began receiving greater ongoing and royalty cash flow on a quarterly basis from its Universal Hands-Free patents that were used in almost a million new vehicles sold to consumers each year by Audi, BMW, Land Rover, Opel, Mercedes-Benz and Volkswagen. With revenues from some of these sales now growing, I could finally concentrate on pursuing additional licensees, not only for our Universal Hands-Free patents, but for our MobileWeb patents as well.

This new phase of business development at Cellport took a sudden and unexpected leap forward one beautiful morning in late September. While I was enjoying a coffee on my porch and reading *The Wall Street Journal*, I saw an article that would make that day one of the most spectacular in years. On the front page of the *Journal* it was reported that Motorola had hired an investment banker to help sell off its telematics business. This was a most fortuitous turn of events for Cellport, which was still reeling from the devastating Ford arbitration ruling a long and painful month earlier. I smiled from ear to ear because I knew that the buyer of Motorola's half-billion dollar telematics business would need to have a new license from Cellport. In short order, I opened dialogue with Mike Kraus and his legal deal-making team at Motorola on how to accomplish a win-win license for the new buyer.

When I called Mike Kraus to remind him that Motorola had a nontransferable license, I could hear him groan. "Yes, I was afraid I would hear from you Pat; the only thing worse would have been a call from Andy." After a chuckle I said, "Please, Mike, you make me feel like a visiting dentist." Mike responded with a combination chuckle-groan: "As a matter of fact," he wryly commented, "my jaw is feeling a bit tense right now." After a few more minutes Mike agreed to open talks with Cellport for a sub-license under Motorola's existing master-licensing agreement for both of Cellport's patent portfolios and for the future buyer of their telematics business. The buyer was yet to be named, but in time we learned that it was Continental AG, a large German conglomerate and one of the leading automobile technology suppliers in the world.

After five months of intense back-and-forth negotiations between Kraus's legal team and Cellport, we agreed to provide Motorola with a valuable and transferable license for the new buyer. On a day I fondly remember in late February 2006, the Cellport Board approved the sub-license package on behalf of Motorola and their buyer and within minutes I counter-signed an 8-digit sub-license agreement and faxed it to Mike Kraus. We received the bank wire the next day and overnight we were debt free — with millions of surplus cash in the bank. This was a recovery unlike anything I had ever experienced.

The Motorola license payment was not only a huge shot in the arm — of cash — but it also helped us regain confidence that there is fairness in the business world and that those of us who relentlessly toil in research labs could ultimately get their rewards (that's if we survive!).

With money in the bank and growing royalty revenues that were giving us good cash flow, we now had time to develop a brand new business plan. I decided to spend a couple of months analyzing the markets and assessing all the opportunities in front of us before committing to a new plan. As it turned out, Cellport's connectivity technologies were becoming ever-more germane given the world-wide adoption of wireless for both voice applications and the bourgeoning number of data applications.

The updraft of the Motorola-Continental license payment, Hiro's research of the Japanese market need for our Link Selection technology and a partnership launch strategy of our CP-Connect technology made the spring of 2006 extremely busy. That summer I took my sons for a visit of northern China. After that, we went to Japan to attend Hiro's son's wedding and to spend a few weeks traveling around Japan with my old friend. My sons got to experience the brilliance of Hiro's hosting skills and listen as he wove into our tour his thoughts on creating a Japan-based partnership that would focus on developing and licensing Cellport's Link Select patents. Hiro's idea was to start a Tokyo based business called Con-X that would pioneer wireless link selection methods between Wi-Fi and cellular services on mobile handsets and PCs. Hiro's market research taught us that data applications would soon swamp traditional cellular networks and that both wireless carriers and subscribers would pay for a technology that optimized network usage and minimized costs. I was so impressed with Hiro's proposal that I gave him the green light to start Con-X and asked him to join the Cellport Board.

Upon my return to the states, I retained our old friend Dr. Axel Fuchs to help advance research that Chuck and I were working on to combine aspects of our Secure Telematics Framework and CP-Connect. It was also time to map out the launch of CP-Connect and our HIS technologies into the market. After extensive discussions and analysis, Axel Fuchs and I agreed to try to create a partnership, inclusive of some of our licensees, to give us better international coverage. After numerous trips to Europe and Asia, we formed a partnership with our close friends Alf Naber and Hiro Sakurai and with one of our licensees, Peiker of Germany. We would call the new partnership Omniport. Its charter would be to commercialize a new universal adaptor and software platform based on our pioneering work with CP-Connect and HIS that we accomplished between 2002 and 2005.

**

After the four tortuous years catalyzed by the Ford cancellation, we were now experiencing amazingly wonderful times at Cellport. Our research was producing record levels of wireless-connectivity innovations, our licensing revenues were growing and a new Board of Directors helped energize our directions. By late 2006 we set up a Colorado-based team with initial funding to launch our new Omniport marketing partnership and we quickly gained market attention. Early interest for the Omniport portable connectivity platform came from an old friend of mine, Danny Bowman, a V.P. at Sprint Wireless. During the first meeting Chuck and I had with him, Danny committed to provide leadership and funding for the launch of Omniport in exchange for Sprint to have an early market launch advantage with the Omniport platform. With much excitement we responded affirmatively and for the next six months we were diligent in selling across the Sprint organization to secure broad support for Omniport funding and its commercial launch.

By summer of 2007 Hiro finally secured an initial round of funding for Con-X from a group of Japanese venture funds and was now able to rent office space in Japan and start hiring software development staff. Chuck and I stayed close to Con-X's market findings and were delighted to discover that the advanced state of Japan's wireless applications was fertile ground for more innovations on the Link Select front. We also learned that Hiro was struggling to find software engineers, so we decided to recruit some talented student interns from the University of Colorado at Boulder (CU-Boulder) to kick-start his design efforts. It was great to see Hiro work so skillfully while building Con-X, albeit I did not envy his challenges; they were formidable in the entrepreneur-unfriendly Japan.

I then turned my interest to rumors out of Europe indicating that Mercedes-Benz (formally Daimler-Benz) had replaced the Motorola-designed and Continental-supplied docking stations for their Universal Hands-Free system. Flying into Germany is usually very productive and for this trip I expected no different. My first meeting was with our licensee and now-Omniport partner, Peiker. When I asked the fellows at Peiker about the changes at Mercedes-Benz, they responded: "Oh, yes, indeed they did replace the docking stations, but the details are Mercedes proprietary; what information we do know we can't share with you because of confidentiality agreements." And when we talked about planning for Omniport promotional progress in Europe, their position was, "Let's make progress with Sprint before we tap into Peiker's design resources and carrier connections in Europe."

The energy of the meeting felt like one of those one-way streets that I work to avoid. Putting it another way, it was a "heads-they-win, tails-Cellport-likely-loses" type of situation. While driving to my hotel after a dinner with Peiker's management, it sunk in: As hard as I tried to work cooperatively, the Peiker team was a risk-adverse licensee that preferred to avoid the bleeding edge of technology and the long lead times of cutting edge business development projects. The next day I went to see Mercedes in the Stuttgart area and found the Mercedes engineers to be delightfully friendly. But when I asked if they would explain the change in their docking station design, they recommended that I visit Peiker for the details of the new system. "Really, I was just there and they said you would be able to tell me the details of the new system," I informed them. "Well," the Mercedes guy said, "since the new system was a Peiker-initiated design change, they are the ones you should talk with regarding the changes." The fellow at Mercedes offered to introduce me to several providers of dashboard screen systems who were working with Peiker, but he warned they'll most likely bounce me back to Peiker as well.

Upon my return to Boulder, more setbacks were waiting for me; so much for all the good progress. In October 2007, Sprint fired their CEO. Our advanced discussions with Sprint Ventures for obtaining funding for the Omniport platform launch were put on the back burner until a new CEO was hired. Danny Bowman and other members of the Sprint team encouraged us to be patient. I assured them we could hang on until early 2008 as long as they stayed committed to the Omniport connectivity platform. The Sprint delay was one event that was very costly. I was convinced that the U.S. economy would suffer a deep recession in 2008 and that trying to find an alternative funding source and launch supporter would not be easy. Hence, a supportive, albeit wounded, Sprint appeared to be our best bet. The combination of a less-than-engaged Peiker and now a big delay with Sprint were two negative variables that weighed heavily on our Omniport ambitions. For an inventor it is hugely frustrating to have innovated a technology that customers proclaim they love, yet for political, financial or partnership motivation reasons, getting the launch progress underway seems to be nearly impossible.

In contrast to all the frustrations on the business front, we had assembled a bright new team of researchers to help us advance our Mobile Multimedia Connectivity invention work. Over the years, Dale Hatfield had introduced us to several professors that were with the Department of Computer Science at CU-Boulder. After countless meetings with various professors, we retained Dirk Grunwald and Doug Sicker, whom both had strong software architectural and security backgrounds, as consultants to our development team. Both Dirk and Doug turned out to be highly stimulating for our "art-of-the-possible" work, especially in security and connectivity challenges that we wanted addressed to further advance our Secure Telematics Framework and CP-Connect. As I learned years ago, framing the right questions in the invention processes can stimulate some of the most powerful creativity. Both Dirk and Doug were fascinated by our expertise in the arcane field of wireless connectivity. The combination of our briefings on state-of-the-art design along with their questions and insights helped push our inventive work at a fabulous pace.

At the start of 2008 Cellport was making progress on both the licensing and invention front, but complex problems were brewing with Peiker. They were not only becoming a reluctant supporter of the Omniport marketing program, but now I had evidence that they were deliberately deflecting my requests for a better understanding of the new Mercedes design. While back in Europe, I visited Panasonic and Harman/Becker International to better understand how the new dashboard head-units they supplied to Mercedes worked with the Peiker phone adaptor system. Both companies claimed to know little about the system and simply said they designed the system with a basic Bluetooth link and screen interface, per Mercedes' instructions. When I pressed them on providing more system details, they blatantly remarked: "Sorry, but that is beyond the scope of the requirements Mercedes gave us."

Now the mystery only grew deeper; I was certain of that there appeared to be some new level of potential patent crossing that I needed to understand and that all roads led to Peiker. Dealing with IdeaJackers is one thing, but when they're also a current licensee and a joint-venture partner on a separate project, the situation becomes a bit too complex for my liking.

When I returned home I decided to go vehicle shopping. Of course, visiting a Mercedes dealer was top on my list. Over a three-hour period of inspecting every model they offered and test-driving several higher and medium-end models, I discovered that Mercedes had a Peiker docking plate in almost every vehicle. A most helpful sales-person tried to explain how the new Peiker-centric system worked; it used a traditional pocket adaptor with a new docking station set of resources. I was suspicious this system was covered under the existing Cellport/Peiker license.

After my visit to the Mercedes dealership, I went next to the BMW dealership in Boulder looking for more unknowns. Within an hour I was test-driving a 535xi and, as I drove, the salesman pitched the vehicle's safety features — including the BMW's slick universal cradle adaptor system. Forget the awesome power train, handling, suspension and exquisite leather interior, I wanted to learn more about this universal cradle adaptor system. The salesman did not know the system details, but promised to have the parts department manager give me a tutorial. That afternoon, while visiting the BMW Parts Department, I saw what looked like another Peiker license violation: Peiker's name was on a BMW universal adaptor and docking station. Unlike the shocking discovery of the Cullmann system at the Frankfurt auto show back in 1999, I was now used to this "cops and IdeaJackers" game. I simply smiled and said to the salesman, "Give me your best shot at pricing a blue 535xi with the Peiker Universal Hands-Free system with an adaptor for my iPhone, and if the price is right, I'll buy it next week." As I drove away I called Andy to report what I believed to be the second license violation by Peiker. "Keep on digging, Sherlock Holmes," Andy replied, "It sounds like great progress, but," he reminded me, "you know they'll want detailed evidence of such big license violations."

At this point in Cellport's history, we had refined the methods of advancing big-idea inventions. We made fabulous progress on the Mobile Multimedia Connectivity front by combining the work of our internal team with help from Dirk Grunwald and Doug Sicker. As a team we were delivering great innovative results to the Patent Office and we had success with early prototypes. Yet what was becoming ever-more time consuming was tracking down initially evasive IdeaJackers. Furthermore, while the IdeaJackers ultimately became obvious, this happened only after a great amount of time-hogging detective work was accomplished. The dozens of IdeaJackers that we needed to analyze in further detail proved to be immensely difficult, especially those that appeared to be crossing our MNT portfolio. We owed our shareholders the financial harvest of royalties we were due, especially given the tens of millions of dollars that we spent on past research efforts. And while we would certainly do our best to accomplish that harvest, this detective work was a completely different business than our traditional, art-of-the-possible invention model.

Advancing our understandings of the Peiker IdeaJacking mysteries took place shortly before a much-needed family vacation. Although I felt relieved that I cracked the mysteries prior to a necessary break, I was not in a great mood. Obfuscation is not my style and I really disliked dealing with the shades of gray when it came to license relationships. Being IdeaJacked, either by discovering a brand new violator or finding a current licensee under-reporting, is very disheartening. During our entire history we prided ourselves on advancing technology architectures via our art-of-the-possible invention methods. Now with so many IdeaJackers adopting our patented works, we were facing a new reality, one that called for the "art-of investigative-detective-work." As I was painfully learning, good detective work takes a great deal of time and a lot of creativity to connect the proverbial dots. However, it does pay off. Besides the benefit of increasing revenues for our shareholders, one major benefit of our detective duties was we gained a better understanding on how to improve our patent work by using claim language that translated into market solutions versus more esoteric technical breakthroughs.

As Cellport's efforts on IdeaJacker detective work was ramping up, the prospects for our Omniport marketing partnership were waning. Two of Omniport's partners, Con-X and Peiker, notified us that they unwilling to invest more money in advancing the marketing partnership. This was primarily due to the long gestation time to launch the Omniport technology platform and the worldwide recession that started in 2008 and now looked to be a prolonged and nasty downturn. I understood their reluctance to continue with an investment in a long-term development project. By the summer of 2008 it became clear that the Omniport marketing partnership with Con-X, Peiker and Alf Naber would be shut down by the lack of funding support and insufficient commitments from Sprint. The shutdown of Omniport was a sad outcome for me as I really wanted the Omniport partnership to succeed, especially for the sake of Hiro and Alf. They both had been long term supporters of Cellport's universal connectivity and open licensing model. I was frustrated that Peiker seemed to have little interest in Cellport's long term development mindset; it became clear that we had a misalignment of business expectations, both timing and marketwise, with the Omniport marketing joint venture. It was also becoming clear that the Peiker-Cellport relationship was becoming strained. The more we discussed with them what we considered violations of our license agreement regarding their Mercedes and BMW supplied products, the more I realized we were in a semantic battle with Peiker that would not end anytime soon.

As Omniport was imploding in the fall of 2008, Ralph Poplawsky called me and asked if there was any pioneering work for him to do at Cellport. After several years working as the CTO of a small test equipment company, Ralph wanted to rejoin Cellport to work on more cutting-edge opportunities. I explained that Chuck had recently presented a significant advancement called M-Tools which, in essence, turned a phone into a Web server and would enable easier application development and device interface. Given the inventive breakthrough with M-Tools and the need for an entirely new product platform and business plan to model the opportunity, I had plenty of work for him. Plus, I could use Ralph's technical assistance to help analyze and document the specifics of what I believed were the Peiker patent crosses and license violations. In the late fall of 2008, the Omniport partnership officially folded and our detective work on the Peiker patent crosses accelerated. The timing of Ralph rejoining our team was most fortunate.

The waning days of 2008 were full of delightful surprises. Ray Sokola, now CTO of Motorola's $11 billion dollar Home Network business, proposed to stop by Colorado and catch up. During Ray's visit, Chuck and I explained our work on turning phones into a Web server using Chuck's M-Tools design work. Ray remarked, "M-Tools is such a big paradigm change that I need some time to absorb its ramifications. Once again," he continued, "Cellport has reshuffled the way wireless connectivity works." Within days Ray called and said, "I love the M-Tools idea. This, coupled with your previous work on CP-Connect and HIS, makes for explosive new opportunities in countless markets. I'd like to help you guys advance this important big idea." Ray said that he would seek permission from Motorola to help us as an advisor. Furthermore, he wanted us to introduce the idea to our old friend Marios Zenios, who was now the head of Chrysler telematics. Ray laughed at his request and remarked, "A meeting with Chuck, Ralph, Pat and Marios would be one hell of a reunion of telematics pioneers."

Within weeks we were on Marios' calendar and his enthusiasm for the growing capabilities of our MMC portfolio (CP-Connect, HIS and M-Tools) was exceptional. Marios had so many ideas on how to use the MMC technology that we knew Ray had pointed us to a good opportunity. Marios' first idea was to turn his Chrysler head-units into a Web browser and enable text messages from any phone to be read aloud to the driver. Then, using voice-to-text technology, the driver could respond to the text without touching the mobile handset. He said once we demonstrate this to Bob Nardelli, then the CEO of Chrysler, support for a rapid launch schedule would be assured. Marios also loved the prospect of Google maps and MP-3 music playlists being exported to the vehicle from the user's mobile phone. That evening, during a classic Michigan snowstorm, Marios greatly warmed my enthusiasm when he said that if Cellport would give Chrysler early launch advantage, he would do his best to make our MMC patent portfolio and software solution the industry leader.

The start of 2009 could not have gotten off on better footing. To add more fire to the reunion flame, my old friend Bob Johnson, who in 1993 played a vital role in Cellport by securing an anchor purchase order from McCaw Cellular/AT&T Wireless, agreed to join Cellport's Board. Bob's career at AT&T Wireless had risen rapidly in the 1990s and he eventually became the COO of the nation's largest wireless carrier. Bob's experience was a perfect addition, not only to our Board, but also to a study team to help launch some of our MMC technologies as a Cellport spin-off. To further strengthen the Board, Nancy Pierce, a well-regarded financier and founder of a Boulder-based public company agreed to join Cellport's Board, adding significant deal moxie to Cellport.

Crafting a new spin-off based on our growing MMC patent portfolio took months of careful strategizing and planning. The rapid growth of smart-phone sales made the importance of the launch of the MMC technology platform enormously critical, especially given that Cellport's skilled CTO Chuck Spaur would lead the technology development in the new company. After months of developing model after model for both the business structure and first product introduction, we finally found a consensus with the formulas. We proposed in April 2009 to the Cellport Board a business spin-off called Obly. It would have Chuck leading the technology road map, Ralph Poplawsky leading the technical operations and an old Boulderite friend, John Hickey, leading the team as president of Obly, a subsidiary of Cellport. To give the Cellport Board additional comfort, Bob Johnson and Nancy Pierce would sit on the Obly Board of Advisors and I would chair the entity. To further the team's commitment, collectively Cellport allocated a couple of hundred thousand dollars in seed capital to launch Obly.

Right after the seed capital was allocated, we planned to secure the advisory services of two ace financiers: our old friend Helena Stelnicki, formally of the Motorola telematics team and who has since founded a banking and strategic advisory firm, and Nancy Pierce to help Obly raise between $500,000 and $3 million in convertible debt. This is certainly an all-star cast, with a hot technology hand and a market seemingly anxious for our Obly solution. Only time will tell just how well thought-out our Obly vision and strategies really are.

The spin-offs of Link Select to Hiro's Con-X business in Japan and now Obly to this all-star cast, full of competent old friends and allies, were good diversification bets for Cellport's shareholders. On a going-forward basis, Cellport needed to do a great deal of work in the patent enforcement arena and continue with several technology advancements. First at bat on the enforcement front was Peiker. After nearly a year of discussions that led nowhere, Cellport filed a lawsuit against Peiker in the spring of 2009 for multiple contract violations based on our Universal Handset Connectivity patent portfolio. I'm hopeful we can settle the lawsuit out of court; otherwise, Cellport and Peiker will have to listen to a court rule in either our favor or theirs. The stakes are high for both companies. For Cellport, filing a lawsuit is an expensive and time-consuming proposition. And if Peiker loses, the judgment for them could be significantly north of eight digits.

In addition to the ongoing Peiker litigation, we are now studying numerous companies that appear to be crossing our MNT portfolio. The process of analyzing all the products, applications and then the detailed functions of their Internet-connected equipment and services is very time-consuming and expensive. The work of patent-crosser analysis is real detective work and for inventors it becomes a major distraction. To a high degree, it is even the antithesis of the invention spirit. From an inventor's standpoint, if all these companies would just honestly license our MNT portfolio, all of our businesses would be far less stressful and expensive, plus we would all have much more time to advance technologies for the betterment of our respective businesses and society in general.

As luck would have it, Danny Bowman, our early supporter of the Omniport product at Sprint, was promoted to become the President of Sprint's Nextel division and in the spring of 2009 Bob Johnson was named President of Sprint's CDMA Cellular division. Both Danny and Bob are high-powered visionaries and big fans of the Obly solution. Hence the Obly spin-off team has supporters in the right positions to help launch the platform. John Hickey, Chuck Spaur and Ralph Poplawsky have a world-class opportunity to turn Obly into the next big thing. Nevertheless, this team of capable business and technology leaders will face countless challenges in building the Obly connectivity platform, from signing on wireless carrier partners, fund raising, hiring and of course dealing with a new set of IdeaJackers lurking behind every nook and cranny. I wish them the best of luck and agility as they work to introduce to the world a wonderful connectivity framework called Obly...

Epilogue

This book is about the pursuit of one of the fundamental tenets of the American Dream: the right to invent and to own one's unique intellectual creations.

It is about the drive to invent, the dramatic world inventors and technology pioneers live in, the immense barriers that stand in the way of new market development and the degree to which established and powerful companies will fight to protect their perceived interests. It is a story about global competition, business friendships and rivalries, lucky breaks, losses that are hard to accept, survival and, fortunately in our case, market and financial success.

When Hiro Sakurai and I came up with our first big idea in 1991 and formed Cellport Labs, we knew instantly that we wanted to protect our idea and that we needed to get a patent for it. As idealistic, young entrepreneurs, it did not occur to us that we would have to carry out a protracted struggle against companies that chose not to honor our patents. Many start-up companies, unfortunately, do not make it through these substantial difficulties, but Cellport is one of the fortunate ones. While we had investors and partners who came through for us when we were in the depths of our most precarious circumstances, I believe we prevailed because we never let go of our belief in our vision and our patents.

If I were to share any of the lessons I've learned with young entrepreneurs who desire to enter the inventive world independent from established companies, I would have this to say: Give very careful consideration to the course you are embarking on and your commitment to it. It is a high-risk and costly field, made even more so by the many-years delay between filing for a patent and the opportunity to fully leverage it in markets. Strive for the art-of-the-possible in all of your work, and that includes your patent strategy: The ultimate goal is to create a portfolio of core inventions that will represent a full and recognizable advancement of the inventive art in your field. Once you are established, continue to invent and to build a contiguous portfolio of patents to extend your contributions and the relevance of your innovations over time. Use an open licensing model if you can; it will encourage others to adopt your technologies, which is most likely why you invented them in the first place. Find and motivate a team of tenaciously committed partners who are considered experts by the experts in their own fields. Stay agile — so agile that you can turn on a dime if business conditions change unexpectedly. And finally, try not to burn bridges: sometimes your adversaries will turn out to be your best partners.

One thing I've learned from Cullmann, Harman/Becker, Motorola, Peiker and others over the years is that building relationships in lucrative, highly competitive markets takes time. These companies had varied motivations for crossing our patents. It wasn't simply a tactic for avoiding having to acknowledge or pay royalties to an American firm, though such sentiments were expressed to me at times. For many companies, IdeaJacking is simply the most expedient way of entering a competitive market because it is a way to short-cut the expensive and time-consuming process of R&D. It's a practical risk they take, in other words. Many IdeaJackers look at royalties as a form of taxes; unfortunately, there is a pervasive culture of tax avoidance in our society that is both selfish and nearsighted.

As much as I have taken the IdeaJacking of Cellport's technologies pretty personally over the years, I know quite well that the problem of idea theft is not unique to Cellport. It is actually very, very prevalent. I would like the story of Cellport's struggles to be viewed within the context of this much larger problem: Intellectual property theft, counterfeiting and under-reporting of royalties are taking place all the time, all around us. Most of it is more deliberate and insidious than the type of idea theft that Cellport struggled with, and it affects us all. A staggering $650 billion in counterfeit goods are sold each year, and that number is sure to grow until changes are demanded [1].

As it is widely known, differing intellectual property rights values and policies among countries participating in international trade have brought this issue to its current levels and made it hard for businesses and artists to enforce their intellectual property rights internationally.

Because of this, a growing body of economists has begun to question the World Trade Organization's current notion of free trade, which in the interest of facilitating trade across borders has in some cases turned a blind eye to the enforcement of intellectual property rights. China is of course the worst violator of this, producing the vast majority of the world's counterfeit goods. Because of the sheer magnitude of their violations, and the well-publicized economic impacts on other countries, the matter of enforcing ethical trade has entered policy debates. I would even go so far as to say that if the U.S. is going to continue to participate in the WTO and open our borders to China we must demand that it effectively crack down on counterfeiting and insist that it enforce ethical trade practices. I believe that if we want to protect the very fabric of our society and economy, we have to take this step.

I am a firm believer in the Schumpeter philosophy of creative destruction, that economic turbulence that churns in society as a result of innovation and the development of new ideas is healthy. But the global trend in counterfeiting and piracy is creating a lopsided balance in unfair trade that has its basis in cheating, and its destructive effects are unhealthy. The many businesses and factories that are shutting their doors in developed countries around the world and the many lower- and middle-class workers who are losing their jobs are paying the price for it. And I fear another effect from high-volume trade in counterfeit products; if counterfeit trade is left unchecked, it could cause the larger community of technology inventors, those who are prone to share their achievements for adoption by others via the patent system, to resort to more secretive methods. It could undermine the value we attach to the patent system and it would be terribly counterproductive to society as well.

I encourage anyone who wants to express their thoughts about the ethical trade problem or get involved to help address the issue and those who might be interested in learning more about intellectual property rights, pursuing a patent, or how to confront the theft of their own ideas to please visit our Innovation and Ethical Trade blog on these topics, www.IdeaJacked.com, or consult some of the other public resources that are listed in an appendix to this book.

Appendices

- Cellport Patent Portfolios and Product Development Evolutions

- America's Most Influential Inventors

- 10 Examples of Other IdeaJackings in Developed Countries

    Automotive Parts

    American Indian Arts and Crafts

    Consumer Electronics Devices

    Cosmetics

    Luxury Watches

    Manufacturing Equipment

    Personal Appliances

    Pharmaceuticals and Medicines

    Refrigeration Test Equipment

    Snowboarding Equipment and Accessories

- The Political and Economic Impacts of Patent Competition and IdeaJacking in the International Arena: A Commentary

    The China Factor

    Europe's Policies

    Weaknesses in the U.S. System

    Conclusion

Handset Connectivity Systems (HCS)

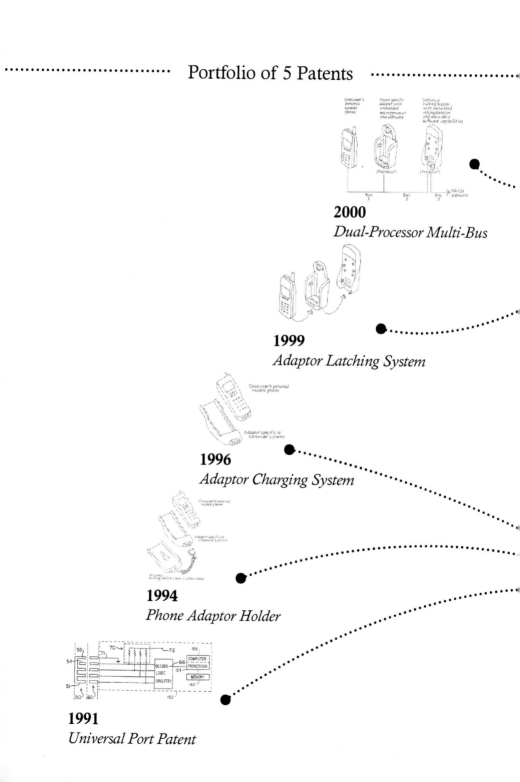

2000
Dual-Processor Multi-Bus

1999
Adaptor Latching System

1996
Adaptor Charging System

1994
Phone Adaptor Holder

1991
Universal Port Patent

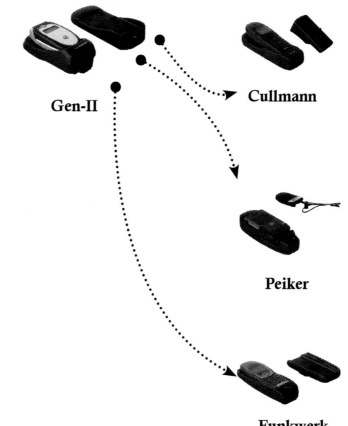

Product Developments ·········· Licensees ············

Cullmann

Peiker

Funkwerk
Dabendorf

Gen-II

Gen-I

Mobile Network Technology (MNT)

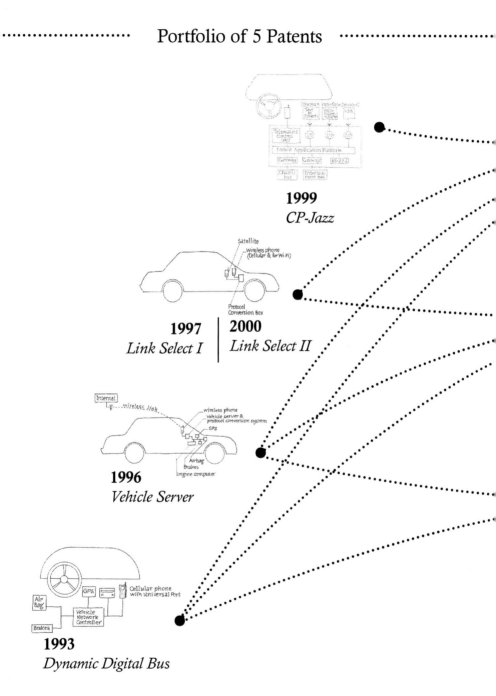

1999
CP-Jazz

1997 | **2000**
Link Select I | *Link Select II*

1996
Vehicle Server

1993
Dynamic Digital Bus

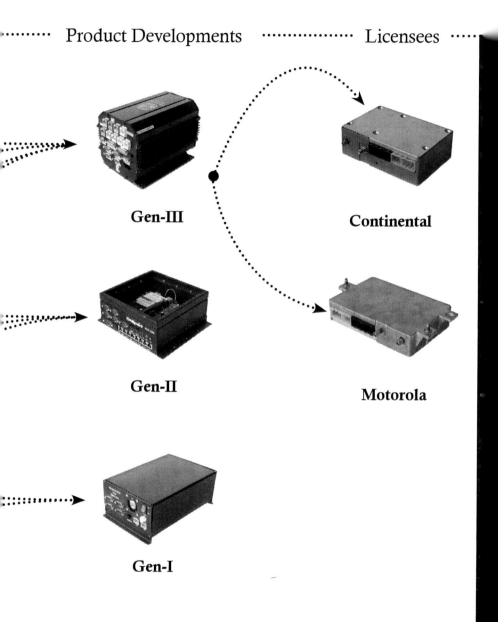

Product Developments ·················· Licensees

Gen-III

Continental

Gen-II

Motorola

Gen-I

Mobile Multi-Media Connectivity (MMC)

Issued and Pending Patent Portfolio

2008
Secure Telematics Framework II
(Patent Pending)

2006
Link Select
(Patent pending)

2005
Human Interface System
(Patent Pending)

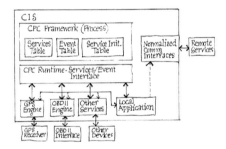

2004
CP-Connect

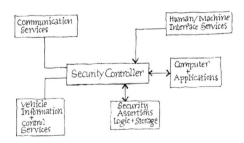

2004
Secure Telematics Framework

MMC Product Model

America's Most Influential Inventors

The U.S. patent system has proven to be a brilliant economic incentive to human capital. In the 215-plus years since the Founding Fathers brilliantly crafted the 1790 Patent Act to give inventors limited-time monopoly ownership rights to their ideas and creative works, the U.S. has issued more than 7.6 million patents. While the country has less than six percent of the earth's population, its people have created a disproportionately large share of the world's most important inventions. These patented ideas have enabled the United States to become the wealthiest and most entrepreneurially vibrant economy in the history of mankind.

To illustrate just how large a role the U.S. patent invention system has played in shaping the country, I've characterized patented inventions that were, in my opinion, instrumental in bringing about significantly positive changes to American economic prosperity and culture — AAA-caliber core inventions, in other words. I received most helpful assistance from Thomas Frey, founder of the DaVinci Institute, in identifying patents that had this type of impact for each 25-year period beginning with 1776, when the country first began formally articulating its philosophy of government. As individuals, the inventors who pioneered these patents have uniquely colorful biographies, but their life stories all resonate with the relentless drive to fulfill visions of exceptional and new technologies that will benefit society. The stories we found described courageous people sustained by tenacity of vision and motivated by personal pride and the desire for personal wealth. None of the geniuses who delivered the AAA core patents described here received support or funding from the industrial incumbents of the time, whose methods or technologies were often displaced or eclipsed by the new ideas.

1775 to 1799: During the founding period of the U.S., Eli Whitney invented a mechanized method for removing cotton seeds that are deeply embedded and entangled in harvested cotton balls. Vastly superior to the manual methods of seed removal, which were the only option at the time, Whitney's cotton gin greatly reduced both human injuries and the cost of producing cotton fiber. It made cotton the most cost-effective raw material for the production of fabrics, eclipsing wool, fur and flax as the most popular fabric resources. Whitney's cotton gin invention, the first AAA-caliber patent issued in the U.S., created vast economic opportunities in agriculture and fiber mill operations and made possible the mass production of clothing, introducing a new notion of affordability for numerous consumer goods. Like every great invention, Whitney's invention delivered huge social and economic benefits long after the patent expired and it continues to bring value to the majority of the world's citizens today.

Whitney never received a dime of development monies or encouragement from the incumbent wool, fur or flax material communities to develop his invention, but he saw a very specific need for mass processing cotton balls into pure cotton bales for export. Unfortunately, Whitney spent a lot of time and money trying to enforce his patent against dozens of IdeaJackers. He had little luck enforcing his patent and collecting royalties due to an immature U.S. court system and the newness of intellectual property case law. Whitney's brilliant cotton gin invention did bring him fame, and many influential people supported his follow-up research, which finally enabled him to continue his entrepreneurial contributions and, eventually, find business success.

1800 to 1824: I could not identify any AAA patents from the U.S. in the 1800 to 1824 time period. The most important inventions during this period were from Europe, where the system was more mature. It is possible that many inventors in the U.S. may have kept their ideas secret or that they could not afford to pursue patents. The extreme difficulties Eli Whitney faced when trying to enforce his cotton gin patent could not have been encouraging.

1825 to 1849: Samuel Morse invented the telegraph system in 1837. Morse was a brilliant individual who had an eclectic background. He studied fine arts at Yale and for a while as a young man made a meager living as a painter traveling around Europe. During these travels abroad, Morse learned of significant advances in electricity measurement and control, which inspired him to pursue the "art-of-the-possible." This inspiration, in turn, helped nurture his invention in the telegraph. Although many telegraph components or sub-systems had been developed by other inventors prior to 1837, the initial work was woefully shy of Morse's system, which he developed through 12 years of work with a diverse invention team that consisted of a physicist, machinist, chemists and linguists. The eventual long distance telegraph system also included the dot-dash code scheme used to send messages. The invention initially accelerated commerce and communications on the East Coast. In a second phase, it helped accelerate the expansion of the western U.S., particularly through its ability to help coordinate train departures and arrivals for railroad system optimization.

1850 to 1874: One of the most disruptive AAA inventions during this period was contributed by Elisha Graves Otis. Although Otis was credited with many inventions, his most famous and important invention was the critically clever improvement to a popular hoisting machine that was commonly used in factories and small buildings. Otis revolutionized hoisting machines with the addition of an automatic lifting cable brake system that later evolved into multi-story elevators systems that ordinary people could safely use without operators. These elevator systems made modern multi-story buildings practical, completely transforming urban life and urban skylines and creating new types of real estate wealth.

1875 to 1899: In 1887, three years after he moved to New York City from what is now Croatia, Nikola Tesla invented a system of alternating current motors, generators and transformers that brought society into the modern electrical era, which in turn fostered the development of new industries and businesses. Tesla is considered one of the greatest inventors of all time. Not only did he create breakthroughs in energy production and delivery that improved people's lives, but he is also credited with inventing the first radio. He envisioned a plethora of applications for radio technology and foresaw its use as a global communications medium. Tesla also used radio waves to remotely control devices, which he called robots. He created the first concepts of radar and the microwave oven and he developed the first X-ray. Tesla was known for his unusual capability to envision entirely new concepts fully in his mind before committing his ideas to paper and building physical representations of his ideas.

Tesla came to New York intentionally to work on electricity projects with Thomas Edison, but later became Edison's rival when the Tesla AC system became recognized as vastly superior to the direct-current electrical system Edison invented, which was the best available at the time. Another rival was Guglielmo Marconi, who won most of the recognition and wealth for inventing the radio, though certain fundamental aspects of his work were later acknowledged to have violated Tesla's patents. Tesla's story is a classic one. He was a man who conducted much of his work independently from large corporations and did not have the financial backing to adequately defend his patents. Some of his disputes with Marconi, for example, were ultimately resolved in Tesla's favor, but not until after Tesla's death.

1900 to 1924: One of the greatest examples of a disruptive technology invention can be credited to the Wright brothers of Dayton, Ohio. The Wrights, successful bicycle manufacturers, were fascinated by the challenge of creating combustion power conversion mechanisms and using this power to enable man to fly. Although flying machine concepts were advanced by numerous French, German and American inventors, including an effort by Alexander Graham Bell in the late 1800s, none of these inventors was able to design and create a machine that actually could fly in a navigable manner. The tenacious and brilliant Wright brothers refined their inventions through obsessive tinkering and clever testing methods, including the use of an advanced wind tunnel to test the performance of key airplane components prior to constructing their airplane. Their most important invention for avionics was the lateral steering control method, in which one portion of the wing tips up while the opposite wing tips down, which is necessary for a plane to turn in mid-air. They had another critical insight that the then-accepted theory for shaping the wing design was wrong, and corrected this error by testing more than 80 wing component designs; through this dedicated work they were able to create a new and highly effective wing contour that provided proper lift for flight. They also used their inventive wind tunnel test lab to optimize propeller shapes to provide enough power to enable to fly the Kitty Hawk, an airplane that employed their brilliant lateral steering capabilities and enhanced wing lift design.

The Wright brothers received their first core patent in the U.S. in 1906, three years after their flight. Unfortunately, they were denied any patent coverage in Germany and France, and therefore numerous European IdeaJackers were able to flagrantly use the Wrights' pioneering and core inventive work that made sustained airplane flight possible. Even in the U.S., the Wrights spent years trying to enforce their numerous patents before earning the substantial royalties that they clearly deserved. They both suffered from exhaustion and lost their motivation to invent as a result of that struggle.

1925 to 1949: Chester Carlson represents the quintessential Horatio Alger story. Raised on the West Coast in near poverty, he was able to obtain work as a printing apprentice in his youth and from there he went on to study physics at the California Institute of Technology. Some years later, he earned a law degree at New York Law School. While working as a young patent lawyer in the mid 1930s, Carlson suffered from nearsightedness and arthritis and found the U.S. Patent and Trademark Office policy of submitting multiple copies of drawings and applications unduly challenging. In a classic case of necessity being the mother of invention, Carlson worked for years in his kitchen, developing an idea he had for a more efficient copying method, one that would use photo-conductivity, a process by which some materials change their electric properties and when exposed to light, to create a mirror-image copy. Because this process did not require ink, Carson called it xerography, from the Greek words meaning "dry-writing."

As many successful inventors learn, finding a partner to commercialize the product was not easy, and after being rejected by IBM, General Electric and RCA, almost 10 years after filing his first core patent application, Carlson finally convinced the family-run Haloid Company of Rochester, New York, to fund the development needed to create a commercial xerography product. It would be another 10 years of cutting-edge development work with Haloid and the filing of dozens of additional patent applications before Carlson, in 1959, would see a commercial product based on his idea. Given the enormous popularity of Carson's invention, the Haloid Company changed its name to Xerox and became one of the world's fastest growing and most profitable companies. Ten years after the introduction of his xerography machine, just prior to his death, Carlson gave away over $100 million of his fortune to various charitable causes.

1950 to 1974: Shortly after the end of World War II, Mervin Kelly, a management strategist at Bell Labs, proposed shifting a significant number of researchers from the company's military-related efforts to a new initiative that focused on solving the problem of slow and expensive telephone switches that were based on vacuum tubes and electromechanical relays. The research group was headed by William Shockley and included John Bardeen and Walter Brattain. Their revolutionary work, which became the core invention of the transistor, earned two Nobel prizes and spurred one of the most profound series of technology advancements in history. Within a decade, the transistor replaced many low power vacuum tube applications and launched the start of the high-tech era.

Ten years later, two gifted engineers, Jack Kilby of Texas Instruments and Robert Noyce of Fairchild Semiconductor, invented the integrated circuit, which was a way of combining many transistors and circuitry on a single piece of silicon. This invention made the high-speed, cost-effective modern computer and minicomputer possible. Kilby's inventive genius led to numerous core patents for his work in the field of semiconductors and derivative products, and in 2000, Kilby was awarded the Nobel Prize for core inventions in the semiconductor field.

During 1968, Robert Noyce left Fairchild Semiconductor with Gordon Moore and Andy Grove to start Intel Corporation. Gordon Moore is famous for "Moore's Law," which predicted that integrated circuit density would double every 18 months. The Moore, Noyce and Grove team at Intel would pave the way for the next industry revolution, which was the Intel 4004 microprocessor chip. The microprocessor made possible a tsunami of ever-more sophisticated digital products and software innovations. Virtually all of today's electronic products use the digital processing power of the microprocessor.

Microprocessors facilitated the development of digital calculator, computers, electronic games, cellular phones, Internet routers and countless others devices that enhance our daily lives. Today this group of semiconductor inventions generates trillions of dollars in revenue annually and greatly enhances all of our lives.

1975 to 1999: In the mid 1990s, inventive genius came out of the research labs of Stanford University and the University of California San Francisco. Dr. Stanley Cohen and Herb Boyer collaborated to discover some of the core aspects of recombinant DNA, and their work began the biotechnology and genetic engineering industry that has revolutionized modern medicine and biology. The two scientists came up with a novel way of swapping DNA between E. coli bacteria that became the basis of a 1973 paper they authored, which was published in the *Proceedings of the National Academy of Sciences*. The three core patents resulting from this work, awarded to Stanford and UCSF, have been licensed to more than 400 companies. This innovative technology caught the traditional pharmaceutical industry flat-footed. When Bob Swanson, a young financier and entrepreneur, partnered with Herb Boyer to start Genentech in 1976, the vast majority of the large pharmaceutical firms thought the West Coast venture was doomed to failure. In spite of widespread skepticism, Genentech and its research partnerships opened a broad and disruptive field of bioengineering research. To convince the most talented scientific and engineering people to join the company, Boyer insisted on publishing Genentech's cutting edge research while preserving the company's future intellectual property equity with multiple patent applications. Today, Genentech, Amgen, Biogen-Idec and other leading genetic engineering firms are creating some of the world's greatest blockbuster drug therapies, delivering cures for millions of cancer patients and sharing many of their genetic engineering innovations via the patent publishing systems.

2000 and Beyond: As we move into the twenty-first century, billions of dollars have already been invested to advance a new material science field called nanotechnology. In a nutshell, most nanotech materials often come in the form of microscopic tube-like structures that are as small as 1/10,000 of the thickness of a human hair. Nanotech will enable a wide range of new technologies and the field's developmental progress and applications coming out of university and private labs already hold the promise for a broad array of applications, from revolutionizing drug delivery to healing specific body organs or tumors, to improving the way we build almost everything and, perhaps most importantly, green energy production. My favorite example of the promise of nanotech is its capability to increase the effectiveness of today's organic polymer solar cells by a factor of two or greater. With nanotech enhanced solar receptors, one could imagine a future in which the entire roof and siding of a home are covered with nanotech receptor skins that effectively turn a home into a solar collection system to generate enough electricity not only for the inhabitants' in-home use, but to power their electric vehicles as well.

A major challenge in nanotech research is advancing the seemingly endless number of prototype designs to complex high-volume production systems. Creating high-volume production systems will most likely take a community of geniuses, much like the community that helped advance basic transistors to the semiconductor and eventually the microprocessor. The development of open invention sharing by gifted AAA inventors of nanotech production technology will depend on the degree to which key world markets are dedicated to protecting patents over the next 10 years. Much like the fellows who started Genentech, who, promulgating their vision, used brilliant science from university research labs coupled with enormous risk capital and energy to catalyze in today's biotech miracle drugs, tomorrow's seminal nanotech pioneers need the same breakthrough-promoting combination of:

- Dedicated visionary leadership
- Design and production creativity
- Funding and legal savvy
- Patent protection

Once these resource alchemies germinate, we should see a turbocharging in the commercialization of emerging nanotech innovation projects, currently percolating in countless research labs.

Ten Examples of Other IdeaJackings in Developed Countries

Automotive Parts

Terrence J. Keating, the CEO of Accuride Corporation, a $1.4 billion company that supplies parts to the automotive industry, was attending a conference held by the Heavy Duty Manufacturers Association in January 2006. At the conference, he came across a Chinese company that was advertising a brake drum that was a clone of an Accuride product. The brake drum was not only a duplicate of the Accuride design, it had the same part number and the brand name, "Gunite," which Accuride gave to the original product.

Keating described this experience in testimony before the U.S.-China Economic and Security Review Commission in July 2006. In his remarks, Keating said that Accuride has been forced to compete against these types of counterfeit products because China does not provide adequate protection of intellectual property rights. While the lost sales resulting from this type of illicit competition obviously adversely affect his company's revenues, the implications go much farther than that. "The product may be a duplicate in style but the quality of some of the imported product falls far short of the standards required to protect the safety of the American motorist," he told the commission.

Keating said that warranty claims filed by customers because of defects in knock-off products that falsely appear to be manufactured by his company underscore the safety issues such products introduce to the market. In addition to the safety issue, he said that the warranty claims and the costs to identify and get counterfeit products off the market have a negative economic impact on the company. "It is very difficult to estimate the negative impact of these knock-off products in lost market share, damage of brand name and overall value, but it is fair to say it is very significant." [1]

American Indian Arts and Crafts

American Indian art is one of the most popular categories of art produced and sold in the United States, and it represents one of the most successful forms of entrepreneurship and economic development on Indian reservations, not to mention the cultural and often religious significance Indian art has to those who create it. While the U.S. has tried to regulate the Indian arts and crafts industry with laws that prohibit the sale or display of any product that falsely implies that it was made by an American Indian or Indian tribe, substantial weaknesses in the laws make enforcement hard to achieve. The market has been flooded with imitation products imported from the Philippines, Mexico, Thailand, Pakistan, China and other countries, as well as a large volume of fakes made here in the U.S. American Indian artisans are believed to lose $400 million to $500 million from these imitation products. [2]

In a survey of 300 American Indian artists conducted by the U.S. Department of the Interior Office of Inspector General, half said they had seen or heard about a counterfeit copy of their own work and more than half said they had seen or heard about a counterfeit copy of another artist's products. [3] The American Indian artists must cut the prices of their own work by as much as 50 percent to compete against the fraudulent items. Some have even had to resort to selling imitations of their own work in order to make an income. "For Indian artisans, the playing field will never be level as long as imitation Indian-style arts and crafts can be manufactured overseas or mass-produced domestically at significantly reduced prices," the OIG concluded in a report on this issue [4].

Consumer Electronics Devices

In 2006 the Japanese electronics company, NEC, concluded a two-year investigation of counterfeit keyboards and recordable CD and DVD disks sold in Beijing and Hong Kong. The company's conclusion was startling: The counterfeiters had not only pirated NEC's products and brand name, but they had contracted with an entire network of factories to produce the goods and set up warehouses and other businesses that used the NEC name. "The counterfeiters carried NEC business cards, commissioned product research and development in the company's name and signed production and supply orders […] they also required factories to pay royalties for 'licensed' products and issued official-looking warranty and service documents," David Lague of *The International Herald Tribune* wrote in an article exposing the audacious counterfeit system. The pirates even went so far as to create some of their own goods that they sold under the NEC brand.

According to Lague, the counterfeiting of NEC operations was orchestrated in Taiwan and the goods were produced in factories in China, Hong Kong and Taiwan. The fake NEC products were sold in these areas, in Southeast Asia, North Africa, the Middle East and Europe [5].

Cosmetics

Unilever Cosmetics International, a New York company that manufactures cosmetics and fragrances for high-end international brands, claimed in late 2001 that law enforcement authorities in Jakarta, Indonesia, had seized a forty-foot shipping container of counterfeit versions of fragrances Unilever produces for brands including Calvin Klein, Chanel, Christian Dior, L'Oreal, Estee Lauder, Valentino and others. The pirated colognes and perfumes had been manufactured in Barcelona and then sent to Jakarta for assembly with Taiwanese components. Unilever has identified Indonesia as one of the leading source countries for counterfeit fragrance products worldwide. The container of illicit fragrances seized in 2001 was just one of many shipped over the previous five years to markets in the Middle East and Latin America and its discovery led to location of additional counterfeit fragrances in Dubai, UAE. Unilever has also found a counterfeit manufacturing operation in the U.S., in New Jersey [6] [7].

Luxury Watches

Some reputations take centuries of work to build and perfect. Consider, for example, the storied history of the elegant Swiss watch industry — a history that led to esteemed brands such as Breguet,

Patek Philippe, Tag Heuer, Audemars Piguet, Omega, Rolex, Tissot and Longines, to name a few. Yet sadly, it only takes a few counterfeit factories to threaten this priceless image and history. "Counterfeiting is a huge problem," stated Yves Bugmann, head of the legal division at the Federation of the Swiss Watch Industry. "It's a question of the loss of reputation to the brand."

But the Swiss Watch Federation is fighting back. In 2008, with the help of allies, they seized some 2 million fakes. However, the murky elements of the Internet and the current economic recession make counterfeits increasingly difficult to monitor. The Internet allows counterfeiters to pose as the real thing, and sell, behind the privacy of a computer screen, fakes to unknowing customers. Meanwhile, the current economic recession might have consumers choosing the cheaper fakes over the genuine products.

Astonishingly, some 40 million fake Swiss watches are produced every year — nearly double the amount of genuine Swiss watches produced every year. Perhaps not surprisingly, nearly 40% of these counterfeit watches originate in China [8].

Manufacturing Equipment

Eastman Machine Company, based in Buffalo, New York, was established in 1892 by a Canadian inventor, George Eastman, who invented the first electric fabric-cutting machine. Eastman's invention revolutionized the clothing manufacturing business in 1892 when it came up with its first cutting invention because the industry until then had only one means — manual labor — to cut fabrics. The company has many patents and today sells more than 100 manual and automated cutting machine products worldwide. Since 1898, Eastman Machine has been owned by the Stevenson family, whose ancestor, Charles Stevenson, was one of the original investors in the company.

Eastman Machine discovered its first clone of its technologies in the 1990s, when it found a Chinese-manufactured copy of one of its most popular products, a manually operated electric-powered cloth cutting machine that has been a mainstay of its business for 50 years. As in the counterfeit Accuride product mentioned above, the cloned Eastman product used the same design, model number and color as the original Eastman device. The only difference, a not-so-subtle one, was that the Chinese manufacturer had changed the machine's name from "Eastman" to "Westman."

In testimony before the House Committee on Ways and Means in April 2005, Eastman's CEO, Robert Stevenson, described the devastating effects the counterfeit machines from China are having on his company. "Over the last ten years, we went from a company that employed 150 union workers and sold 20,000 straight knife machines worldwide, to a company that now employs only 58 union workers and sells fewer than 8,000 of these machines. Today, we are almost a non-player on Mainland China, where 75 percent of the world's cutting machines are to be found and over 100,000 pirated Eastman-clones are sold annually," he testified.

Stevenson said in his remarks to the committee that as his company has watched the sales of its manual machines plummet it invested millions of dollars in research to create new, automated and computerized cutting technologies that have, once again, revolutionized the cutting process in manufacturing facilities. Yet he fears that its new techniques are vulnerable as well. "We are truly afraid that our research and development efforts — all the hard work and effort to bring these machines to market — will shortly be pirated as well as we start to sell these machines in the Chinese market" [9].

Personal Appliances

In an age when many American companies are outsourcing their manufacturing jobs to China, Farouk Shami, creator of a $1 billion company that creates hair irons, is doing just the opposite. Shami, inventor of the popular Chi hair iron, decided to move his production of personal appliances from China to Houston after struggling to fight countless counterfeits of his product — most of them pirated in China.

Farouk Shami believes the move back to the States will help his company, Farouk Systems Inc. — which spends about $500,000 a month battling the fake products — better control production and distribution. "We'll make more money this way," stated Mr. Shami, a Houston resident, "because we'll have better quality and a better image." A swell of counterfeit Chis has dragged down prices and posed difficult questions for Shami, who in early 2008 sent 16 engineers to the Fenda Electrical Company, his company's Chinese supplier, only to learn that the company representatives were suspiciously denied access to parts of the factory. Shami says most personal appliance irons returned to his company for refunds are defective fakes. But, thanks to the move, Shami will have production right on his doorstep — a shift that will render any imported irons suspect.

Surprisingly, his move is not as unconventional as it might seem. As Daniel Meckstroth, economist at the Manufacturers Alliance/MAPI pointed out, "I think you're starting to see more manufacturers rethinking outsourcing," in reference to a speech made by the CEO of General Electric, Jeffrey Immelt, stating that U.S. companies needed to increase domestic manufacturing as outsourcing is out of control[10].

Pharmaceuticals and Medicines

Based in Switzerland, Novartis International is one of the world's leading producers of patented and generic pharmaceutical drugs, vaccines, and over-the-counter medicines. The company has operated a worldwide anti-counterfeiting program for many years and has participated in hundreds of investigations of counterfeit drugs in more than 30 countries.

In testimony before the U.S. House of Representatives in June 2005, James Christian, Novartis' vice president and head of global corporate security, described a very pervasive and dangerous threat from counterfeit drugs that is growing more serious by the day because the counterfeiters have become so sophisticated that they are expert at packaging fake products in ways that make it impossible for consumers or investigators to tell if a product is authentic. "There can be no doubt that drug counterfeiters present a severe and growing threat to the health and safety of U.S. citizens," he said in his testimony.

Christian said his company has extensive proof of drug counterfeiting activity on many continents. He described Russia as a country in which drug counterfeiting activities are essentially ignored and the country has therefore become a "paradise" in which to make fake drugs for distribution via Poland to European countries. Some of these counterfeit drugs have been found in the U.S. He described China as a country in which counterfeiting businesses are conducted by the country's most successful, publicly traded companies. Enforcement is difficult against these companies, he said, because many have "health, regulatory and law enforcement officials as shareholders." Countries in Central and Latin America are producing enormous quantities of counterfeit medicines; in Colombia alone, Novartis shuts down an average of one counterfeit drug lab every month. Novartis has found counterfeit drugs made with "raw materials" such as boric acid, floor wax, and lead-based paint and counterfeit injected drugs contaminated with feces and bacteria. Patients have been hospitalized and many, including many children, have died after taking these medicines [11].

The counterfeit drug problem is spiraling out of control and as it does so, its implications on human health are increasing. According to a February 2007 article by Donald G. McNeil, Jr. in the New York Times, fake medicines are believed to cause "tens of thousands [...] to 200,000 or more" deaths per year. Drugs used to fight malaria — which causes one million deaths annually — have become one of the most popular counterfeiting opportunities, tragically preventing many people who need these medicines from getting the treatment they need. So far, the use of the fake malaria drugs has had most of its impact in Asia, where more than half of the products sampled in a recent study were found to be counterfeit, however the influx of these products into Africa is now being realized [12].

Refrigeration Test Equipment

Uniweld is a small family-owned manufacturing company based in Ft. Lauderdale, Florida that manufactures testing instruments used by technicians in the refrigeration industry to determine the condition of air conditioning and refrigeration systems. The company, founded in 1949, began selling its products into the Middle East and in time became the leader in its particular market in the region.

Uniweld has registered its trademark in six countries in the Middle East and in 17 other countries in the world, but is finding that the trademark registrations are not protecting it against illicit copies of its products. The company is now losing $1 million a year in sales due to counterfeit products that are manufactured in China and sold in Saudi Arabia and the United Arab Emirates. The products were packaged just like the originals and used Uniweld's name, part numbers, address and instruction sheets that included Uniweld's name, address and phone number and an image of the American flag. The products sold in the UAE were offered in retail shops at half the price Uniweld charges its distributors.

"Not only are we losing business, but also the quality of the counterfeit product is so poor that our hard-earned reputation for producing a quality product is being destroyed in one of the most promising market places in the world," David Pearl, Uniweld's executive vice president said in testimony before the House of Representatives in June 2005, where he represented the National Association of Manufacturers [13].

Snowboarding Equipment and Accessories

Burton Corporation, based in Vermont, the leading manufacturer of snowboard equipment, is credited with the popularization of snowboarding as a legitimate sport. The company traces its roots to the late 1970s when its founder, Jake Burton, began trying to figure out how to make and manufacture snowboards while working out of a barn in Vermont. He built his first production prototype in 1977, launching the snowboard sport and industry. Today, through several subsidiary companies, Burton has expanded to now offer boots, bindings, helmets, clothing, and accessories that it sells through dealers worldwide. The company holds patents around the world for its snowboard technology and associated products and has more than 60 registered trademarks in the U.S. and several other countries in Latin America and Asia.

Despite these precautions, Burton has encountered counterfeiting problems in the U.S. and in Asia. It characterizes the problem in the U.S. as small-scale manufacture and sale of its products on eBay, where it says unauthorized goods carrying the Burton brands, including products it manufactures in limited editions, can be found "almost continuously."

The company has encountered a significant and increasing intellectual property theft problem in Asia, where it has found counterfeit versions of its clothing and accessories in Hong Kong, Taiwan and Thailand. In testimony before the U.S. Senate Judiciary Committee, Vanessa Price, Burton's intellectual property specialist, said the company fully expects that the counterfeiting problem will increase dramatically as its brand continues to grow.

"As a smaller company, Burton is deeply concerned about the rise of theft of our intellectual property since we do not have the resources it takes to combat or offset the effects of large-scale counterfeiting," she said in her testimony [14].

The Political and Economic Impacts of Patent Competition and IdeaJacking in the International Arena: A Commentary

Several unfortunate conditions in today's global trade arena are making gifted inventors and creators of the arts fearful that the integrity of their work cannot be protected. If left unchecked, I worry that these circumstances could very well motivate inventors to keep their critical ideas and creative works secret and proprietary, which would in turn deny the knowledge transfer that derives from the patent publishing and copyright processes and stifle the advancement of inventions and the creative arts.

I would like to call attention to three of these threats that are particularly serious and should be dealt with quickly by diverse groups from the international community.

The most serious and by far the biggest threat is China's cavalier intellectual property philosophy that combined with a lack of commercial trading ethics and judicial integrity in the country has created a global business crisis. The second threat comes from Europe, where policies allow granted patents to be challenged, prior to the issuance of a final patent award, at little cost or risk to protesting companies. This practice allows entrenched and powerful businesses to suppress and potentially squash the introduction of brilliant AAA ideas and even helpful grade A or grade B inventions. A third threat is brewing here in the U.S., where the U.S. Patent and Trademark Office has created a multi-year backlog of patent examinations, prompting a new generation of U.S. computer technology oligarchs to seek the establishment of a public review system of patent applications. As it has in Europe, this approach will put innovators of disruptive technologies at a complete competitive disadvantage against the incumbent oligarchs.

Indeed, one of the primary reasons the U.S. is a world leader in per capita wealth has been our innovators' culture of creating a continuous stream of mega-revenue generating companies like IBM, Xerox, Intel, Genentech, Qualcomm, Cisco, Amazon, eBay and Google. These companies, as well as tens of thousands of others, have succeeded in great part because of confidence in the American judicial and patent system. These companies have prospered because we have historically enjoyed a trusted system of inventive ownership and judicial enforcement of contracts, especially public intellectual property rights (such as patents, trademarks and copyrights) and non-public or proprietary intellectual property. The multi-trillion dollar question: Can we sustain our historical system of inventive ownership in a world swamped with ethical-trade challenges?

The China Factor

China, representing its 1.3 billion people, has become both a large and significantly difficult trading partner for the developed economies of the world. It is no secret that despite its membership in the World Trade Organization (WTO) since 2001, China has conveniently ignored most of its ethical trading commitments, yet it is happily taking advantage of global market access and the privileges that WTO membership brings. The country has enjoyed a greater-than-7-percent economic growth rate that is unleashing dynamic forces of progress and destruction in the global market. The country has accumulated a currency reserve of nearly $2 trillion dollars from its staggering merchandise trade surplus, which in 2006 exceeded $223 billion with the U.S. alone [1] [2], and used its cash to buy billions of dollars worth of U.S. mortgage-backed securities and Treasury bonds, which helped American consumers to continue to buy cheap and oftentimes IdeaJacked Chinese consumer goods. We have fallen into this self-perpetuating cycle at a cost to our own jobs and economy. During the past few decades Americans have often been shortsighted and foolishly over-consumptive; I am hopeful the 2008 and 2009 economic reset will rebalance the country in a more progressive and less-consumptive direction.

Cellport has spent more than 18 challenging years investing in and advancing pioneering wireless and telematics industry technologies. With three portfolios of core intellectual property under our belt, I feel strongly about just how critical it is for all WTO member governments to protect the private ownership of intellectual property and to enforce penalties for unethical trade practices that IdeaJackers introduce to the system. China's exporting of and internal consumption of IdeaJacked goods and technologies is out of control. The country is widely recognized as by far the worst violator in the $650 billion [3] in trade of counterfeit goods globally. Unfortunately, that number continues to grow.

The hundreds of thousands of businesses and factories in developed countries that have shut their doors or suffered reduced profits and the many lower- and middle-class workers who are losing their jobs because of this problem are paying the price for China's trade in IdeaJacked goods just as that illicit trade has helped fuel the rapidly growing Chinese economy. Another negative consequence that many IdeaJacked companies also suffer is what I call DoubleJacking. The practice is common: First, the company suffers the loss of its product designs to a counterfeiter. Then it realizes it has lost its customers, too, to the pirates who used the stolen designs to win the original company's domestic and international customers. DoubleJacking forces the entrepreneur who produced the original design to lower their prices — and profit margin — to compete against the lower-cost pirated products. The reduced profits, in turn, diminish the entrepreneur's ability to invest in future innovation. Being DoubleJacked is a world-class nightmare of diminished expectations for the company, employees, suppliers and for the host government; being IdeaJacked has a very unwelcome ripple affect.

IdeaJacking has a big impact at the societal level, in the form of decreasing tax revenues paid by companies and employees to their governments, which in turn affects their countries' abilities to sustain educational, healthcare, military and other governmental services needed to provide for the quality of life and safety people desire.

The Chinese government does know how to stop piracy and to respect intellectual property, when that property is its own. In 2002, China was awarded the 2008 summer Olympic Games and shortly after that announced a logo for the2008 Beijing games. Within days of revealing the Beijing Olympic Games logo, street merchants throughout China were selling t-shirts, key chains and mugs decorated with the logo design. Aghast at being IdeaJacked, the Chinese government quickly passed a special law protecting the Beijing Olympic logo against unlicensed copying and within days after the law went into effect, the merchandise disappeared from the streets. Strict enforcement by the communist government officials put a halt to the practice. By the time the 2008 Olympic Games began, merchandise adhered to very stern licensing requirements and used anti-pirating devices such as holograms and radio ID tags to prove its legitimacy for sale [4].

I observed this first hand during the summer of 2006 when my sons and I shopped Beijing's famous Silk Market. I asked a shopkeeper there where I could purchase some Beijing Olympic Games trinkets as souvenirs and was told that the items are available "only from licensed companies, those products are restricted." Yet this very merchant was selling counterfeit Louis Vuitton and Gucci hand bags.

One of the major obstacles the Chinese government has in addressing intellectual property rights issues, counterfeit products and unethical trade practices is its judicial system, which is widely acknowledged to be highly corrupt and in need of radical reforms. The legal system in the country is a byproduct of the old Chinese Communist Party (CCP), which has historically had tight control on the creation of laws and the management of the judicial system. For years, judges in China were appointed by the CCP and serve at the whim of the CCP officials, so it is no surprise to anyone that political considerations are often favored over the integrity of judicial decisions [5]. Historically, China's judges were usually former military officials who have Communist Party ties to central government and who needed little to no legal training. While the country began introducing reforms in 2002 to improve its courts, judicial reform, promised since 1979 in the country, is still in its very early infancy in the country. Given the inadequacy of its legacy legal system, the country's legal infrastructure is not expected to gain a fully effective measure of sophistication for some time [6] [7] [8] [9].

Prior to the 1980s, China's court system handled only two types of legal cases, criminal and marital. Contract disputes were handled administratively and there were no intellectual property laws whatsoever [10]. I believe that if the CCP had wanted to bring its legal system up to Western standards it could have done so in the late 1990s after it took control of Hong Kong, which had a well respected judicial system developed under the British. Historically, the CCP has not wanted to upset the friendly and malleable judicial system that it carefully built based on rules of cronyism and convenience. As of 2000, only 10 universities in the entire country offered Juris Doctorate degrees [11]. New training curricula and a new certification test for judges, prosecutors and lawyers, introduced in 2002 to help improve the caliber of legal professionals, reveal the magnitude of the problem: only 7 percent of the 360,000 who took the first of these exams, in 2002, passed the test, and in some courts, no judges received a passing score. Less than 50 percent of the participants had a university-level law degree [12].

In 2004, China's chief justice filed a report with the National People's Congress that discussed the rampant judicial corruption that plagues the country and stated that 461 judges had been convicted of corruption the previous year [13].

Today the CCP faces a plethora of problems from this lack of legal grounding as it tries to manage fairness in the courts within the context of the immense success and wealth building in its own country. For a variety of reasons, the CCP's leadership in Beijing has lost some control over local party members, who are growing more independent as their revenues increase from new land lease agreements created for growth development projects. Local party leaders, who also influence the regional courts, have little incentive to rein in violations of the intellectual property and commerce laws from other countries. Per textbook communist ideology, in which private ownership is not acknowledged, it appears that stealing intellectual property is considered a legitimate way of striking back at neocolonial oppression and western power that many CCP leaders detested for decades. Given the poor condition of the Chinese judicial system, the prospect for contract disputes or intellectual property violations to be reasonably adjudicated in China today is remote, especially by a foreign firm. The ethical trade crisis caused by Chinese IdeaJackers and China's immature judicial system is just starting to heat up. This crisis could prove far worse if any source of internal disruption manages to shake the CCP's role in governing China.

The first source of potential disruption is the internal economic and political corruption that has created growing social unrest, especially among an ethnically-diverse rural peasantry of roughly 800 million people. As the peasant populace seeks a new cause to replace the beliefs of old, many are both converting — at a startling rate — to Christianity and becoming restless over corruption and economic disparities in their country. Recent work by the CCP to address rural unrest issues through policy, tax relief and better revenue sharing should be applauded. If the Chinese government leadership does not move fast enough to address corruption, the prospect exists for a disruptive revolt in China, either by the peasants or other segments of Chinese society, which could bring about unwelcome instability worldwide [14].

Another internal problem could come from the well-educated Chinese youth, whose vast numbers are beginning to realize that the current judicial system and the historical lack of respect for intellectual property creations limits their prospect of building innovative ecosystems for the future. This hinders China's most creative minds and forces them to toil in a low profit margin economy that, perpetuated by pervasive IdeaJackings, does not reward innovative research with higher margin enterprises. In fact, there is little opportunity for creative engineers, scientists or entrepreneurs to invest in proprietary innovations. Today, very few companies, except for large government-owned enterprises, can get credit from the state-controlled banks or China's capital markets to fund risky yet groundbreaking product development. Furthermore, typical Chinese companies are not motivated to take on complex and precarious innovation projects because they, too, can't be assured that their intellectual property rights will be protected [15].

In the near future, millions of ambitious and educated Chinese youth will come to realize that their government's policies of not protecting creative and inventive contributions, both domestically and internationally, will undermine China's own investments in its gifted and motivated human capital. I believe that China's emerging educated and creative minds will assert their desire and need to work in an environment in which their ideas, products and trade are ethically protected. Recent progress by the Chinese government to roll-out more intellectual property laws and increase the staff at their patent office is encouraging — let's hope that they deliver a more trusted environment for all.

The last likely near term consequence of China's IdeaJacking behavior is that our global trading system is likely to become more isolationist due to growing levels of distrust stemming from the Chinese commercial trading behavior and disregard for intellectual property ownership. A growing body of savvy economists has begun to question the notion of the current WTO policy of free trade, especially when not all participants share the same ethical trade and judicial values. Unfortunately, in today's China, free trade is not synonymous with ethical trade [16]. And while China is certainly not the only rogue trading country to skirt WTO rules, it must, for the long-term benefits of its 1.3 billion eager people, turbo-charge judicial reform to reach a reliable platform of ethical credibility. What happens if China's annual revenue haul of hundreds of billions of dollars from counterfeit goods and DoubleJacking practices continues to grow unabated into the trillions? Already the combined economic and social costs of China's current practices are nearly impossible to calculate. And what will the future hold for global citizenry if our rate of innovation diminishes because future AAA inventors make their knowledge proprietary?

It is critically important for leaders of the developed world to address the need to preserve and build on the inventive network motivated by patents and other forms of intellectual property ownership for gifted inventors. Fortunately, given the sheer size of the Chinese IdeaJacking costs, the issue of ethical trade enforcement is becoming increasingly important and part of the everyday political debate in many countries. The ethical trade issue is likely to affect elections and political directions in the developed world for the foreseeable future — especially during the current economic reset — and it should. It is that vital.

Europe's Policies

The second threat, one that undermines two key drivers of our patent invention system —inventor motivations and the publishing of the inventive art — is a European Patent Office policy that allows for a patent, granted to the inventor by the Patent Office, to be reviewed and protested by any company before the patent is finally issued.

Over the years, numerous European entrepreneurs (Wolfgang Cullmann, for one) have told me that America's inventive and entrepreneurial ecosystem is far superior to their own and described the challenges they face trying to launch new technology businesses in Western Europe because of the European Patent Office policy allowing granted patents to be reviewed and protested by large oligarch companies or small rival firms. The European patent environment is extremely distracting and expensive for those innovative entrepreneurs who are striving to create disruptive technologies and to stay focused on commercial delivery.

A recent literature survey on intellectual property rights, which compared the patent processes in Europe and the U.S. in the early 1990s, observed that European companies do not build their business strategies around their intellectual property as frequently or as effectively as U.S. companies do [17]. It also found that Europeans had a lower propensity to patent than Americans; the latter's higher tendency to patent was believed attributable to the "lower cost of patenting in the U.S. than in Europe" and to the efficacy of patent-encouraging reforms in the U.S. [18]. In 2004, the European Patent Office ranked fifth in the number of patent applications filed worldwide, following, in order of ranking, Japan, the U.S., the Republic of Korea and China [19]. This same study found that Europeans in 2004 filed only 57 patents per million inhabitants in the region; the U.S. filed 654 per million inhabitants. The average number of patent applications per million people in countries for which statistics are available was 148 [20].

We have seen the discouraging effects of the European system for ourselves at Cellport, having spent roughly $90,000 in legal fees, for each patent we have been granted in Europe, to respond to challenges from oligarchs or competitors. Even if a patent is eventually awarded as the outcome of this process, and aside from the legal costs, these procedures significantly delay our ability to enforce our patent and generate revenues from our idea.

If European patent delay policies had not helped allow the region's companies to counterfeit our first- and second-generation Universal Hands-Free designs, Cellport would have likely received profitable orders from automotive producers and the Cellport Global Partners program, which we developed to help push Universal Hands-Free products to the market at a more affordable cost. Cellport would have profited and automobile drivers all over the world would have been safer sooner. And if Mercedes-Benz had given us credit for the first Internet-connected vehicle that they built with our product's technology and design assistance, Cellport would not have fallen into its highly distracting cash crisis that lasted from late 1997 throughout 1998.

Today we are experiencing a growing number of large European companies protesting our MobileWeb patents as they are granted by the European Patent Office. The patent protestors in Europe are acting protectively for their shareholders and clearly not for the good of an inventive ecosystem that drives a more inventive and wealthier future. It is no great surprise that the vast majority of the companies protesting our core telematics patents are companies that will likely owe us license royalties once these patents receive a final issuance certificate. Unfortunately for those European industrial oligarchs challenging our patents, Cellport has both the capital strength and intellectual determination to fight off these tactics.

Weaknesses in the U.S. System

The final cloud that currently threatens innovation is the backlog at the U.S. Patent Office for application reviews. In the 1990s, Cellport's patent application submissions typically spent about 18 months in the Patent Office "first action" review; after a series of negotiation exchanges between our lawyer and the patent examination staff, we would typically receive the final issued patent in 24 to 36 months. Unfortunately, the patent application process today is taking double to triple the time it took then. For example, in mid-2002, our research team began developing the Secure Telematics Framework architecture and after a tremendous amount of time and dollar investments, we submitted the initial patent application on this technology in early 2003. This patent application was finally issued in 2008, more than four years from its original submission date!

Much like the delays and costs the European patent system can add to the patenting process, a slow U.S. patent review process generates a similar human capital diseconomy by retarding the pace of inventive developments and the delivery of financial rewards to investors that fund upstart commercial technology entrepreneurs. The patent office's backlog of applications slows down technical innovations much like a constrained money supply slows down the economy. The other undesired consequence of slow patent reviews is that more U.S. inventors will decide to do less public patenting and in turn stay private with ideas.

The U.S. Patent and Trademark Office is, of course, well aware of this problem and in 2007 began trying out a new solution that will open up the patent examination process to peer review. A program, called Community Patent Review, introduced a Web-based system through which any interested party can submit information relating to a patent application, such as examples of previous, similar inventions, for consideration in the review of that patent. Peer reviewers also have opportunities to rate claims and to comment on patent applications and to evaluate other reviewers who are commenting. The peer-review system is intended to help weed out inferior patents before they are granted (and thus cut down on the number of lawsuits prompted by low-quality patents), help expedite patent review and build a Web repository of information that will help patent examiners in their work.

The USPTO has developed the system in close collaboration with the New York Law School, which introduced the concept with IBM, and it has found several of the country's leading patent-holding companies to volunteer to have to submit their patents for evaluation in a year-long pilot test of the Community Patent Review process that began in April 2007. Companies participating include Computer Associates, General Electric, Hewlett-Packard, IBM, Intel, International Characters, Microsoft, Oracle, Out of the Box Computing and Red Hat [21] [22].

While I appreciate the USPTO's attempt to get its arms around the patent-backlog problem, I fear this community review process will in fact undermine our patent system by opening up opportunities for competitors to interfere with the patent approval process and to derail applications from innovatively disruptive young firms, much like we've seen occurring in the European Patent Office's review process.

Today the U.S. Patent and Trademark Office does have the revenue to address the backlog without going this route; the agency actually operates as a profit center for the U.S. government, though much of its profits are siphoned off to other political ambitions. It is vitally important for the U.S government to make the inventive engine of this country a bigger priority; a good early step would be to address the resource needs at the Patent and Trademark Office.

Conclusion

There are a countless number of inventors, entrepreneurs, managers, researchers, investors, economists, judges and government employees who understand in painful detail the ominous economic and social challenges our creative artists and inventors are facing. From the unethical behavior exhibited by the IdeaJackers out of China, to the tactics European industrial oligarchs employ to slow down or derail disruptive new technologies and raise costs with their pre-issuance protest system, and now the patent application backlog and the new review system introduced to the U.S.'s own Patent Office, I believe it is safe to say that launching future innovations with the confidence of protection will undoubtedly become increasingly more difficult.

Unfortunately, when I meet with young innovators, I advise them to consider very carefully the opportunity costs associated with building a meaningful patent portfolio of inventive art. Was this the same warning message that was given to the inventors in the early 1800s after Eli Whitney's cotton gin invention was IdeaJacked and he experienced little support from a very immature U.S. judicial system for his efforts? At the very time when the world needs to encourage the invention of many AAA breakthroughs and the public dissemination of those ideas to build healthier economies and greener world technology innovations, it lacks the ethical trade and critical patent office policies and services needed to feed those efforts. Without remedies, we may, unfortunately, be headed into an innovative dark age at the very time society needs a technological renaissance that's green in orientation.

Chapter 1

[1] "Nokia Mobile Phones Becomes First European Manufacturer to Access Japanese Cellular Market," press release published by Nokia, Jan. 30, 1992.

[2] "Portable and Personal," by Maxine Carter-Lome, in *Cellular Marketing*, Dec. 1992, Vol. 7; No. 12, page 16.

[3] The subscriber figures were reported by CTIA-The Wireless Association, in its Semi-Annual Wireless Industry Survey, published at www.ctia.org, on April 1, 2009.

Chapter 2

[1] *Foundations of Intellectual Property*, by Robert P. Merges and Jane C. Ginsburg. 2004. New York, New York: Foundation Press, pages 13-14.

[2] *Encyclopedia of the American Constitution*, Second Edition. Edited by Leonard W. Levy, Kenneth L. Karst, and Adam Winkler. 2000. New York, New York: MacMillan Reference Books, page 1880.

[3] *Innovations and its Discontents: How Our Broken Patent System is Endangering Innovation and Progress, and What to do About it*, by Adam B. Jaffe and Josh Lerner. 2004. Princeton, New Jersey: Princeton University Press, page 8.

[4] Isaac Ehrlich in a lecture given to the Conference of Human Capital at the University of Buffalo, October 27, 2007, hosted by the University of Chicago Press for the launch of the *Journal of Human Capital*. Erlich often cites Russia as a country that offers a strong example of the need for an effective patent system. Russia, he says, has some of the world's brightest mathematicians and scientists, yet comparatively few commercial products or wealth to show for all the intellectual capabilities its society has to offer.

[5] *Encyclopedia of the American Constitution*, page 1801.

[6] *Innovation and Its Discontents*, page 1.

[7] Ibid., page 17.

[8] *WIPO Patent Report: Statistics on Worldwide Patent Activities*, 2006 Edition, published by the World Intellectual Property Organization, Oct. 16, 2006.

[9] The mobile operator was Grupo Iusacell. The company was bought by Verizon Communications and Vodafone in 2001; at that time it was Mexico's second-largest cellular phone company, with 1.5 million subscribers.

[10] There are two types of patents: utility and design. A utility patent, which is the most common and the type Cellport has, teaches either the "means" or "method" of how an electronic and/or mechanical innovation enhances the workings of a physical phenomenon. Design patents are limited to the specific "design" aspects of a product and can be fairly easily circumvented.

Important concepts in the patent community are "skilled in art," "non-obvious," "novel" and "teaching," which are used frequently to qualify a patent application for actual patent issuance. An acid test for utility patents is to ask if one who is skilled in the art or has other expertise can be taught a non-obvious and novel method of accomplishing an intangible creation, compliments of the teachings in the invention's claims.

A patent application document has two primary components: a "specification" section that describes the background leading to the invention and how the invention works, oftentimes described with both text and drawings. The other key component of a patent is the "claims" section, which describes in very legalistic language the actual novel and non-obvious patentable aspects of the invention. The claims section is exclusively a text description. It is often supported by drawings that appear in the specification section.

[11] Cellport sold the product distribution business to Tessco, one of the oldest wireless products companies in the U.S. It sold its part of the Cellular Solutions de Mexico Mexican partnership to Iusacell.

[12] The company in the wireless industry that was famous in the late 1980s and early 1990s for using the closed licensing model was Telular Corporation. Telular owned a patent on the "faux" dial tone used for mobile and portable phones, which do not have traditional dial tone capability. I sold their products at Cellular Solutions and saw first-hand how their royalties, which were reported to exceed $100 for a device that sold for $300, delayed the industry's ability to adapt cellular phones for novel uses, such as home alarm systems. Telular's royalty fees provided great frustration to early cellular phone companies such as McCaw Cellular and GTE, which found Telular's technology too costly to support.

Chapter 3

[1] Southwestern Bell was the company that failed to support the study.

[2] CDPD was a revolutionary technology because it was the first commercial wireless system to utilize TCP/IP, the protocol used to send data over the Internet, to cellular networks. Several carriers, including AT&T Wireless and Verizon Wireless eventually introduced CDPD services commercially and law enforcement agencies, which used the technology to give police officers a means to send and receive data from devices installed in their patrol cars, became one of the technology's primary users. The cellular carriers decommissioned these networks by early 2006, when new and more powerful digital cellular networks made CDPD obsolete.

Chapter 4

[1] "Trends in the Evolution of the Public Web," by Edward T. O'Neill, Brian F. Lavoie, and Rick Bennett, in *D-Lib Magazine*, Volume 9, Number 4, April 2003.

[2] "Internet Access and Usage and Online Service Usage: 1997 to 2004, and by Characteristic, 2004." Table 1146, in Statistical Abstract of the United States: 2006, U.S. Census Bureau.

[3] Both John Deere and Union Body Truck Company eventually discontinued this work because of insufficient CDPD coverage in the U.S.

[4] "Auto Industry Embraces Wireless to Help Head Off Safety Issue," by Jerry Blake, in Radio Communications Report, Jan. 27, 1997, page 10.

[5] "Daimler-Benz to Exhibit an Early-Stage Internet Car," by John Markoff, in The New York Times, April 29, 1997, Section D, page 2.

[6] From "Listening Post" to Trendsetter, Ten Years of Research for the Vehicles of Tomorrow: DaimlerChrysler Research and Technology North America, Inc. No author. Daimler Chrysler High-Tech Report. 2005. Issue 1, pages 46-50.

Chapter 5

[1] Unwired Planet was one of the first companies to develop servers and micro-browser technologies to allow live interactive use of Internet applications on mobile phones. It later became phone.com and now uses the name OpenWave.

[2] For more on links and hubs, see Linked: How Everything is Connected to Everything Else and What It Means, by Alberto-Laszlo Barabasi. 2003. New York, New York: Plume.

[3] Another option considered by the automotive industry was to use Bluetooth, the short-range wireless networking technology that was just being standardized, to avoid the need to provide a handset-docking device to connect to vehicle systems in the manner of Cellport's technology. Bluetooth continues to struggle as a link between cell phones and vehicle networks, however, because of software constraints, because it does not accommodate the power requirements of increasingly feature-rich mobile phones, and because it doesn't pro-

vide the interface between the handset and the automobile antenna.

Chapter 6

[1] "Tech Firm's Korean Growth Raises Eyebrows," author unknown in *The Wall Street Journal*, Aug. 8, 2000.

Chapter 7

[1] An independent claim is a sole point or aspect of invention that's related to over-all patent filing. A dependent claim relates to the independent claims in a patent and essentially extends those claims, usually in some marginal way.

[2] By this time we had applied for patents in the primary European vehicle-producing countries: France, Germany, Italy, the United Kingdom, and Spain. Between 1999 and 2005 Cellport received seven patent grants in Europe, and two were issued. Five of Cellport's patent grants fell victim to protests by Volkswagen. Here is how the system works: The European patent office rejects or grants a patent application. If a patent is granted, it is kept open for nine months, when it can be protested by anyone. Volkswagen's systematic protest of Cellport's patents put patent enforcement on hold for at least two years while we responded to the European patent office's questions. The process cost Cellport at least $40,000 in legal cost per challenge, and of course enforcement is impossible during the protest period. This protest mechanism brings great difficulties to small companies and feeds very well into large European companies' desires to suppress competition and disruptive technologies. I believe Europe's patent policy is one of the reasons that Europe lags the U.S. in starting new companies and economic growth.

Chapter 8

[1] *U.S. Department of Transportation, Bureau of Transportation Statistics, National Transportation Statistics 2004*, Washington, DC, U.S. Government Printing Office, February 2005, page. 40.

[2] "Gartner Group's Dataquest Says Mobile Phone Sales Increased 65% in 1999," press release, Feb. 8, 2000.

[3] "Gartner Dataquest Says Worldwide Mobile Phone Sales Increased 46 Percent in 2000," press release, Feb. 15, 2001.

[4] Michael Frendo served on the Cellport Board of Directors for one year. He was followed by Greg Pelton as Cisco's representative on the Board.

Chapter 9

[1] "Togetherness: A Balance Sheet," in *The Economist*, Sept. 30, 2000.

[2] Germany's Neuer Markt was an early and smaller equivalent of the NASDAQ. It eventually shut down.

[3] The names of James Mayhew, Alexis and Stephanie are pseudonyms.

Chapter 10

[1] By May 2001, Ford would delay the Wingcast launch from late 2001 to mid-2002, acknowledging that the technology was complicated and that it needed additional time to develop it. "Ford Delays Launch of Wingcast Telematics Service," published online by *Automotive Fleet* magazine on May 21, 2001.

[2] Indeed, it later became clear that Motorola was working a three-way deal with Cellport, GM's OnStar and Verizon Wireless. Ray Sokola had introduced Cellport's Dynamic Digital Bus and Vehicle Server technologies to OnStar in 2000, but they couldn't fund a next-generation design due to budget constraints. Therefore, in 2001, Ray architected a three-way deal that proved to be a master stroke: He talked Verizon's senior management into providing approximately $25 million in funding to move OnStar to the Cellport Vehicle Server architecture, which Motorola would build. For this huge commitment of development funding, Verizon in turn got OnStar to phase out its

old analog services and deliver its services on Verizon's new third-generation digital wireless network, and to sign a long- term commitment to use that network. Motorola came out of the deal with a very sizeable, cash-funded project that assured the company market leadership in telematics, and OnStar received free R&D and other benefits as well. Before Sokola could consummate this three-way, $25 million deal, however, he wanted to secure a license to use Cellport's patented Internet connected vehicle technologies. The catch was that Helena had to manage the licensing process without revealing the identities of Motorola's customer. We had much more leverage then we ever knew during these negotiations in 2001.

[3] Cellport was in the position of being one of those rare companies that can set its own share prices. Our shares were always comparatively expensive and we usually had to convince our investors that Cellport's value would indeed grow over the years. Patent portfolio investments are very high risk and extremely long term investments, but if your work is truly a pioneering core technology that creates a large new market, you can enjoy essentially 90-percent margin royalty streams for 10 or more years. I typically compared our company to patent-holding companies that had proven to be these kinds of survivors, such as Qualcomm, SanDisk and Immersion Corporation. Because their patents were generating substantial cash, these companies had extremely high multiples.

[4] Ford had promised us a $58 million dollar program. Nissan had ordered $8 million in products for a 2002 launch and the BMW Mini Cooper had forecasted ordering $7 million to 10 million in products. From the expectations we were given by these three customers, our backlog was over $70 million.

Chapter 12

[1] Cellport had funded the Nissan and Mini-Cooper programs, which in retrospect were two of our larger mistakes. While Wolfgang Cullmann had advised me to insist on pre-pay contracts with automotive companies, our automotive sales team convinced me that suppliers fund engineering projects in the automotive market. While in fact this

is the way Detroit dictates to tier-one suppliers, Cellport need not have taken on this role with Nissan and Mini-Cooper. These mistakes obviously imploded on us.

[2] Visteon was one of two suppliers that Ford had contracted with to build the Wingcast units. The other firm was Denso, a Japanese company. Visteon's behavior made it obvious, to me, that this former division of Ford knew something about Ford's real intention for the Cellport product.

[3] Donnelly was later acquired by Magna International.

[4] We learned, later on, that during this time period Delphi was negotiating with Ford to buy Wingcast. The deal collapsed.

[5] *Worldwide Telematics Summary*, spreadsheet, TRG Telematics Research Group, Inc. Copyright 2004-2006.

Chapter 13

[1] The credit reduction and credit payment scheduling negotiations that Andy conducted with these various creditors provided fascinating glimpses into the philosophies of the different companies and the character of their decision-makers. Elcoteq, for instance, which was our primary manufacturer and biggest creditor, could have forced us to sell our entire business to satisfy our debt, which was nearly $3 million. Yet it took the high road and gave us time and flexibility to pay it off. Elocteq's President, Doug Brenner, was an accomplished inventor in his own right; he understood the potential value of pioneering core patents in a young market like telematics. He was willing to trust that Cellport would get back on its feet and fulfill its obligations to his company.

[2] One of the great benefits of the patent system is that a patent award itself becomes an objective document that an inventor can use to prove the specific claims of the invention and to establish, in time, when the invention was filed and awarded. Yet a patent award does not address the amount of time, energy and money that goes into

developing the innovation and as inventors, we found that one of our greatest challenges was effectively characterizing, to our prospective licensees, the 11 years of effort it took to create our MobileWeb and Universal Hands-Free design innovations.

One favorite trick IdeaJackers use during licensing discussions with a patent owner is to obfuscate who contributed what to the design evolution and when. With Motorola this was not an issue for Cellport, because our technology transfer sessions with that company coincided with its investment due diligence efforts; all of the history between our two companies was well documented. Further, as an institution, Motorola had its own history of inventing groundbreaking and sophisticated technologies and it nurtured invention as part of its corporate culture; its executives both understood and respected the efforts and investments needed to develop a portfolio of core intellectual property. Ray Sokola, who was a tenured and gifted inventor in his own right and a business leader at Motorola, embodied these values and thus took the high road with Cellport. Omron, also a large and mature institution that considered pioneering technology inventions as part of its core business strategy, was another example of a company that believed in maintaining good corporate relationships with fellow inventors. The licensing challenges that Cellport had encountered to date were mostly with small entrepreneurial companies in Europe that tended to look at patent licensing differently: They viewed licensing as a greed tax.

Chapter 14

[1] Schumpeter, Joseph A. *Capitalism, Socialism, and Democracy*. New York: Harper & Row Publishers. Third edition. 1950. Pages 81-87.

[2] THBury, despite the recommendation from its Chicago-based lawyers, refused to settle and take a license. We ultimately had to file a suit against its customer, Porsche, which forced a THB settlement. Porsche then cancelled THB as a supplier. Needless to say, after suing two German companies, Cellport's popularity in Germany has not been enhanced.

The Political and Economic Impacts of Patent Competition and IdeaJacking in the International Arena: A Commentary

[1] "What Should China do with its $1 Trillion in Foreign-Exchange Reserves?" by Keith Bradsher, *The International Herald Tribune*, published online March 5, 2007.

[2] "Paulson Optimistic on U.S. Economy," by Associated Press, published in *Forbes.com*, March 4, 2007.

[3] "Worldwide Market for Counterfeit Goods: $650 Billion," *Trade Fact of the Week*, email newsletter published by the Progressive Policy Institute, June 14, 2006.

[4] "For Sponsors, China's 2008 Olympics Have Already Begun," by Geoffrey A. Fowler and Wendy Lee, *The Wall Street Journal*, Tuesday, Aug. 8, 2006, pages B1-B2.

[5] "China Attracts and Challenges," by David Manners, in *Electronics Weekly*, April 21, 2004, page 13.

[6] "Justice, Chinese Style," by Robyn Meredith, in *Forbes*, June 21, 2004, Vol. 173, No. 13, page 114.

[7] "China: Lessons for the Bench," analysis published by The Economist Intelligence Unit, Ltd., November 5, 2001. No author.

[8] "China's Legal Reform at the Crossroads," by Jerome A. Cohen, in Far Eastern Economic Review, March 2006, republished by the Council on Foreign Relations at http://www.cfr.org/publicatoins/10063/chinas_legal_reform_at_the_crossroads.html.

[9] "Justice, Chinese Style," Meredith. Page 114.

[10] "China: Lessons for the Bench."

[11] "The Structure of Legal Education in China," by Huang Jin, Wuhan University Law School, China, presented May 24-27, 2002, at

The Association of American Law Schools' Conference of International Legal Educators in Florence, Italy.

[12] "Judicial and Legal Training in China: Current Status of Professional Development and Topics of Human Rights," by Vincent Cheng Yang, PhD, a background paper for the United Nations Office of the High Commissioner for Human Rights, presented August 2002 in Vancouver, Canada, at the China-OHCHR National Workshop for Judges and Lawyers. Pages 3 and 20.

[13] "Best Prepare Yourself for Legal Quirks When You Carry On Business in China," by Arthur Loke, letter to the editor published Nov. 4, 2005, in The *Financial Times*.

[14] Several articles describe the unrest, include the following:

"Bulldozed by Growth, Stonewalled by Government; Pleas by Peasant Farmers for Fair Payment for Land are Left Unanswered," by Edward Cody, in *The Washington Post*, March 26, 2006, page A12; "Farmers Being Moved Aside By China's Real Estate Boom," in *The New York Times*, Dec. 8, 2004, page A1; "Who Should Own the Good Earth of China," in *Christian Science Monitor*, March 15, 2006, page 8; "China to Assuage Discontent While Fueling Economy for Building Harmonious Society," from the Xinhua General News Service, March 7, 2005 [no page number]; "Chinese Farmers Escape Harvest Tax Paid for Centuries," Rob Gifford and Renee Montagne, National Public Radio Morning Edition, August 26, 2005; "Best Prepare Yourself for Legal Quirks When You Carry on Business in China," letter to the editor by Arthur Loke, in *The Financial Times* Asia Edition 1, Nov. 4, 2005, page 12.

[15] "To Innovate, China Must Change," by Mike Clendenin, in *EE Times*, September 25, 2006, page 4.

[16] Please visit www.ideajacked.com to follow and participate in an ongoing discussion of free trade versus ethical trade.

[17] Intellectual Property Rights Business Management Practices: A

Survey of the Literature," by Petr Hanel, in *Technovation, The International Journal of Technological Innovation, Entrepreneurship and Technology Management*, Amsterdam, The Netherlands: Elsevier Ltd. August 2006, page 35.

[18] Ibid., page 13.

[19] *WIPO Patent Report, 2006 Edition, Statistics on Worldwide Patent Activities*, published by the World Intellectual Property Organization, 2006. Page 7.

[20] Ibid., pages 15, 39, 40

[21] "Community Patent Review Project Summary," published by the New York Law School Institute for Information Law & Policy, February 2007. Published online at http://dotank.nyls.edu/communitypatent/p2p_exec_sum_feb_07.pdf

[22] "Open Call From the Patent Office: Agency Web Site Will Solicit Advice," by Alan Sipress, in *The Washington Post*, March 5, 2007.

About the Author

Pat Kennedy has been an executive and entrepreneur for more than 25 years. In the early 1990s he founded Cellport Systems, a research lab whose work has now yielded three families of inventions that enable wireless phones to interoperate with automobiles and other devices. He has been awarded 11 patents and has numerous others pending. Kennedy has a BA in international economics from the University of Buffalo. He speaks frequently on technology, intellectual property and global trade topics, and sits on academic and corporate Boards.

In addition to his book, IdeaJacked, Kennedy hosts a blog at www.ideajacked.com that is devoted to the topics of innovation and ethical trade. The site includes discussion rooms that readers can use to exchange ideas and register their own experiences with global product misrepresentations and IdeaJacking.